"I like this book a lot. Mike Horton and I are *friends*. And friendship is what we need a lot more of right now. In this critical moment gripped by fear, we desperately need this message. When we lose a good fear of God, all kinds of bad fears rush in. But when we see other people from God's perspective, they're gifts and not threats. This book has come at just the right time."

—**John M. Perkins**, author, *Let Justice Roll Down* and *One Blood*

"We are living in a day when the media relentlessly exploits our fears, while social media puts us in an echo chamber of strongly held opinions, working together to create division and confusion. In *Recovering Our Sanity*, Michael Horton provides a biblical and historical foundation for developing (and perhaps changing) our thinking about the most polarizing issues of our day. We need more than someone's hot take in 280 characters. We need reasoned argument grounded in Scripture and gospel hope centered on Christ, which is exactly what this book provides."

—**Nancy Guthrie**, author and Bible teacher

"Yet again, Michael Horton has written a book that Christians across the nation—and around the world—need to pick up and read today. Clinging to God in fear and faith is the antidote to the fears we have of everything and everyone else right now. If sanity is going to be recovered, it needs to start in the church. Horton's message is not only timely and critical—it's also a great comfort."

—**Ben Sasse**, U. S. senator (NE) and author of *Them: Why We Hate Each Other—and How to Heal*

"With his usual yet uncommon balance of biblical, theological, and historical wisdom, Horton offers not only a penetrating analysis of our current fear-driven cultural moment, but also provides a way forward that is both transcendent and timely. He reminds us that we are made by God and for God, and only in that recognition and reality can we drive out fear and find true rest and peace. Do you need help and encouragement navigating the stormy seas of life? Then take up and read this important book."

—**Julius J. Kim**, president, The Gospel Coalition

"We're all afraid of something: sickness, death, or loss (of loved ones, a job, our rights, or our status). Additionally, as Christians, we fear persecution, oppressive government, and corrupt culture. The media, politicians, and even pastors and ministry leaders use those fears to increase clicks on their websites and social media; drive up book sales, conference attendance, and fundraising; and spur us to the polls on election day. The result is not just a divided nation, but a divided church. In *Recovering Our Sanity*, Michael Horton wants to put an end to this division by helping us overcome irrational (insane) fears. Instead, he argues, 'the fear of God drives out the fear of everything else.' So, whether you're a church leader or a church member, do yourself a favor and pick up this book. Gather a group for discussion. Give away a copy for free. It's time to stop the insanity that divides us and embrace the sanity that comes from the fear of the Lord."

—**Juan R. Sanchez**, senior pastor, High Pointe Baptist Church, Austin, Texas

Recovering OUR SANITY

Recovering OUR SANITY

HOW THE FEAR OF GOD CONQUERS THE FEARS THAT DIVIDE US

MICHAEL HORTON

ZONDERVAN REFLECTIVE

Recovering Our Sanity

Requests for information should be addressed to:
Zondervan, *3900 Sparks Dr. SE, Grand Rapids, Michigan 49546*

Zondervan titles may be purchased in bulk for educational, business, fundraising, or sales promotional use. For information, please email SpecialMarkets@Zondervan.com.

ISBN 978-0-310-12793-2 (hardcover)
ISBN 978-0-310-12794-9 (ebook)
ISBN 978-0-310-12795-6 (audio)

Cover Design: Micah Kandros Design
Cover Photo: Shutterstock
Interior Design: Sara Colley

Printed in the United States of America

22 23 24 25 26 27 28 29 30 /LSC/ 12 11 10 9 8 7 6 5 4 3 2 1

To Leslie Wilson for her clever mind, big heart, and example of loving and serving everyone around her.

At the end of the days I, Nebuchadnezzar, lifted my eyes to heaven, and my reason returned to me, and I blessed the Most High, and praised and honored him who lives forever,

for his dominion is an everlasting dominion,
and his kingdom endures from generation
to generation;
all the inhabitants of the earth are accounted
as nothing,
and he does according to his will among
the host of heaven
and among the inhabitants of the earth;
and none can stay his hand
or say to him, "What have you done?"

—Daniel 4:34–35

CONTENTS

Foreword ix

1. A Pandemic of Fear 1

PART 1: THE FEAR TO END ALL FEARS

2. What Does It Mean to Fear God? 21
3. Eyes toward Heaven 41
4. The Wisdom in Fear 58
5. Fears Relieved 74

PART 2: FACING OUR FEARS WITH EYES RAISED TO GOD

Our Longing for Life

6. The "Sting" of Death Removed 97
7. Suffering Isn't Bad Karma 124

Our Daily Bread

8. A Secure Future 141
9. Stewards, Not Saviors 156

Confronting Our Fear of Each Other

10. Why We Fear Each Other 183
11. "Christian America" versus the Body of Christ 202
12. Religious Liberty: Cancel Culture and Persecution 222
13. LGBTQ+ Fears: People over Positions 238
14. Racial Fears: Redefining "Us" 255

Conclusion: Walking Each Other to the City of God 287

Acknowledgments 289

Notes 290

FOREWORD

Citing statistics that show the number one reported fear of people is public speaking and that the number two fear is death, the American comedian Jerry Seinfeld would famously mock the ordering of these phobias in his stand-up routine. "Does that sound right?" he would ask. "That means to the average person, if you go to a funeral, you're better off in the casket than doing the eulogy." The joke elicited laughs because the statistics, in this case, aren't lying. Virtually everyone fears one of those two realities—and most people fear both. We can obviously understand—at least at the most natural level—why people fear death. But what is the fear of public speaking? In this, people are not afraid of the dynamics of putting together a speech or of the vibrating of their vocal cords into microphones. What they fear is the humiliation or rejection that will come if they jumble their words, or if they don't have anything to say at all. The fear is not of the speaking itself, but the audience. More specifically, what they fear is the judgment and rejection that will come from other people—especially from people they know. For some of you, even the idea of speaking in front of others causes you to cringe, perhaps the way you might when you see someone poorly singing in front of a panel of judges on a reality television talent show.

Now, perhaps it's cruel and a bit dismissive for a celebrity known to the world because he speaks in front of people for a living to make fun of that widespread fear of public speaking. Isn't this, after all, the equivalent of Michael Jordan making fun of people who are clumsy on the basketball court or Jeff Bezos laughing at the fear of making the payment on next month's rent? Maybe—but probably not, since many of those who speak publicly for a living know exactly what the fear of public speaking is like and grapple with it every time they approach a stage. Even when this struggle is not present, though, everyone—no matter how articulate and professional—knows what it means to fear the judgment of other people. Fear is a universal human experience. And everyone—even those who believe that life is merely a meaningless absurdity—knows what it means to be afraid to die. That, too, is universal. Evolutionary psychologists would tell us that this happens because those early human beings unafraid of death wouldn't have survived to pass on their genes, while the Bible would tell us that this "fear of death" is part of the "lifelong slavery" from which Jesus has come to free us (Heb 2:14–17).

The truth is, though, that these two fears are related. We fear "judgment" from other people because it has been a consistent pattern that for most of human history—and in many places in the world even today—to be alone, without the support of one's tribe or neighbors, is a sentence of death. Added to this is the fact that most human beings do precisely what the philosopher Blaise Pascal wrote centuries ago—distract ourselves from the fear of death with "diversions." The primal fear of death, the Bible reveals, is, at root, far more than just a survival mechanism for a nervous system. This fear is not of extinction as much as it is of judgment. We suppress what our conscience knows—that we will stand before a living God to whom we must give an account (Rom 2:15–16). Because we psychically hide from that Judgment Seat, we find ourselves consumed with all the little judgment seats we see all around us—whether they are represented by people we know or by anonymous masses on social media. In the middle of the last century, T. S. Eliot wrote in his poem "East Coker": "Do not let me hear of the wisdom of old men, but rather of their folly, / Their fear of fear and frenzy, their fear of possession, / Of belonging to another, or to others, or to God."[1] Although most of us can hardly imagine living in Eliot's time of world war, we can certainly understand what it means to live among a population fearful of frenzy, of belonging to, of losing, of others or of God, or of fear itself.

In this book, Michael Horton shows us that we do not displace fear with the absence of fear, but with the presence of a different kind of fear. We drive out the fear of others, the fear of the future, and even the fear of death itself with the fear of God. As this book explains, this fear is not the trembling of demons before One who will condemn them, but an altogether transformed sort of fear—the awe and reverence of a holy God who loves us and who sent his Son to the Place of the Skull in order to put us—and the universe itself—right with him. This means that we reorient our lives around a cross that shows us a God who both judges sin and justifies sinners (Rom 3:26). That fear is grounded not in anxiety and shame but in the freedom that comes with the hearing of Good News.

In so doing, Horton walks us through various aspects of the fear that threatens to paralyze us—from the cosmically apocalyptic to the quietly personal to the sometimes disorienting nature of the social, the cultural, and the political. One need not agree with all of Horton's diagnoses of all of these various aspects of fear to learn from him how to identify and fight against fear—how to supplant the quivering of a limbic system with the adoration of a heart set free.

This book is, ultimately, not about categorizing and refuting fears as much as it is about pointing us to the One who has walked for us through the Valley of the Shadow of Death—and who walks through that same Valley with us now. This book is meant to shake us out of our fears of that which (and those who) cannot ultimately hurt us by showing us the gravity and glory of a God before whom we will all one day stand. We learn to quell our fears not by reassuring ourselves that there is nothing in the darkness, but by coming to the Light that shines in the darkness, and has overcome it (John 1:5). That God in whom is life is not afraid of death. And, come to think of it, that God who revealed his Word to us is not afraid of public speaking, either. As you read this book, I pray that you will hear the two phrases repeated numerous times each in the Scriptures—"Fear God" and "Do Not Be Afraid." And I pray that as you do you will see that these are actually not two contradictory commands but one coherent message, a message that we need to hear once more if we are to recover our sanity in an insane time and recover our courage in a culture of fear.

Russell Moore

Chapter 1

A PANDEMIC OF FEAR

Driving home late one night, I suddenly came across a deer positioned directly in front of me, trying to cross the road. Stunned, the animal stood frozen, the reflection of my headlights flashing from its eyes. Thankfully, I swerved just in time to miss it. It was a literal "deer-in-the-headlights" moment.

But let's imagine a scenario in which the deer population fell victim to a mental illness that made them react to *every stimulus* as if it were an oncoming vehicle. Their daily habits of trotting through the brush in a cheerful herd, sipping at a gentle brook, biting off berries and leaves (and flowers from my aunt's garden) would cease. They would now look at every cracking piece of underbrush—and each other—as if a semi were speeding head-on toward them.

How much worse it is for human beings, made in God's image, to experience life as one giant catastrophe-about-to-happen. If we responded as these deer, the other deer would appear to us as automobiles—threats to be avoided. We might band together in organized groups of deer-vigilantes, anticipating the traffic and chewing off battery cables in parking lots. However, perhaps this metaphor is not too absurd. Indeed, many of us live each day in constant fear. And our smartphones are the headlights, freezing and immobilizing us.

Don't get me wrong: adrenaline is a gift. Fear can save our lives. God equipped us with this amazing instinct to flee oncoming cars and tsunamis. For example, I'll never forget the time I went scuba diving on the Big Island of Hawaii. It began as a beautiful and tranquil experience—until one ingenious buddy decided to spear an ono fish, dragging his quarry to the shore while several hungry sharks pursued us. I quickly found myself standing on an outcropping of lava rock, doing my best to avoid being eaten. This shows that we have a necessary instinct for survival, and God has blessed us with incredibly smart reactions in these situations. No deliberation is necessary. No calm conversations, no need to read experts. We just do what comes naturally.

God equipped us with endorphins to face fears with a flight-or-fight response. However, he did not design us to live in a perpetual state of emergency. Nevertheless, that is how many of us are living today: bracing ourselves for the next gale, the next catastrophe. Some even go looking for the next crisis like a tornado chaser searching for a storm. But this is not healthy for individuals or for the communities we live in. When people live like a deer frozen in the headlights, our natural flight-or-fight instinct subverts our fact-gathering (and fact-checking), causing careful deliberation, logical thought, and empathy toward others to all take a holiday.

Sadly, this exceptional instinct has become our routine way of life.

Like you, I have some fears. I'm an optimist by nature, but there is always something going on—something that demands a response. I worry about my kids growing up in a world that is incredibly different from the world I knew as a child. Since the rise of the internet, smartphones, and social media, the standard generation gap has grown to the size of a canyon. Things that my parents considered unthinkable were experimented with by my generation, and today those same attitudes, behaviors, and lifestyles are not only normal but celebrated. I'm most anxious about the unknown effect this technology will have on our thinking and our relationships. Millennials and younger generations have never known a world without social media. It's a grand experiment, and our children are the guinea pigs. Sure, there are upsides to this revolution, but there are plenty of downsides as well.[1]

According to one survey, Americans right now fear government corruption the most (74 percent), closely followed by threats to the environment, loss of income, a loved one's serious illness or death, and medical bills.[2] We are cursed with unhealthy fears—fears of death and disease. We long for security and comfort and fear the loss of certainty about the future—fears of unemployment and changes to our planet. And many of our common fears today are rooted in a fear of the unknown—a fear of those who are culturally and politically different from us.

Let's take a closer look at these three types of common fears.

I. Our Longing for Life

We are told that Boomers are afraid of getting old, Millennials are concerned that they're not special, and members of Generation Z are worried about everything. Illicit drug use and alcoholism are on the rise, and suicide is now the second leading cause of death among children, adolescents, and young adults aged 15–24.[3] During 2020, approximately 93,000 drug overdose deaths occurred in the U.S.[4] There are myriad causes of such conditions, but fear and anxiety are major drivers. Nearly 1 in 5 U.S. adults will have a diagnosable mental health condition in any given year.[5] Disability payments for mental illnesses have skyrocketed in comparison with those for cardiovascular, respiratory, and other chronic conditions, which have remained fairly steady.[6] Of course, fear is not the only driver of mental illness; genetic and brain chemistry also play a significant role. Yet fear pours fuel on the fire.

On March 11, 2020, "COVID-19" passed from being an "outbreak" to a "pandemic," according to the U.S. Center for Disease Control.[7] Deaths escalated frighteningly, with the U.S. bearing the lion's share. A majority of Americans have said that the global pandemic had a significant impact on their mental health. I have no expertise to weigh in on the highly politicized debates surrounding government regulations, and I won't comment on the medical facts regarding this novel virus. But COVID-19 was undoubtedly an international emergency, and the world eagerly awaited the production and release of vaccines with hope. Sadly, on both sides the tragedy of this virus became yet another opportunity to put our politics on display. Behind every mask or no-mask decision was an ideology that had little concern with neighbor-love. For many, the virus was yet another chance to judge if a person belonged to Them or to Us.

Fear drives many people to worship science and government. We have been trained to expect a comfortable blanket of comfort and security provided by technology and the advances of modern medicine. Monarchs of the past could not have imagined the extent to which an average person can control the temperature of a home, let alone the wonder of a modern automobile. However, fear has also driven other people into suspicion of science and government as part of a worldwide conspiracy.

2. Our Daily Bread

In 2019, *The Atlantic* reported an "unprecedented surge in fear about climate change." A Yale–George Mason University study found that seven out of ten Americans now say that this concern is "personally important" to them—up nine points from the previous year. The reason, many expressed, was that they personally perceive changes in the climate. However, although a majority believed that climate change would affect their own lives, 70% said they would not give $10 a month to slow it.[8] Thus, there seems to be a gap between anxiety and personal responsibility. And we also totter between two insecurities: the environment (which can seem pretty abstract) and work-and-wages (which doesn't). Perhaps, like the deer in the headlights, we're paralyzed by the urgent calls to "save the planet." And the more frequently experts, media, and politicians hit the high beams, the more stupefied we feel. What difference could I possibly make?

Given such statistics, it cannot be only progressives who are worried about the climate. But when we hunker down in our hermetically sealed silos of partisan politics, we often hand over our own thinking and responses to surrogates who bear our collective anger, guilt, and actions. Like all the anxieties we're engaging, the fear of environmental disaster is highly politicized.

Like their neighbors, Christians typically fall into party positions regarding the problem and the solutions on this issue. I am not qualified to weigh in on either. So, like you, I try to find the most reliable and least partisan sources for the facts. Here is what I have found, though I realize that experts in the field may offer adjustments, elaborations, or corrections.

As weather patterns change significantly, especially with droughts and wildfires in the Southwest, more intense hurricanes in the Southeast, and rising water levels in all coastal areas, many Americans—regardless of political bent—are becoming more anxious. According to the Intergovernmental Panel on Climate Change (IPCC), consisting of 1,300 scientists from around the world, temperatures will rise 2.5 to 10 degrees Fahrenheit over the next century.[9]

The result, according to NASA: rising temperatures, a longer growing (frost-free) season, and changes in precipitation, with some regions experiencing more than average rainfall and others less. We can expect more droughts and heat waves, even more intense hurricanes, and sea levels rising 1–8 feet over the century, with the Arctic becoming ice-free in summer before this century's midpoint. The crisis is not in the future, but in the present. Carbon dioxide levels have risen 416 parts per million and global temperatures 2.1°F since 1880. The Arctic ice minimum is being reduced by 13 percent per decade, and the Arctic ice sheets are losing 427 billion metric tons of mass per year. Finally, the global average sea level is going up 3.4 millimeters per year.[10]

The questions are, how much human activity is responsible for this serious crisis, and what, if anything, human beings can do about it. According to experts, extremely high levels of carbon dioxide along with deforestation have played a large role. Major volcanic eruptions emit massive amounts of CO^2 into the atmosphere, but their output is nothing close to the everyday emissions from fossil fuels.[11] God designed and created a world in which the whole ecology is interlocked. So, when humans tinker with one part of it, we affect the whole ecosystem. Why can't we talk about these issues without igniting partisan firestorms?

Speaking of firestorms, in the West we now have what are called "megafires." The breadth of devastation grows annually. In San Diego, the Cedar Fire in 2003 was the largest recorded conflagration in California history at that time, with 273,000 acres burned. (I especially remember this one because we had to evacuate and it seemed certain that our house would be lost.) Fourteen years later, it was surpassed by the Thomas Fire, at 282,000 acres. However, in 2020, in California alone, more than 4 million acres burned—the majority of this in just a little over a month. Just a single megafire—the August Complex—devastated over 1 million acres. So far in 2021, 2.5 million acres have scorched California.[12] And we have more concerns than just fires—each year heat waves break previous records, while hurricanes pummel the Gulf Coast as the water warms.

It seems reasonable to ask: How much have such threats grown due to forest management and population and property density in fire- and storm-prone regions? And are we just more aware of these events because of constant, global, and immediate media reporting?

Regardless, the environment is on the minds of many of us who used to regard it as a secondary or even nonexistent issue. The facts are real. They are also more complex than polarizing rhetoric suggests. Yet, as Francis Schaeffer argued in his 1970 book *Pollution and the Death of Man*, Christians should care about life on this planet for the same biblical reasons that they care about the lives of the unborn, ill, or aged.[13]

Adding to the uncertainty which people feel about the future is the ever-present reality of unemployment. As of the fall of 2020, unemployment numbers were the worst since the Great Depression thanks to the COVID-19 pandemic. As the situation worsened, Jerome Powell, the chair of the Federal Reserve, commented that the U.S. economy was deteriorating "with alarming speed."[14] We have seen how quickly a virus can cripple national economies. Around the world, iconic brands shuttered their stores and many small businesses filed for bankruptcy, leaving millions unemployed.[15] Airlines slashed operations and employees, and the U.S. deficit began skyrocketing by trillions of dollars.

Even before the pandemic, the nonpartisan Congressional Budget Office forecasted that at then-current rates taxpayer debt would rise from 78% of GDP in 2019 to 144% by 2049.[16] But in 2020 and early 2021, the federal government granted trillions of dollars in modest relief aid. How would you feel if your personal debt were around $250,000? That is roughly what we are talking about for *every working taxpayer* today. How will this burden be borne by our children and grandchildren?

As worrisome as the national economy might be, where we really feel the pain is in our own daily lives. Layoffs coincide with rising medical costs and fears of inflation. But there are larger and longer-term issues, too. In my parents' generation, a worker would ordinarily expect to hold the same job with the same employer until retiring with a decent pension. That is a vanishing horizon. We now have to prepare for having many different jobs and working for various employers.[17] You may not necessarily be experiencing this now, but your children will definitely come to know job-shifting as a real and potentially anxiety-provoking way of life. Of course, those most affected will be in sectors where mechanical labor eliminates human workers, but this phenomenon is more extensive. For example, the Biden administration pledges a burgeoning job market in green technologies, but this will eliminate a lot of other jobs. That is because the labor market will rapidly change regardless of who occupies the White House.

As with the other fears that haunt us, I am not qualified to explain these factors, and I don't pretend to offer any solutions. I simply acknowledge that these fears stoke anxieties which God's wisdom addresses. We all feel the impact of these changes, some more than others. Even right now, there are many people who are afraid of being told, "Your services are no longer needed here," or of being so sick that they can no longer be part of the workforce, at least for now. If they do return, they resume wondering if they can ever get back on the freeway during rush hour as everyone speeds past. God gave us callings as part of our sense of identity, meaning, and purpose. When we lose a job or worry about the possibility of being "let go," it's not just about making ends meet. It has wide ramifications for our physical, emotional, and spiritual health.

3. Fearing Each Other

If our hopes indicate that what we value most is what keeps us going, then our fears reveal the same in reverse. What do we need (or think we need) so much that we would be unable to go without it? And what do we believe in so much that we would become totally disillusioned if it doesn't come through for us? For example, if our choice was between "a famine of the Word" (Amos 8:11) and overturning *Roe v. Wade*, which would we choose? Or if the choice was between gathering with the Lord's people and protesting mask wearing by staying home? What if you just affirmed same-sex marriage in exchange for security and cultural acceptance?

Or what if you yielded complete obedience to a president in exchange for social and political security? Christians have always been faced with various versions of this Faustian bargain. For early Christians, the choice may have been more obvious: pinch a little incense to Caesar or go to the lions. I am not suggesting that such imaginary choices are equal to what these martyrs faced, just that they provoke us to consider what we value—and fear—most highly.

Fear is such a powerful drug that it is easily exploited. Not only hucksters but sometimes even medical, pharmaceutical, and insurance companies along with investment marketers and public scientists sell fear. CNN and FOX could hardly survive without it. Tyrants, whether political leaders or employers, create a culture of fear to rise to power and then to tamp down dissent.[18] The recent conspiracy-mongering associated with QAnon is just an extreme version of the broader trading in fear on the left and the right alike. We are becoming accustomed to living every minute under the tickertape of "Breaking News" banners. Everything is urgent, demanding our immediate reaction. We all have to make a comment, with or without relevant facts. We think that we're expressing ourselves, but often we're actually following the script of whatever talking head we've come to trust for the take on everything. Instead of being exposed to challenging points of view, our biases are often simply confirmed.

According to various studies, conservatives have a bias toward negativity.[19] In one sense we have more information and access to differing views than ever before. Yet, sitting in our own social media silos, we're actually less informed. We may know more about what Our Team already thinks (especially about Their Team), but we don't really know much about topics, viewpoints, or events beyond our increasingly reinforced echo chamber.[20] Each side runs verbal flags up a pole: Woke, SJW (Social Justice Warrior), Homophobic, Intersectionality, Anti-Women, CRT (Critical Race Theory), LGBTQ+, and many other buzzwords. Both sides in the culture wars invoke these terms, often utilizing dubious credentials or research, as if they could cancel each other by simply throwing out epithets. Anger drives us to identify our neighbors and their particular life experiences and convictions with either Us or Them so that instead of listening, understanding, and engaging we can just cheer or jeer.

According to our side, we must not only disagree, but must be *afraid* of Them. This is what the myriad political pundits on the right and the left do every day to gin up our fear-and-anger meter. In fact, if you disagree with the right-wing guru, you might not be a patriot or a Christian. And if you disagree with the left-wing agenda, then you must be "canceled." A good word for this is bulverism: assuming that alternative voices are wrong and then presuming to explain this error on the basis of their motives. Just read the direct-mail letters of political parties and special interest groups and you begin to realize: They must really think we're so stupid that we cannot make a decision without being motivated by fear. The ultimate beneficiaries of our fear are the media empires looking for ratings and advertising dollars.

In fact, though, fear is the weakest motive. It works for a while. But how many times can you see daily catastrophes from around the world without getting jaded? Over time the fear factor actually demotivates because everyone, on the left and the right, becomes immune to the drug. Surely, even deer couldn't keep the adrenaline going in the midst of perpetual shock. No wonder we've become tired and younger generations are especially cynical about there being any ultimate truth beyond the cacophony of sound bites and hashtags.

We Long to Be Happy and Fear Being Unhappy

Perhaps all of our anxieties can be reduced to the fear of being unhappy. There is a fear of losing a certain "quality of life." In spite of the poor ways we often treat the elderly, Americans spend more money per capita on extending life—except for unborn children who are perceived as impediments to our happiness. Often the slightest inconvenience can jar us, throw us off track, and make us fearful about our long-term happiness.

For a long time now, many preachers have marketed God as a product. "And if you're not completely satisfied, simply return the unused portion for a full refund." What if you have been promised that God exists for your happiness? That you can have your best life now? What happens when the investment *doesn't* work and you get sick or divorced or laid off? The same me-centered worldview that makes *my* happiness the goal of God's existence can easily justify abortion-on-demand—at least in *my* circumstances. Surely God can't be against my *happiness*?

If you have a human-centered philosophy of life, then it doesn't matter whether you vote Republican or Democrat. Old people, sick and incapable of contributing to my "flourishing," are problems. A spouse blocking the way to my happiness is a problem. The unborn are problems. Homeless and mentally ill and alcohol- or drug-addicted neighbors are problems—until perhaps we find ourselves in their ranks. If only we could be freed of these burdens, life would be good or at least better. It doesn't matter whether we side with the police or the protesters—we demonize and dehumanize them while idolizing ourselves and our allies.

Even as we lament the crumbling of society, we are worried about our own marriages and about raising children in a decadent society. As I said earlier, I get this. I worry about it, too. However, like our neurotic deer, we often find ourselves frozen in fear of the Others who threaten to take away our happiness and sense of security. Our individual narcissism draws us into an ominous social tribalism.

Often these fears are stoked from the pulpit by constant cultural jeremiads. You would think that our present society is the most godless ever to come down the pike. A historical perspective (and a more robustly biblical doctrine of sin) would relieve us of that apprehension. Yet, for many, this seems like a distraction from the feeling we want to have that we are the most important generation living on the verge of Armageddon.

This response to a decadent culture contrasts sharply with that of the ancient church. One of the reasons for the success of Christian evangelization of Romans was the radically different ethic that was *practiced* by believers, not just preached. For the most part, the early Christians were not wringing their hands or protesting the paganism of, well, pagans. They knew that they were a strange colony of Christ's kingdom in a fading age that glorified sin and mocked righteousness. Instead of parading their values, Christians practiced them quietly and communally and shared the saving message of "Christ crucified" for sinners. Given the shoddy state of today's churches and Christian leadership,

Protestant as well as Roman Catholic, it is not surprising that even conservative Protestants (evangelicals) have become comfortable with their own sins. Expecting unbelievers to surrender their autonomy and narcissism while we reinforce these vices with human-centered preaching and practice is a hypocrisy that is not lost on the public today.

Decisions about the value of human life are made long before bills are passed or courts offer rulings. Since *Roe v. Wade* in 1973, there has been a steady decline in abortions after the initial spike following that fateful decision. By 2017, rates of abortion were lower than they were *before Roe*.[21] This sounds strange, but it shows that politics is downstream. Culture is not shaped by politics, but by the theological and moral universe of actual human beings. It is also shaped by economic and social factors, but we are most essentially *religious* creatures. Made by God for God, we cannot help but yearn for meaning, identity, and salvation. Laws, courts, and constitutions along with self-crafting, group-identity, and virtual communities have not determined who we are. Rather, God has assigned us a value and identity that trumps everything else. But we have twisted this into idolatry ever since the fall. And since we have made ourselves god, we fear anything and everything that we perceive as a threat to our reign. However, in all of these cases, the extent to which we have lost the fear of God will increase our fear of everyone and everything else.

If someone buys the worldview that says that the chief end of human existence is personal peace, prosperity, and security, this demand for satisfying immediate felt needs will override whatever scruples one might have against abortion, divorce, abuse, or racism or just about anything else. At least secularists are living more consistently with their nihilistic convictions. But, in my experience, much of the message among American evangelicals is just as human-centered. There are threats to my happiness. I'm scared of . . . (fill in the blank). I need to find other people who are scared of the same things. Then we'll express our group narcissism in chat rooms, vicariously through the screeds of favorite pundits, and then finally in the identity politics that has little concern for the common good.

But what if God is against my "happiness," as I define it, because it is shallow and short-sighted and rebels against his design? In our fallen condition we're so befuddled that we do not really know what makes us or each other happy. God does not exist for my happiness, but I exist for his glory. And when I am glorifying God, I am also enjoying him. Worshiping God *is* the flourishing of ourselves and those around us. So it is only in communion with him that I find genuine satisfaction which can weather unhappy circumstances. I don't naturally know this because I'm a sinner. Rather, I have to be confronted with God in his holiness and majesty, accept that I am the problem, and then flee to his mercy in his Son. And then he unites us also to each other as members of his body—gifts instead of threats. That is what Christians *should* be saying. Maybe I'm living on an island, but I just don't hear enough of this.

Hypochondria Makes Us Lose Our Minds

We are so used to—perhaps even addicted to—the adrenaline rush of fear that we have to invent a crisis even when things are relatively calm. There are, of course, very real and justifiable fears. But our society exhibits a sort of emotional hypochondria that spawns hyperbolic rhetoric. Therapeutic hypochondria about victimization belittles individuals who actually *are* victims of dangerous people and relationships. It also keeps us from actually understanding serious issues that need to be worked out, because we are perceiving the Other as completely demonized, irredeemable, and evil. These people, who hold different political views from us, are not only, well, people who hold different political views from us, but are dupes or drones of a sinister conspiracy. They threaten our very existence and flourishing and must be *cancelled*—what used to be called "treated rudely." They cannot be allowed to speak their mind because they are really bad people.

Shutting people down is a kind of real *oppression*. Yet, ironically, it is justified usually by a sort of whining about being *abused* by someone simply expressing an alternative viewpoint. On the surface it seems assertive and self-confident, but just under the skin it reveals a fragile ego that cannot defend its own beliefs and so merely parrots the highly-charged emotional memes and shibboleths of Group Think. It seems that everyone wants to get in on the act of being a victim. Yet such hypochondria belittles the real abuse, oppression, and toxicity that some have actually experienced. And this makes us all sick and insane. We lose our minds, our fears driving us to think irrationally and blame others.

Pundits like atheist Bill Maher love to correlate conspiratorial thinking with religion in general. After all, as he said in one TV episode, once you put your confidence in what you really, *really* believe, then why not entertain the possibility that the 2018 fires in California were started deliberately by Jews operating a space-laser?[22] Does the emotional intensity of our believing compensate for the lack of arguments and data?

In a panel discussion I participated in, Bill Nye ("The Science Guy"), like Maher, reduced all of religion to what I call the Realm of Fuzzy Things, like teddy bears and comfy blankets. Fear of death is religion's fuel, he argued, following a long line of atheistic apologists. Or maybe it's like fake headlights to scare us into a blind leap. Regardless, it's all basically wishing upon a star, Nye argued. There's no need to engage specific beliefs—just dismiss the whole religion thing with one easy stroke.

"Yes, I agree with almost everything Bill has just said," I responded, to the astonishment of the mostly secular audience. "Now could I mention the resurrection of Jesus Christ?" For the next thirty minutes I laid out the historical case, and Bill, for all his erudition, had no answer. He was visibly frustrated. He had come with a stump speech dismissing religion as the "opiate of the masses." He wasn't prepared for historical arguments, much less scientific ones. Any Christian could have made the case that I laid out that day, and many do make it every day. It was totally unremarkable on my part. But when it comes to religion, secular fundamentalists are as ill-prepared for logic, reason, and historical argumentation as their real or imagined religious counterpart. For both, the world is a very simple place. No deliberation, nuance, or reasoning is necessary, since *We* are smart and *They* are stupid.

When it is not perverted by culture warriors on the right and the left, Christianity is inherently oriented to making reasonable arguments rather than emotional blackmail. Christianity is not based on feelings or on moralistic platitudes and political visions of grandeur ensuring that Our Team can stay in power. Its symbol is a cross, planted in the middle of history, with a resurrection three days later as the beginning of the new creation. That is either true or false, but it's not fantasy. We like being the underdogs. We are at our best when folks think they have us in the secure half nelson wrestling hold. They don't—not because we are smarter or better, but because the facts are on the side of Jesus Christ.

However, many Christians today are as likely as others to substitute arguments for enthusiasm. With notable and refreshing exceptions, reactionary emotionalism and instinctive flight from reason and arguments dominate our public discourse. When you have to pull at the levers of power, playing the game of Washington insiders—or invading outsiders—you have already lost the hearts and minds of a lot of people. It's an act of desperation, a knee-jerk reaction to whatever "headlights" (or headlines) extremists of one sort or another project on the wall.

Looking Up, Looking Out

We do have some legitimate anxieties. I will be exploring some of them and striving to sympathize with people who are facing serious trials. I experience many of them as well. However, my thesis is that *the fear of God drives out the fear of everything else*. And, to begin, we will turn to God's Word for wisdom. We do not have a stern Father who just tells us to brush off our wounds and move on. He binds our wounds—even ones he inflicts—to save us, like a doctor who cuts out a malignant tumor.

My goal in this book is not to take sides in cultural and political debates. Instead, it is to raise our eyes to heaven so that our sanity can be restored, as Nebuchadnezzar experienced in Daniel 4.

In many ways, this story reprises the fall of our first parents in Genesis 3. Instead of giving their ear to God's word, they wanted to grasp here and now for themselves what they could see and possess. This was nothing less than Satan's lie, "You will be like God." Well, they *were* like God—his image and likeness, in fact. But they did not want to be reflections of *his* glory; they wanted to be autonomous (self-ruling) sources of glory themselves. *God* was originally their security and goal for a blessed life; the one whose sovereignty, goodness, love, and faithfulness provided a rich and healthy environment of variety and abundance; the one who promised everlasting life upon fulfilling his covenant; the one who made their work a meaningful partnership in his kingdom, and whose friendship with Adam and Eve made them trusting mates to each other. But they lost the fear of their Maker, and all sorts of wrong fears rushed in.

The fall brought a curse on all of these blessings. Adam and Eve began to die, the ground was cursed and subjected to vanity along with their work, and childbirth became a chore. Even they began to blame and resent each other for the curse. As early as Cain and Abel, we see the outworking of the perennial war between Satan's persecuting "offspring" and the "seed of the woman."

And yet God did not let his rebels have the last word. Even in the midst of these curses, God proclaimed his promise to govern nature and history. He delayed Judgment Day so that humanity could have the opportunity to be justified through faith. Work was no longer a sacred commission to extend God's kingdom of holiness, but it remained under the blessing of God's common grace. Marriage was still blessed: Adam and Eve did stay together, after all, and raised a family. Also, God still allowed humans to eat and drink from *his* storehouse—even if by the sweat of their brow. Finally, even through the pain of childbirth, God graciously elected a woman to bring forth his messianic Seed for redemption from the curse.

I want to help us shift our whole focus from a human-centered obsession with saving ourselves through false securities and promises of immediate gratification to the "solid joys and lasting treasure [that] none but Zion's children know."[23] From that perspective, we can be joyful even when we are unhappy, hopeful even when the hype fails us, and persevering and growing even in and through fearful trials.

Part 1

THE FEAR TO END ALL FEARS

The antidote to our fears is the fear of God. The proper fear of God leads us to Christ, our only mediator, so that the improper fear of God—anxiety about whether he is our terrifying Judge or merciful Father—can be settled once and for all. Spreading its domain, the proper fear of God also conquers our fears of false gods that we often take too seriously as if they had the last word over our lives.

Chapter 2

WHAT DOES IT MEAN TO FEAR GOD?

Why the *fear* of God? For many of us raised in conservative churches, it seemed that God was primarily a judge, evaluating our performance. In reaction to such a solemn requiem, many churches turned the channel to easy-listening. It seems that over the last few generations there has been a shift away from "the fear of God" being something positive to a condition ranging from inappropriate to troubling neurosis. We are so afraid of sounding like a hellfire-and-brimstone preacher that the last emotion we think we—and especially seekers—should experience is the fear of God.

I have written elsewhere at length about how a human-centered society turns God into a supporting actor for our life movie. Whether as a personal therapist, life coach, entertainer, manager, or mascot in the culture wars, God exists for us. We might say that the chief end of man, in contrast to the first question of the Westminster Shorter Catechism, is to *use* God and enjoy *ourselves* forever. The picture of God as "a consuming fire" (Heb 12:29) seems quite foreign even in churches where we can express our fears for just about anything and everything except the fear of God. Fear just doesn't seem like the right emotion at all when we are talking about a god who exists for our happiness. How could the fear of God contribute to our well-being and flourishing?

Even in more conservative contexts today, the reading of a "fear of God" passage is often quickly followed up with an explanation, dying the death of a thousand qualifications. The upshot is that fear doesn't really mean "fear." In such widespread dismissals we are not only failing to give God his due but are depriving ourselves and each other of the only antidote to the crippling fears that haunt us.

The only way to conquer the *wrong* kinds of fear is to embrace the *right* kind. I am not saying that the fear of God is the only thing we need. However, "The fear of the LORD is the beginning of wisdom, and the knowledge of the Holy One is insight" (Prov 9:10) and the wisdom of God *in person* is Jesus Christ (1 Cor 1:30). The fear of God leads to trust, and trust bears the fruit of the Spirit, producing a harvest of blessings for ourselves and for others. Fear really is worship—we *fear* what we believe is *ultimate*, what we think has the last word over our lives.

The problem is that we fear "gods" that are not God. We either live under crippling subservience or we smash or divorce our idols when they fail to give us the satisfaction we can only have with the triune God. In either case, we are fearful in the wrong way because we give up our hopes and dreams to lords that cannot liberate. We worship what we cannot live without. It's ironic: by nature, since Adam's fall, we want autonomy—to be gods ourselves—and yet we realize that this doesn't quite work. We find ourselves gravitating toward *other* gods, instead of going back to square one and entrusting ourselves to the only true God. We may worship our spouses as protection against loneliness or insecurity, until they inevitably fall short of the deity invested in them. Or children, for the joy they bring—until they disappoint. Or a job, for giving us identity, meaning, and dignity—until we're demoted, laid off, or feel compelled to quit because the job doesn't give us ultimate meaning and satisfaction. It may be comfort a person cannot live without. We all have our sweet tooth for some idol or another, depending on the main fear from which we trust it to save us.

The fear of God, running from Genesis to Revelation, must once again fill the horizon of our thoughts, imaginations, hearts, and lives. As this happens, we find ourselves able to stand back and identify the idols of our hearts, saying with the prophet,

> Thus says the LORD, the King of Israel
> and his Redeemer, the LORD of hosts:
> "I am the first and I am the last;
> besides me there is no god.
> Who is like me? Let him proclaim it.
> Let him declare and set it before me,
> since I appointed an ancient people.
> Let them declare what is to come, and what will happen.
> Fear not, nor be afraid;
> have I not told you from of old and declared it?
> And you are my witnesses!
> Is there a God besides me?
> There is no Rock; I know not any." (Isa 44:6–8)

But first something should be said about why the fear of God seems alien today.

The World Became Flat

As John Lennon's "Imagine" has it, the outlook of our society today, including many Christians, is implicitly secular, as if there were no

God and no heaven above or hell below—above us there is only sky. There are myriad subplots in the story of how experiencing God came to be more remote, if not completely off our radar.

Imagine a hanging mobile. Its various pieces are suspended from a single point at the top, with concentric hoops or rings, each smaller than the other. Remove the mobile from its hook and the whole thing collapses into a flat set of hoops on a table. Something like that has happened over a long period in our modern world. Premodern Christians just assumed that all of reality—we and everything around us that we can see, touch, hear, and smell—is suspended from above itself by God's free speech: "By the word of the LORD the heavens were made, and by the breath of his mouth all their host" (Ps 33:6). Spoken into being by God's word, nature replies accordingly: "The heavens declare the glory of God, and the sky above proclaims his handiwork" (Ps 19:1). That meant that the most insignificant creature could raise our eyes to God. Even ants could teach us something about wisdom (Prov 6:6).

Human beings were the only creatures who decided one day not to bear witness, instead imagining that they were autonomous. I think this is what Ecclesiastes means when it talks about life "under the sun." Living "east of Eden," we try to find meaning in each of those concentric circles, but in vain. Only when the mobile is suspended again from its proper Anchor do our world and our own lives have depth, richness, coherence, and beauty. Now it is life under *the* Sun, our triune God.

Once upon a time in Western nations, people used to ask, "How can I be right before a holy God?" This question made sense when the mobile was hanging. But now we ask, "How can I have my best life now?" There may be "transcendence"—higher experiences, places, and entities—*within* this world, but meaning is "immanent"—that is, it's just one natural occurrence after another. Often we seek this transcendence *within ourselves*. That's part of what people mean when they tell pollsters that they are "spiritual but not religious." Even in many churches, the biggest problem seems to be peace of mind or with ourselves, perhaps even with each other, rather than peace with God. When our greatest fear is subjective shame rather than objective guilt before God, or threats to a long life instead of everlasting life, we live in a flat world.

Joining others in the singing of the national anthem draws us together and taps our deepest loyalties. A baseball game, a kiss, or a ballet may bristle with intimations of the sacred. Cresting the summit of a glistening granite peak may fill one with an overwhelming sense of the sublime. Joining a march may charge one's soul with the exhilaration of being part of something larger than oneself, participating in the arc of history that bends toward justice. But all of these quasi-mystical moments are not being confronted or even accosted by an eternal God who breaks into time. The experience is not of someone or even something that transcends us but of our own inner psyche. Like a pinball, our affections are shot from one bell-ringing score to another, but always under the glass of the pinball machine itself. As has been pointed out frequently, even when we are with other people we are often alone together.[1] We express ourselves, but nobody is even listening since they are expressing themselves too. This can happen even at church, where we basically have private experiences in the same room with other people. These experiences may be shared with others, but they remain uniquely individual—like being alone together. Such events may trigger a *new consciousness* of the always-and-everywhere "miracle" of nature, but there is little expectation of a personal God intervening in history and showing up on our doorstep, as it were, to do a *new thing*.

In 1348–1350, when the Black Death struck, the Church of England called for a period of prayer and fasting. However, in response to the HIV/AIDS crisis in the 1980s it called for more public funding for medical research.[2] On both the Left and the Right, many churches seem to think that the most relevant thing they have to announce are public policy prescriptions. However, the world doesn't need the church for that. There is indeed a place for talking about more aid for research, but the church has a very unique commission from Christ the King of all creation. In fact, the church is the society he is forming, by his Spirit through his Word, into a communion that experiences, proclaims, and models the fear of the Lord. If the church gives the impression that this world's problems and solutions are the most significant challenges for it to face, it might as well close up shop and transfer assets to its preferred political party, pharma company, or tech firm. The sense of a genuinely transcendent God, qualitatively distinct from creation and yet the one in whom we live and move and have our being, is waning if not eclipsed in an era that reduces the horizon of desire to what we can access with a smartphone.

This new experience of the world is not defined by any political shift. The culture wars are mere aftershocks of a deeper shifting of the tectonic plates beneath us. And it is not as if we stand on one of those plates, drifting farther and farther apart from our secular neighbors inhabiting the other. Culturally speaking, we're all on the same plate. We *pray*, "Give us this day our daily bread," but we *know* that bread comes from Costco. As believers, we know that God is the giver of all good gifts. Yet how do we *experience* this truth? The answer begins with the fear of God.

But what exactly *is* the fear of God? It is an emotion, to be sure, but it does not bubble up inside of us. Rather, it is provoked when we are confronted with the God who exists outside of our inner psyche. The short definition of the fear of God is *sanity*. The diseased deer who mistake each other for oncoming headlights are behaving insanely. Refusing to leave my room because I'm convinced that hungry panthers are waiting outside is not living with the grain of reality. No less unreasonable is the assumption that I am "my own person," the only one who decides what and who I am, without any authority, accountability, or need for salvation outside of myself.

My day job is teaching apologetics along with systematic theology. I make light work for myself at the beginning by telling the new class of seminarians, "Everyone already knows God, without any arguments." Then I spend the rest of the class helping to equip them with arguments. Why? Because human beings "by their unrighteousness suppress the truth" (Rom 1:18). It is not a revelation problem, as if some people just don't believe God exists because they do not have enough information. God is not hiding from us (Acts 17:26–27). In fact, "his invisible attributes . . . have been clearly perceived, ever since the creation of the world, in the things that have been made. So they are without excuse" (Rom 1:20). We offer arguments and evidences to help these people see that they are misinterpreting the knowledge that they already have and, of course, to announce the good news that they do not know by nature.

So it is not the case that people first have to become convinced that there is a God before they can worship him.

> For although they *knew* God, they did not *honor* him *as* God or *give thanks* to him, but they *became futile in their thinking*, and their *foolish hearts* were darkened. Claiming to be wise, they became fools, and exchanged the glory of the immortal God for images resembling mortal man and birds and animals and creeping things. (Rom 1:21–23, emphasis mine)

We twist and rationalize in order to defend ourselves against the God who created us, judges us, and saves all who call on his name. Our corrupt heart guides us to use our reason and sense observation for weaving webs of half-truths, distorted truths, and untruths. So we do not start with ignorance and come to truth, but begin with truth and, as Calvin put it, "deliberately befuddle ourselves."[3] We are created as worshiping creatures. If the knowledge and indeed even some sense of fear of God did not exist, then there would be no idolatry and no false religion.

How far will we go in denying what common sense, reason, and observation naturally yield? First, Paul goes on to say, we will exchange the worship of God not only for the worship of human beings but even of images of animals. Then we will exchange natural relations for unnatural ones that even basic anatomy testifies against. We live against the grain of nature—even against what we know as true from science (general revelation). The essence of the fall is idolatry—specifically, the serpent's false promise of autonomy: "You will be like God." After their fall, Adam and Eve no longer used their reason and experience of the world as God's gift leading them to himself. Instead, they would know—or rather, construct—"Good and evil" for themselves, without any dependence on external authority.

The fear of God is living with the grain of reality. As we will see, it is sanity. Go against the grain of a piece of wood and you will get splinters. Defy gravity and you will not break a physical law; you will break yourself against it. We did not make ourselves, so it is insane to live as though we could be whatever and whomever we choose. We do not belong to ourselves, but to God. As believers, we know that we belong to God by right of creation and providence and doubly by right of election and redemption. "You did not choose me, but I chose you and appointed you that you should go and bear fruit and that your fruit should abide" (John 15:16). We do not adopt ourselves, but have been adopted by God into his family by grace. These are the facts of life.

Living with the grain of reality is to accept the truth instead of trying to run from it, hide it, distort it, or bury it so we don't have to deal with it. It is the acknowledgment that God is dreadful in majesty, the author of our existence and the judge of our lives. Ever since our first parents, we have sought autonomy—that is, self-rule, imagining that we could re-write the story with ourselves in the starring role. If God wants to have a supporting role, he needs to make sure that it's to make us happy. He can empower, encourage, comfort, and inspire us in our life projects, but he doesn't *own* us. We own ourselves. And if anyone is going to judge or save, we'll be the ones to do it ourselves. No one's going to tell me what I can do with my body or with my money, what to believe, or how I should live. It's my car and I'm in the driver's seat.

We want to be God, but we are not good at it. Soon we find that it is just too much. Overwhelmed, we become crushed by the burden of pretending that we could take God's place.

It is one thing to accept the grain of sanity intellectually, and another to live daily with it. On Sunday we sing, "Know that the LORD, he is God! It is he who made us, and we are his; we are his people, and the sheep of his pasture" (Ps 100:3). But on Monday it is so easy to settle back into familiar patterns and imagine that we can craft our own identity and justify ourselves by "likes" and "friends." All of the things we're afraid of have something to do with the fear of losing our autonomy. We are afraid of each other because we think our own identity is threatened.

The Beginning of Wisdom

Wisdom is sanity. Knowing, experiencing, worshiping, and trusting in God is the beginning of recovering our sanity. "The fear of the LORD is the beginning of knowledge; fools despise wisdom and instruction" (Prov 1:7). Locating the right object of our fear is Priority Number One. Tell me what you fear the most and it's fairly easy to discern what idolatry you are prone to. My greatest fear is the future of my kids in this Salvador Dali painting we're living in right now. Will they know the Lord? Because of this fear, I have sometimes behaved irrationally. If my wife Lisa and I just catechize them, take them to church twice on the Lord's Day, are consistent in evening devotions, and check a few other boxes, it will work—right? It's like you put in a dollar, press A7, and a Snickers bar drops. I can *say* that I trust in God's faithfulness to keep his promises, but I am still *living* against the grain of reality.

Now, when parents ask me if they think they should feel responsible for whether their kids are walking with the Lord, I—a teacher of God's Word—immediately tell them, "No, it's up to God, right? We do what he has called us to do, using the means he has promised to bless. But we cannot change a heart." I really do believe this. But a part of me, deep down, often doesn't feel it. So I can pray and believe as if everything depended on God, and then act toward my kids as if everything depended on me. This attractive idol is Control—specifically, controlling the outcome of my children's relationship with the Lord. Not only is this a sin against God, but it *always* has the opposite effect on relationships from what I want. When I really "get" the fear of God—*feel it deep down*, I relax and everyone benefits. It's fun to see God at work when I get out of his way.

What do you fear most? Is it getting sick or dying? Or perhaps insecurity? Then you might gravitate toward a god who looks more like Moloch than Yahweh. These are your typical gods of the underworld, demanding constant sacrifices—even of children—to satisfy their hunger for revenge.[4] But, if pacified, these gods will make sure that you are secure. The danger in Israel was always to worship "Yahweh" according to the characteristics of foreign gods. And that is our problem, too. Maybe you fear persecution?

Then you will easily reach for any savior who will keep you from having to face it, even if he, she, or it is a phantom demanding your loyalty in exchange. Maybe you'll still call him Jesus—but it's a demon. If your greatest fear is the destruction of the environment, have you made the government and the collective, global action of the nations your hope? Whatever we fear has a corresponding idol that we trust to alleviate that fear. Also, like the Israelites with the golden calf, we are really good at even worshiping the *right God* in the *wrong way*.

Some might assume that I'm saying that believers are idolaters, and that our fear reveals that we are a church beholden to other gods. But I do not believe this. "Such were some of you," Paul says (1 Cor 6:11), indicating that a real change had occurred in the Corinthian believers. As a Christian, I am no longer an idolater, and I repent of my presumption of control. In Greek, "repentance" means changing your mind, and the result is a U-turn—something I'm all-too familiar with, even though I have a GPS to guide me. We're always making U-turns, but there is a decisive U-turn we make in bending our knee to the Lord. We say, "I am not entitled to believe whatever I want or live however I want. I am not my own, but I belong to God. He made me and he redeemed me." Every genuine Christian has made that decisive U-turn. No true believer says, "I accept Jesus as my Savior, but I've decided to stay on the path that leads to destruction." It's a contradiction.

So we have made the decisive U-turn, but we still lose our way sometimes, like John Bunyan's "Pilgrim." Even on the path of everlasting life, we veer into ditches and ignore traffic signals. We not only wrestle or struggle *with* idolatries of various sorts, but *against* them in the power of the Spirit and on the basis of God's gracious redemption in Christ. Whatever idolatry you wrestle with right now, part of that wrestling involves repenting of it and considering it misguided. But you and I are still tempted by idolatry—and we still commit acts of idolatry. And that is because there still lurks in us a fear that something or someone else can meet our needs and satisfy our desires better than God can. Instead of fearing God as the Lord who *speaks*, we fear the circumstances that we *see* and put our trust in ourselves and our idols.

No Fear of God

Think of the top ten worst sins in today's world that come to your mind. Like me, you probably picked symptoms, not the root illness. In the Bible, the worst thing that can be said about a people is that they "did not fear God" (Deut 25:18). Active rebellion against God is not the root but the fruit of failing to take God seriously: "Transgression speaks to the wicked *deep in his heart*; there is *no fear of God* before his eyes" (Ps 36:1, emphasis mine). "There is no fear of God before their eyes," Paul repeats in his diagnosis of the human condition (Rom 3:18). Did you know that it's possible to live an outwardly pious life, thanking God that you're not like the godless secular humanists, without any genuine fear of God in you?

In a Google search for "Fear of God," the first link I found was to a hipster clothing line with the slogan "Fear God" stitched or printed on the front or back—a vivid example of how nothing is sacred. Instead, holy things are fashion accessories and marketing gimmicks. When God's name is mentioned today, it's often part of a comedy routine or an expression of vulgarity.

But the worst vulgarity is not what we hear on the streets or see when we stream movies online. It is the vulgarity of the church trivializing or misrepresenting God. The more heinous blasphemy is not when comedian Bill Maher plies his wit to outright mockery, but when evangelist Paula White tells viewers they will not receive a blessing unless they send a large check to her ministry. It is egregious when God's name is used by false prophets to justify a religion of greed and selfishness, promising prosperity now if you'll follow their steps and instructions. God's wrath is kindled against such people:

> "I have heard what the prophets have said who prophesy lies in my name, saying, 'I have dreamed, I have dreamed!' . . . Let the prophet who has a dream tell the dream, but let him who has my word speak my word faithfully . . . Behold, I am against those who prophesy lying dreams, declares the LORD, and who tell them and lead my people astray by their lies and their recklessness, when I did not send them or charge them. So they do not profit this people at all, declares the LORD." (Jer 23:25, 28, 32)

More subtle than the person whose speech is filled with profanity is the "smooth talk and flattery" that Paul says celebrity-preachers were promoting in the church (Rom 16:18). You can be sure you're meeting an idol, even if it is called God or Jesus, when it says nothing but "'peace, peace,' when there is no peace" (Jer 6:14). In the political sphere, false prophets profane God's name by using it as a credit card for whatever policy, candidate, or party they believe best contributes to human flourishing. Yet the entire system is human-centered, using God to accomplish our own agenda. Here's the key: The fear of God is not a means to an end, but the end itself. We don't use the "fear of God" as a slogan for national revival, personal well-being (even spirituality), moral crusades, or social justice. We don't use God to make a point—God *is* the point.

Using God, even the fear of God, for our own ends is nothing new, of course. In older days the fear of God was also used to manipulate people. A preacher might go to elaborate extremes to describe the horrors of hell, using his own graphic imagination to fill in details left out of the Bible. Debates over how we are saved from hell were important because people took God seriously, or at least they took hell seriously—and that is the danger of using hell as a stick. But being afraid of hell is not the same as being afraid of *God.* Hell *is* God's face set against us, giving us what we deserve—apart from a mediator. The fear of God is the beginning of wisdom because it gives us the sanity to see the reality of our condition and our need for Christ.

In generations past you might have heard someone referred to as a "God-fearing" person. But today *fear* is probably the last emotion that people associate with God, if they consider him at all. And that is precisely the problem: we do not take God seriously. Whether we turn God into a cruel sadist, as past generations did, or into today's benign Santa Claus, we trivialize God instead of taking him seriously.

As I say, sentimental portraits of God are often a backlash against scolding ones. You get the impression that God is annoyed with humanity—or perhaps irritated—but it's a sort of nagging, like what teens feel from their parents. According to these portraits, God is never angry *with us* but rather with the *pain* that sin causes us. If we would only try a little harder to do things his way, we would be happier, our marriages would be better, and our society would be improved. You can find this idea in the psychobabble of popular preachers who defend traditional morality on the basis of how useful it is to human beings. But if you start with that utilitarian and human-centered premise, then it is quite easy to say, "But I'm *not* fulfilled by these prescriptions and I do not feel liberated at all. Instead, this other 'community' I'm listening to affirms my deep-down feeling about what would free me to be a happy person."

The tragedy here is that God's moral will really *is* satisfying. It really and truly satisfies and fulfills us. It gives us meaning and purpose, because that is how God made us. First and foremost, God made us *for himself* and we cannot be truly happy when we decide for ourselves what makes us happy. *Sanity sanitizes.* Fearing God brings health. But we fear God not just because he promises us happiness—even ultimate happiness—but because of who he is.

Sometimes, instead of hearing about the fear of God, we are told that our sins (or "mistakes") let God down. God is sad and we shouldn't want to make God sad. This just makes a portrait of God as Man-Writ-Large. But imagine if God *were* like us, affected by offenses the way we are. Every sin against him and each other would fill him with such grief and anger in his essence that he just could not move on. He would be a glorified mood ring, changing colors every time someone somewhere did something good or bad. Or he'd get so tired of it all that he would wipe us off the map. The nation of Israel was constantly courting this sort of disaster by its disobedience through the constant cycles of idolatry and spiritual prostitution. Yet God made it clear that he was in charge and would keep his promise, saying, "For I the Lord do not change; *therefore* you, O children of Jacob, are not consumed" (Mal 3:6, emphasis mine). It is good news that God does not change and that he is not affected emotionally by us and our failures to fear him. Instead, he stands by his eternal resolve to save his people. We are not in a state of grace one day, only to lose it the next. We do not let God down. In fact, it's more serious than that. Rather, we have all merited God's judgment. And "our God is a consuming fire" (Heb 12:29).

At least the "Don't make God sad" approach is still concerned with God, even if it is wrong-headed. Worse is what we often hear today: "God doesn't want you to *let yourself* down. He doesn't want *you* to be sad. He wants *you* to be all you can be." Recall the picture of the hanging mobile. In this case, the mobile is not suspended from God, but flattened out on the table in concentric rings—or actually turned upside down. I may have sinned against myself or even against my neighbor, perhaps even against creation. But, according to Scripture, even these offenses are ultimately derivative of my greater transgression against God. Every good that we find here below is anchored in a greater goodness above. And every evil that we commit is made even more evil when we see that it is another attempt to unhook ourselves from the Anchor. Even when David sinned violently against Bathsheba, he confessed to God, "Against you, *you only*, have I sinned and done what is evil in your sight, so that you may be justified in your words and blameless in your judgment. Behold, I was brought forth in iniquity, and in sin did my mother conceive me" (Ps 51:4–5, emphasis mine). David's sin against Bathsheba was made *more* sinful by virtue of its vertical assault on God's goodness, majesty, justice, and holiness.

We do all sorts of things—not just *wrong* things, but outwardly *good* things—that fall short of this proper fear. We may perform good works because we want to be noticed by other people. Or because we want God to take note. We may still have fear, but it is fear of not being noticed, not having a good reputation, not being "liked" on Facebook, or not being in the right group. We may even fear hell or the loss of rewards. But before God this means that "our righteous deeds are like a polluted garment" (Isa 64:6). The true fear of *God* moves us into a completely different framework of thinking and feeling. First of all, it fills us with dread. Instead of being cajoled into "doing better" by feeling sorry for God or for ourselves, we lose all hope of appeasing God ourselves. And this godly fear rightly drives us to Christ, in whom we find a complete Savior and Mediator. The fear of the God of glory and grace, whom we know only in Christ, is the antidote to the fear of the *wrong* God. Only when God shows us that all other doors are closed and that there is no alternative safe access to his mercy do we see the splendor of the one Door—our Savior Jesus Christ.

Fear Is More Than Respect

In churches today, many of us might be surprised to hear a sermon on the fear of God. If we come across one, as we do with any regular reading and preaching through the Bible, it is sometimes said that "fear" doesn't really mean *fear*. We are told it means "respect." And while it is true that respect and awe are involved, the Hebrew noun *pa-had* means "dread, a sort of panic." It means the same thing in Greek, where the word is *phobos*, from which we get the word "phobia." The fear of God is a form of xenophobia—a fear of the stranger, or, in this case, the One who is utterly strange and altogether different.

The fear of God is not primarily a fear of *something* (for instance, judgment) but of *someone*. It is God himself who provokes our phobia. He is different from us, not only because we are mere creatures, but because we are sinful. This is what is sometimes called the *sublime*. We experience small-scale intimations of the sublime in nature. Describing tornados and hurricanes, storm chasers alternate between being terrified by their devastating power and exhilarated by their majesty. The same is true of massive fires and earthquakes or being tossed at sea in a storm. Survivors speak of "respect," to be sure, but it is always more than a sense of deference due. It is being gripped by a deep awe that makes you want to simultaneously get closer and run away.

Whenever God revealed himself to people in Scripture, they were afraid. A sure disproof of a reported vision is hearing it described as a casual conversation. In the Bible, God or his messenger has to say, "Do not be afraid" (and, for some, repeat it) because they *are* afraid, hiding their faces from the glory of the holy God. This fear is a disorienting experience, the recognition one has in sensing that he or she is not in charge. There is no protocol for this sense, as if one could get back on the horse and ride confidently again in the saddle of emotional calm. Abram, Moses, Joshua, David, and the rest simply fell down in worship. While beholding a vision of God's majesty, with even the mightiest heavenly creatures covering their faces and feet, Isaiah reports,

> And one called to another and said:
>
> "Holy, holy, holy is the LORD of hosts;
> the whole earth is full of his glory!"
>
> And the foundations of the thresholds shook at the voice of him who called, and the house was filled with smoke. And I said: "Woe is me! For I am lost; for I am a man of unclean lips, and I dwell in the midst of a people of unclean lips; for my eyes have seen the King, the LORD of hosts!" (Isa 6:3–5)

Again, this fear is a species of xenophobia because *there is not anyone like God.* I am not saying simply that we acknowledge him as unique, but that he *is* unique. God is not just a supreme being at the top of the ladder. He's *above* the ladder he created.

I respect all sorts of people, but they don't render me speechless in their presence. Yet one is simply dumbfounded at the absolute otherness of this Stranger. He does not reveal himself *to* scare us. When angels show up, they have to calm their listeners down and assure them that they come with *good* news. And that's just the natural reaction to angelic servants. But the majesty of the One is overwhelming to all creatures—and this was only a vision, not a direct sight of God in his blinding glory. Isaiah may have thought he was as good as the next guy—until he saw God.

A similar episode occurs in Matthew 8:23–27. Even when God clothes himself in our humanity to hide his blinding glory, his sublimity provokes fear. Jesus and his disciples are in a boat and a megastorm (*seismos megas*) suddenly arises. Terrified of imminent danger, the disciples wake an inexplicably sleeping Jesus: "'Save us, Lord; we are perishing!' And he said to them, 'Why are you afraid, O you of little faith?' Then he rose and rebuked the winds and the sea, and there was a great calm. And the men marveled, saying, 'What sort of man is this, that even winds and sea obey him?'" (vv. 25–27). "Marveled," as most English translations have it, doesn't quite capture the original: *ethaumasan*, from *thamazô*, which means "astonished out of one's senses." We find they similarly "marveled" in Mark's account, but the Greek more accurately reads, "They feared (*ephobethesan*) with great fear (*megan phobon*)" (Mark 4:41).

The fury of the natural elements—the sublime in its most terrifying aspect—provoked the disciples to ask Jesus for salvation. Like the rest of us, they were afraid of an imminent *natural* threat. There may have been some hint of the sublime in this tempest, but it was mostly raw fright. But in that moment when Jesus by sheer command brought the terrifying storm to an end, they were more afraid of Jesus than they had been of the storm. The full presence of the Sublime was too close to them in that moment. For a split second the disciples may have felt relief that Jesus was with them in the boat, but then they feel that disorienting awe! During the storm, they knew that he could save them from mortal danger—and he did. But now they feel a sense that *he* is the greater threat!

In another boating episode, Jesus tells the disciples to throw over the net after a day of fishing failure. Now, this is Peter's boat. On land Jesus might be respected as the wise rabbi, but now he is part of the crew and hardly in a position to give orders to the veteran captain. Nevertheless, Jesus takes command—and when they pull the net back in, it is so full they can hardly heave it into the boat. "But when Simon Peter saw it, he fell down at Jesus's knees, saying, 'Depart from me, for I am a sinful man, O Lord'"

(Luke 5:8). As in Isaiah 6 and Matthew 8, Peter here has that sense of the Sublime—that awful beauty—that simultaneously repels and beckons. What is so striking in these episodes is the fear that accompanies the words and deeds of Jesus even though his blinding majesty is hidden in our human flesh.

God is not our buddy, an indulgent grandfather, a life coach, or a golf partner. He is the sovereign Creator of heaven and earth, demanding an account from each of us for our sins—first of all against him, but also against our neighbors and the rest of the creation that he has made.

And this is the real crisis confronting us. It is this crisis that should make us all afraid: "For the wrath of God is revealed from heaven against all ungodliness and unrighteousness of men, who by their unrighteousness suppress the truth" (Rom 1:18). Only against this backdrop can we be struck by the force of that precious title, "Friend of Sinners."

Chapter 3

EYES TOWARD HEAVEN

Why do we fear God? First and foremost, because of *who he is*. Anything that is good, true, or beautiful in this world is but a reflection of God. To fasten our love upon or place our faith in anything or anyone less than the Author of all good gifts is not only an offense to God; it is also unreasonable, living against the grain of reality (Rom 1:25). Fearing or loving idols contradicts our own best interests. After luring us with their semblance of goodness, truth, and beauty—a false sublime—these idols slowly but surely chew us up and spit us out.

One day, the Lord will return to judge the living and the dead. All who sought justification, acceptance, peace, and security from their idols will be thrown into confusion when they discover that only Christ, the God-Human, restores his sinful brothers and sisters to the Father. We also fear God, therefore, because he will take his throne one day on the earth to judge the living and the dead. The prophets call this "the day of the LORD."

Let us go back to the eighth century before Christ. It was a significant time of change for many nations. The first Olympiad occurred in 776. Homer's *Iliad* and *Odyssey* are dated toward the end of this period. The Neo-Assyrian Empire was rapidly expanding and would soon add Israel to its ever-growing list of conquered people. However, just before that fateful event we have the reign of Uzziah of Judah and Jeroboam II of Israel. Israel and Judah are at peace with each other—a rarity during this time—and, worse, they have both become conceited. They have developed a false sense of security and are seeking self-fulfillment rather than pursuing the Lord. An unknown shepherd from Tekoa, five miles from Bethlehem, is sent by God to call his people to repentance—before disaster overtakes them.

God first pronounces disaster upon the nations, and then turns his judgment toward Israel and Judah. Three times a "woe!" (that is, a curse) is pronounced by the prophet Amos, each woe focusing on a different charge God brings against Israel for its broken covenant. The people are cursed for: (1) thoughtless and paganized (though cheerful) worship, while oppressing others in their daily life (5:18–27); (2) complacency (6:1–3); and (3) self-indulgence and self-righteousness (6:4–7). These woes are quickly followed by the announcement of coming destruction (vv. 8–14).

God has his day in court with Israel, prosecuting the nation's social injustice (4:1–3). But all of this social and personal sin is caused ultimately by the false religion and worship of the people. The first table of the law (loving God) is the foundation for the second (loving neighbor). God's description of the nation's false religion is shockingly similar to Paul's description of false worship in later times, as "having the appearance of godliness, but denying its power" (2 Tim 3:5).

Moreover, the nation refuses correction (Amos 4:6–13). In spite of God's repeated shots across the bow, Israel refuses to listen or change course. So God composes a lamentation:

> The virgin of Israel has fallen;
> She will rise no more.

> She lies forsaken on her land;
> There is no one to raise her up.

For thus says the Lord God:

> "The city that goes out by a thousand
> Shall have a hundred left,
> And that which goes out by a hundred
> Shall have ten left to the house of Israel"
> (5:1–3 NKJV).

Even in her own land, Israel is an alien.

Turning from prosecution to pleading, the Judge cries out, "Seek the Lord and live!" (5:4–15). This is a gracious invitation, that even in captivity God is the Savior of all who simply call on his name. "It may be that the Lord, the God of hosts, will be gracious to the remnant of Joseph" (5:15). "It may be" is a frequent phrase in the prophetic books. Free and sovereign in his mercy, God is not obligated to save anyone. Nevertheless, as God says, he may be gracious "to the *remnant* of Joseph." Even if the nation as a whole forsakes him, God will ensure that there is a remnant chosen by grace, even to the end of time (see also Rom 11:2–5).

After a time of reprieve for repentance, we finally come to the Judge's verdict (5:16–6:14). This final judgment is often called in Scripture "the Day of the Lord." The people go around talking about "the Day of the Lord" as if it were an event they should be eagerly anticipating. Israel's enemies will be defeated, the nation will be vindicated, and there will be peace and prosperity. But there is a problem. It's not only the wicked enemies of Israel that God has in his sights. *God's own people* have failed to take him seriously. "There is no fear of God before their eyes" (Rom 3:18).

So why do the people imagine that God's descent in judgment

will be a good day for them? The people of God assumed God was on *their side*—something like a national mascot. After all, they had God's Word, his law. They heard it regularly. But did they? Really? A day after hearing it read they were back at their old ways, living as if God didn't exist and thinking he would not notice their immoral, idolatrous, and unjust ways. Claiming moral superiority because of their "Judeo-Christian values" (or at least the Judeo part), they were only making their judgment that much greater. They were treating God lightly, failing to take him at his word and blaspheming his name by their hypocrisy. Paul makes exactly the same point in Romans 2:

> Do you suppose, O man—you who judge those who practice such things and yet do them yourself—that you will escape the judgment of God? . . . [Y]ou then who teach others, do you not teach yourself? While you preach against stealing, do you steal? You who say that one must not commit adultery, do you commit adultery? You who abhor idols, do you rob temples? You who boast in the law dishonor God by breaking the law. For, as it is written, "The name of God is blasphemed among the Gentiles because of you." (vv. 3, 21–24)

Israel and Judah have not abandoned temple worship—far from it! They love the ritual, the sacrifices, and the songs. It's all a very patriotic thing, as they celebrate Israel as the apple of God's eye. But there is no fear of God before their eyes. Like Adam, cast out of Eden, Israel will soon be cast out of God's land "and I will send you into exile beyond Damascus" (Amos 5:27). Nobody believed God when he spoke this through Amos, because at this point Assyria wasn't a threat. But we see this fulfillment recorded in 2 Kings 17.

Centuries later, John the Baptist came preparing the way for the Judge to descend and hold court himself (Matt 3:1–12). The Messiah's cataclysmic intervention into history consists of two principal actions: redemption and judgment, his first and second advents. As the culmination of all the past "days of the LORD," this Day of the Lord dawns with Christmas and reaches its afternoon heat in the final judgment. "I have not come to judge the world, but to save the world," says Jesus (cf. John 3:17). But John's preparatory ministry is not to announce salvation, but to proclaim the separation of the wheat from the chaff. If his hearers do not repent, the Day of the Lord will consume them. "Repent, for the kingdom of heaven is at hand!" (Matt 3:2). After centuries of the people demanding another monarch, God is finally Israel's King again. Whereas John's message was, "The kingdom is near," Jesus's message was, "The kingdom is here!" (cf. Luke 17:20–21). For a time it is a kingdom of grace, barely noticed by the world, but one day it will be a kingdom of glory. The judgment placed in the hands of the incarnate Son will be decisive: salvation for all who trust in him and death for all who reject him.

For the time being, we are living in the period described in Scripture as "the day of salvation" *before* "the Day of the LORD." "[I] must work the works of him who sent me while it is day," Jesus said, for "[the] night is coming, when no one can work. As long as I am in the world, I am the light of the world" (John 9:4–5). And yet, because he has ascended and sent his Holy Spirit to make us his people, we too are the light of the world. The concentric circles of judgment that we read about in Amos (the nations, Moab, Judah, Israel) are reversed in redemption (Jerusalem, Judea, Samaria, and the uttermost parts of the earth).

Today we are living in the daylight, and this can similarly give opportunity for the rise of the false security that marked the church of Amos's day and of Jerusalem in our Lord's time. As in the days of Noah, "the great and awesome day of the LORD," as Joel called it, will come by surprise (Joel 2:31; cf. 1 Pet 3:20; Matt 24:37–39; Luke 17:26). Don't mistake God's kindness and patience as a sign that he is either unable or unwilling to unleash his wrath. Even now, there may be some reading this who have lived around Noah's ark all your life, so to speak. You have camped around it and played in its shadow and on its scaffolding, even as this barge of salvation was being built. But you have never entered the ark. Like an old coin, your religion is something you carry around in your pocket. It even has an image of Christ, but this image has lost its embossing and is now faded. That coin is familiar to you—so familiar that the Day of the Lord sounds like pie-in-the-sky thinking. "[Know] this first of all," says Peter, "scoffers will come in the last days with scoffing, following their own sinful desires. They will say, 'Where is the promise of his coming?'" (2 Pet 3:3–4). Like rain falling into a dammed lake, danger hardly seems imminent, but when the Judge appears and the dam breaks, all who are not safely hidden in the ark of Christ's body will be swept into the fiery lake whose smoke rises forever.

Before the assembly of philosophers in Athens, the apostle Paul boldly declared, "The times of ignorance God overlooked, but now he commands all people everywhere to repent, because he has fixed a day on which he will judge the world in righteousness by a man whom he has appointed; and of this he has given assurance to all by raising him from the dead" (Acts 17:30–31). Let us all take to heart Paul's warning that "the day of the Lord will come like a thief in the night. While people are saying, 'Peace and safety,' destruction will come on them suddenly, as labor pains on a pregnant woman, and they will not escape" (1 Thess 5:2–3 NIV). Let us heed these warnings as they lead us into the fear of the Lord and the reception of his mercy, because comfort will quickly follow. The God of awful and holy majesty also reveals himself as the God of grace:

> But you, brothers and sisters, are not in darkness so that this day should surprise you like a thief. You are all children of the light and children of the day. We do not belong to the night or to the darkness. So then, let us not be like others, who are asleep, but let us be awake and sober. For those who sleep, sleep at night, and those who get drunk, get drunk at night. But since we belong to the day, let us be sober, putting on faith and love as a breastplate, and the hope of salvation as a helmet. For God did not appoint us to suffer wrath but to receive salvation through our Lord Jesus Christ. He died for us so that, whether we are awake or asleep, we may live together with him. Therefore encourage one another and build each other up, just as in fact you are doing. (1 Thess 5:4–11 NIV)

Let us not presume that because of the Lord's mercy judgment is indefinitely postponed. We must not sleep, but rather be awake and sober, building one another up in the twofold reality of coming judgment and our merciful salvation in the Lord.

Recovering Our Sanity

For a long time I have been struck by the conversion of Nebuchadnezzar in Daniel 4. It's sometime during the 570s BC, in what is today known as Iraq. Nebuchadnezzar II had just achieved several mighty victories across the region, vanquishing Egypt, Jerusalem, and, most recently, conquering Tyre and plundering its wealth. Babylon is now more than a great city; it is the world superpower, now holding the place that Egypt and Assyria once had in the region. Like Adam and Judah, Babylon is recalcitrant, wanting to be the ultimate sovereign rather than the servant of Yahweh. Yet, from God's perspective Nebuchadnezzar is his to command, designated "my servant" (Jer 25:9; 27:6) by the Lord. He is not autonomous, nor is he able to challenge or change God's purposes. Even while Nebuchadnezzar is the enemy of God and his people, God is at work fulfilling his plans through him.

Eventually, Babylon exceeds God's mandate of measured judgment of Judah in exile and the saints sing joyfully of Babylon's downfall in the future, in terms that echo her own treatment at Nebuchadnezzar's hands (Jer 50:2). Isaiah highlights Babylon's pretensions to universal sovereignty by personifying the nation in terms reminiscent of Lucifer: "You said in your heart, / 'I will ascend to heaven; / I will raise my throne / above the stars of God; / I will sit on the mount of assembly / on the heights of Zaphon; / I will ascend to the tops of the clouds, / I will make myself like the Most High'" (Isa 14:13–14 NRSV). But Yahweh has the last laugh: "'But you are brought down to Sheol, / to the depths of the Pit'" (v. 15).

Nebuchadnezzar is shamelessly narcissistic, setting up a huge gold statue and demanding that when the band plays everyone fall to the ground and worship this image. Shadrach, Meshach, and Abednego refuse to do this and are thrown in the fiery furnace, but God joins them there and none are even singed. At this point, Nebuchadnezzar seems to acknowledge the power of Israel's God, but he retains for himself the presumed sovereignty of an autocrat: "Therefore I make a decree: Any people, nation, or language that utters blasphemy against the God of Shadrach, Meshach, and Abednego shall be torn limb from limb, and their houses laid in ruins; for there is no other god who is able to deliver in this way" (Dan 3:29 NRSV).

If Yahweh is in control of nature, as demonstrated in the fiery furnace, then surely he has "the whole world in his hands." It's ironic. While the people of God had forgotten the signs and wonders he performed for them long ago and were eventually carried into Babylonian captivity, the king of Babylon actually does see and recognize these mighty works. God delivers his people who call on his name, so one had better be among those who call on his name. There is no hint that Nebuchadnezzar wanted to switch mascots to make Babylon great again (it was already great) or to find some additional moral uplift and peace of mind—God simply showed up and proved his incomparable majesty. Yet, still, Nebuchadnezzar himself is "large and in charge," as they say.

Then the king has his second dream and calls Daniel to interpret it. Nebuchadnezzar had seen a great and strong tree with its top reaching to heaven, visible to the whole earth. He then saw a "holy watcher" (angel) "coming down from heaven and saying, 'Chop down the tree and destroy it, but leave the stump of its roots in the earth, bound with a band of iron and bronze, in the tender grass of the field, and let him be wet with the dew of heaven, and let his portion be with the beasts of the field, till seven periods of time pass over him'" (4:23).

Daniel may well have been thinking, "Don't shoot the messenger," as he explained the meaning of this dream to the king:

> "This is the interpretation, O king: It is a decree of the Most High, which has come upon my lord the king, that you shall be driven from among men, and your dwelling shall be with the beasts of the field. You shall be made to eat grass like an ox, and you shall be wet with the dew of heaven, and seven periods of time shall pass over you, till you know that the Most High rules the kingdom of men and gives it to whom he will. And as it was commanded to leave the stump of the roots of the tree, your kingdom shall be confirmed for you from the time that you know that Heaven rules. Therefore, O king, let my counsel be acceptable to you: break off your sins by practicing righteousness, and your iniquities by showing mercy to the oppressed, that there may perhaps be a lengthening of your prosperity." (vv. 24–27)

King Nebuchadnezzar experienced the complete fulfillment of this prophecy. On exactly the day God had appointed, "he was walking on the roof of the royal palace of Babylon," crowing, "'Is not this great Babylon, which I have built by my mighty power as a royal residence and for the glory of my majesty?'"

> While the words were still in the king's mouth, there fell a voice from heaven, "O King Nebuchadnezzar, to you it is spoken: The kingdom has departed from you, and you shall be driven from among men, and your dwelling shall be with the beasts of the field. And you shall be made to eat grass like an ox, and seven periods of time shall pass over you, until you know that the Most High rules the kingdom of men and gives it to whom he will." Immediately the word was fulfilled against Nebuchadnezzar. He was driven from among men and ate grass like an ox, and his body was wet with the dew of heaven till his hair grew as long as eagles' feathers, and his nails were like birds' claws. (vv. 28–33)

For some, this may bring to mind the story of Howard Hughes, proud Hollywood mogul and captain of the aviation industry. Though he was numbered among the rich and powerful, the stress became too great for him and he lost his sanity, living out the rest of his life in secret hotel rooms covered in plastic, fearful of germs. His hair and fingernails went uncut and he lived the rest of his days in total isolation from society, away from business partners and the famous stars who had basked in his sunlight.

Even more recent analogies to Nebuchadnezzar's experience can be found, of course. But my point is that this is *all* of us. Living against the grain of reality is the epitome of insanity. Not accepting reality makes us crazy. No matter how things appear, the reality is that from God's vantage point we are all ants scurrying here and there, sometimes leading but mostly following, imagining that our brief life is about us.

But, as I said, this is a story of conversion. It turns out well in the end for Nebuchadnezzar:

> At the end of the days I, Nebuchadnezzar, lifted my eyes to heaven, and my reason returned to me, and I blessed the Most High, and praised and honored him who lives forever,
>
> for his dominion is an everlasting dominion,
> and his kingdom endures from generation to generation;
> all the inhabitants of the earth are accounted as nothing,
> and he does according to his will among the host of heaven
> and among the inhabitants of the earth;
> and none can stay his hand
> or say to him, "What have you done?"
>
> At the same time my reason returned to me, and for the glory of my kingdom, my majesty and splendor returned to me. My counselors and my lords sought me, and I was established in my kingdom, and still more greatness was added to me. Now I, Nebuchadnezzar, praise and extol and honor the King of heaven, for all his works are right and his ways are just; and those who walk in pride he is able to humble. (vv. 34–37)

When Nebuchadnezzar gave in to his narcissistic tendencies, focusing attention on himself and demanding that everyone else do the same, he lost his sanity. Yes, this was a direct divine judgment in this case, but it also happens naturally whenever we try to live against the grain of reality.

Americans are known for the rugged individualism that built a great nation. Yet the dark side of that individualism is a tendency for each of us to become a little Nebuchadnezzar. Walt Whitman represents this spirit in his poem, "Song of Myself":

> I CELEBRATE myself, and sing myself,
> And what I assume you shall assume,
> For every atom belonging to me as good belongs
>   to you. . . .
>
> Creeds and schools in abeyance,
> Retiring back a while sufficed at what they are, but
>   never forgotten,
> I harbor for good or bad, I permit to speak at every
>   hazard,
> Nature without check with original energy. . . .
>   [Section 1]
>
> Divine am I inside and out, and I make holy
>   whatever I touch or am touch'd from,
> The scent of these arm-pits aroma finer than prayer,
> This head more than churches, bibles, and all
>   the creeds.
>
> If I worship one thing more than another it shall be
>   the spread of my own body, or any part of it,
> Translucent mould of me it shall be you! . . .
>
> I dote on myself, there is that lot of me and all
>   so luscious,

Each moment and whatever happens thrills me
with joy,
I cannot tell how my ankles bend, nor whence the
cause of my faintest wish,
Nor the cause of the friendship I emit, nor the cause
of the friendship I take again.

That I walk up my stoop, I pause to consider if it
really be,
A morning-glory at my window satisfies me more
than the metaphysics of books. . . . [Section 24]

I know perfectly well my own egotism,
Know my omnivorous lines and must not write
any less,
And would fetch you whoever you are flush with
myself. . . .

Sermons, creeds, theology—but the fathomless
human brain,
And what is reason? and what is love? and what is
life? . . . [Section 42]

I ascend from the moon, I ascend from the night,
I perceive that the ghastly glimmer is noonday
sunbeams reflected,
And debouch to the steady and central from the
offspring great or small. [Section 49][1]

Whitman captures so well the insane self-centeredness of Nebuchadnezzar—a narcissism that is endemic to humanity. Yet Nebuchadnezzar repents, and with eyes turned away from himself and upward to God, the king acknowledges reality and his sanity is returned to him. It was never primarily an issue of his power or wealth (although these can be temptations). But the real issue was his heart. He failed to acknowledge his prosperity as a gift to be stewarded wisely on behalf of his people, seeing it instead as a personal achievement and his own property—Nebuchadnezzar Empire, Inc. He did not look up to God in faith or outward to his neighbors in love, but his vision had turned inward. His period of humiliation may seem to us a rather extreme medicine, but it worked. The Lord brought him back to sanity by graciously helping him to realize he was not the center of the universe. And the king praised God for exactly those things he had before attributed to himself: an eternal, universal, and sovereign dominion. And notice that he adds to his praises that it is also a *gracious* dominion (Dan 4:37). I wonder how that radical, sanity-giving, reality-embracing fear of God changed Nebuchadnezzar's manner the next day. Instead of throwing his weight around, with servants cowering in the corner, he must have seen himself now on their level before God. This is what happens when we look *outside of ourselves*: up to God in faith and out to our neighbors in love. Reconciliation occurs—first with God, and then with each other. That's sanity.

The book of Daniel unfolds the prophecy of the great civilizations of this world, each falling to the next, until one day the kingdom that cannot be shaken buries the last, the vast Roman Empire. This kingdom rises not by arms and propaganda, but by the reign of Christ the Messiah through his Word and Spirit to the ends of the earth. Along with Ezekiel, Daniel is in many ways the template for the book of Revelation.

God makes pagan nations his allies in bringing down Israel and Judah in their pride, then brings these allies low when they break away in their own arrogance. Yet there is a surprising note of grace even in the midst of this humiliation. There is conversion, repentance, and deliverance—even for the wicked. This will happen on a global scale in the future kingdom of the Messiah, with a highway uniting Assyria, Babylon, and Israel and all three peoples being named the "people of God"—even those who were originally "no people" (Isa 19:24–25; cf. Hos 2:23).

In the short term, the Persian Empire under Cyrus would conquer Babylon and send a remnant of the Jewish exiles back to Jerusalem to rebuild its ruins—with supplies, including gold, for the rebuilding of the temple. It is God's promise, rooted all the way back in Genesis 3:15, that keeps history moving forward in spite of his unfaithful servants. One day, we learn, there will be a king greater than Cyrus—in fact, greater than David—who will build the end-time temple made without hands. He will humble the haughty and comfort those who mourn in exile. After listing in detail the genealogy from Abraham to the deportation to Babylon and from there to Christ, Matthew says, "So all the generations from Abraham to David were fourteen generations, and from David to the deportation to Babylon fourteen generations, and from the deportation to Babylon to the Christ fourteen generations" (Matt 1:17). We see God's grand plan moving forward to accomplish his purposes.

When a young woman in Nazareth received the astonishing news that she would bear no less than God incarnate, this promise of a true King whose dominion is eternal, universal, and gracious was realized. Stringing together various passages of Scripture she likely knew by heart, Mary exclaimed,

> "My soul magnifies the Lord,
> and my spirit rejoices in God my Savior,
> for he has looked on the humble estate of his
> servant.

For behold, from now on all generations will call
me blessed;
for he who is mighty has done great things for me,
and holy is his name.
And his mercy is for those who fear him
from generation to generation.
He has shown strength with his arm;
he has scattered the proud in the thoughts of
their hearts;
he has brought down the mighty from their thrones
and exalted those of humble estate;
he has filled the hungry with good things,
and the rich he has sent away empty.
He has helped his servant Israel,
in remembrance of his mercy,
as he spoke to our fathers,
to Abraham and to his offspring forever."
(Luke 1:46–55)

Unlike Whitman's "Song of Myself," Mary's "Magnificat" was an anthem of praise to the God who kept his promise.

As Nebuchadnezzar learned the hard way, the fear of God is sanity—it is taking God seriously. Like the ancient king of Babylon, many of our neighbors assume that the *real world* is godless. They believe there is no story except the one we write for ourselves. We are the author of our own script, giving ourselves the starring role. Religion is the *illusory world* invented once upon a time to control the masses or provide some inner peace. People can believe whatever they want about this inner, illusory world, as long as they accept that in the real world there is no God who lives and acts and intervenes in history, who is Lord of nature, and who works everything around his purposes for his own glory. However, the story of Nebuchadnezzar reminds us that we have things reversed. The *real world* is the one in which the triune God is the central character in nature and history, and the illusion is that we're in charge. It's autonomy that is the myth—and the sooner we raise our eyes to heaven, the sooner our sanity will be restored.

Chapter 4

THE WISDOM IN FEAR

It takes a lot of good words to indicate what *fear* means in relation to God. And one of these good words is "sublime," to which I alluded earlier. Have you ever stood on a bridge over a massive waterfall, wondering what would happen if you jumped and were swept away? On the plains of the Masai Mara in Africa, from a jeep a yard or two away, I watched, listened, and even smelled with terrified wonder as eight lionesses took down a zebra with incredible force. Prior to modern technology, people had a deeper and more routine sense of the sublime—such as in magnificent lightning storms. When everything is ordinary and within our ability to comprehend and manage, we can choose what we will do. We are, for the most part, in control, and there is no need to fear anything. We can choose to hold something close or keep it at arm's length. We can drive away our fears by explaining its natural causes. But when we experience the sublime, we become aware that we are fragile, tiny, and insignificant. We sense that we could as easily be the prey as the partner in a shared experience.

There is a wonderful feeling of the sublime in a poignant scene of C. S. Lewis's *The Silver Chair*. Eagerly following a rushing sound after hours of searching for water, young Jill has finally discovered a stream, but she is startled by the presence of the Lion, Aslan, guarding it.

> "Are you not thirsty?" said the Lion.
>
> "I'm *dying* of thirst," said Jill.
>
> "Then drink," said the Lion.
>
> "May I—could I—would you mind going away while I do?" said Jill.
>
> The Lion answered this only by a look and a very low growl. And as Jill gazed at its motionless bulk, she realized that she might as well have asked the whole mountain to move aside for her convenience.
>
> The delicious rippling noise of the stream was driving her nearly frantic.
>
> "Will you promise not to—do anything to me, if I do come?" said Jill.
>
> "I make no promise," said the Lion.
>
> Jill was so thirsty now that, without noticing it, she had come a step nearer.
>
> "*Do* you eat girls?" she said.
>
> "I have swallowed up girls and boys, women and men, kings and emperors, cities and realms," said the Lion. It didn't say this as if it were boasting, nor as if it were sorry, nor as if it were angry. It just said it.
>
> "I daren't come and drink," said Jill.
>
> "Then you will die of thirst," said the Lion.
>
> "Oh dear!" said Jill, coming another step nearer. "I suppose I must go and look for another stream then."
>
> "There is no other stream," said the Lion.[1]

Meeting the sublime is not something you could have planned for, because you are not in control of the situation. Preachers can *tell* us to fear God, and Scripture certainly *commands* this appropriate response. Nevertheless, we only fear God when we *experience* him. As God reveals his character in narratives and unpacks them through doctrinal exposition, wisdom, prayer, and praise, we lose our sense of being in charge and surrender to the reality of the majestic Mystery. Fear is not something that we conjure in ourselves but is the natural response to a supernatural presence. And God is present with us *in mercy* in his Word and sacraments.

In this scene from *The Silver Chair*, Jill is certainly caught between a rock and a hard place. Her natural response would be to flee, but she knows that she cannot outrun the Lion. Besides, she knows that she needs the water. Similarly, we are caught between the dreadful majesty of God and our own need for salvation. C. S. Lewis tells us that the Lion disclosed his power, not as if it were boasting, "nor as if it were sorry, nor as if it were angry. It just said it."

God is not like the Wizard of Oz, who turns out to be an old man manipulating smoke and mirrors behind a curtain to scare everyone into submission. I enjoy occasionally jumping out in front of my kids to startle them, but it is not like that with God. He does not *try* to frighten us; it is just who he is: utterly unique, singularly beautiful, good and powerful, majestic, and shrouded in an unfathomable depth of glory whose mere outer rays blind us unless he condescends to meet us clothed in our language and, eventually, our humanity.

This experience of God as sublime is reflected over and over again in Scripture, and it is marked by paradox. There are many things that instill fear in us because they are evil or simply threatening. The sublime, however, is different. It simultaneously attracts and repels. It is the beauty and light that is overwhelming, not ugliness or darkness. With God we encounter a power that could destroy us but can also save us from destroyers. There is a purity of righteousness, holiness, justice, goodness, and love that simultaneously beckons and scares us. God is our problem, but he is also our solution. Though with one strike he could end our life, he protects those who take refuge in him like a mother bear protects her cub.

It is this paradoxical reality that we find in Hebrews 12:28–29: "Therefore let us be grateful for receiving a kingdom that cannot be shaken, and thus let us offer to God acceptable worship, with reverence and awe, for our God is a consuming fire." We fear God because he is not like us. We do not comprehend him, so we cannot manage him. We cannot anticipate his actions in this relationship, apart from what he deigns to tell us in his Word along the journey. We cannot fathom his plans:

> Oh, the depth of the riches and wisdom and knowledge of God! How unsearchable are his judgments and how inscrutable his ways!
>
> "For who has known the mind of the Lord,
> or who has been his counselor?"
> "Or who has given a gift to him
> that he might be repaid?"
>
> For from him and through him and to him are all things. To him be glory forever. Amen. (Rom 11:33–36)

Two Words of Wisdom: The Law and the Gospel

As Paul tells us in Romans 1 and 2, there is a wisdom God has planted in our human nature. Many of the biblical proverbs find parallels in non-biblical literature. But the highest wisdom comes not from "looking around" or "looking within," but from being driven outside of ourselves—what we feel, assume, imagine, or do—by just hearing God's Word, especially his gospel. Here there is no speculation—no more chattering within ourselves about what we might believe. The gospel is a strange announcement of news brought from a herald. It's based not on timeless principles but on the resurrection of the God-Man in history. "So faith comes from hearing, and hearing through the word of Christ" (Rom 10:17). It is not something you ascend to attain or descend to bring up from the dead (vv. 3–16).

The external Word comes to us through a herald communicating the most concrete thing of all: God in a manger and hanging on a cross. That is why "the cross is folly to those who are perishing," as Paul says in 1 Corinthians 1:18. "Where is the one who is wise? Where is the scribe? Where is the debater of this age? Has not God made foolish the wisdom of the world?" (v. 20). Paul is not here taking back everything he has previously said about Gentiles being aware of general revelation. Nor is he rejecting the wisdom that the Spirit himself distributes to pagans in his common grace. Rather, he is saying that even though the *law* makes sense to our human wisdom, the *gospel* does not. It is a foolish message to our ears.

It seems ridiculous to say that God justifies the wicked. Paul knew this firsthand, as confirmed by the published critiques of Christianity by Roman philosophers. But the religious leaders of Israel had also come to find it offensive, despite the testimony of Abraham (Gen 15:6) and numerous other passages. And yet, God's "foolishness" has turned out to be wiser than the greatest philosopher. After all, Christ is not the greatest philosopher who ever lived, but is the Redeemer who actually brought salvation from death and hell. "And because of him you are in Christ Jesus, who became to us wisdom from God, righteousness and sanctification and redemption, so that, as it is written, 'Let the one who boasts, boast in the Lord'" (1 Cor 1:30–31).

"The fear of the LORD is the beginning of wisdom" (Prov 9:10). As we've seen in Romans 1 and 2, the root of human rebellion is that "they exchanged the truth about God for a lie" (Rom 1:25). Gentiles became proud. No longer thankful for receiving their existence outside of themselves, as Paul says, "their foolish hearts were darkened" (v. 21). "Claiming to be wise, they became fools" (v. 22), looking for rest in someone or something other than the only God who made them for himself. And the tragedy in Paul's day was that his own people, Abraham's physical descendants, had done the same.

The fear of God—reverence for his name, the humility of a covenant servant rather than an autonomous master—is the beginning of true piety. It reveals God's existence and character. But it is not enough. By itself, in fact, it is the blinding glory of God's holy majesty that holds us accountable and sentences us to death. God's law doesn't reveal God's *saving* will in Jesus Christ. Paul continues his argument in Romans:

> Now we know that whatever the law says it speaks to those who are under the law, so that every mouth may be stopped, and the whole world may be held accountable to God. For by works of the law no human being will be justified in his sight, since through the law comes knowledge of sin.
>
> But now the righteousness of God has been manifested apart from the law, although the Law and the Prophets bear witness to it—the righteousness of God through faith in Jesus Christ for all who believe. For there is no distinction: for all have sinned and fall short of the glory of God, and are justified by his grace as a gift, through the redemption that is in Christ Jesus, whom God put forward as a propitiation by his blood,

> to be received by faith. This was to show God's righteousness, because in his divine forbearance he had passed over former sins. It was to show his righteousness at the present time, so that he might be just and the justifier of the one who has faith in Jesus. (Rom 3:19–26)

This is why Paul could say that Christ is the summit of true wisdom in 1 Corinthians 1:30. He not only instructs us in righteousness, but he *is* our righteousness; he not only inculcates holiness by his example, but *is* our holiness. He not only shows us the path to the good life, but he *is* our immortality.

The fear of God which leads us to faith in Christ is not mere abject terror, but is inseparably rooted in how God reaches out to us: "If you, O LORD, should mark iniquities, O Lord, who could stand? But with you there is *forgiveness, that you may be feared*" (Ps 130:3–4, emphasis mine). Not only by reason of our creation, preservation, and all the blessings of this life; not only because of his righteousness, holiness, justice, and majesty, but *because of his forgiveness*, God is feared above all the idols.

What is your greatest fear? Even if it could be relieved, could it relieve the burden of your guilt before a holy God? None of our idols can do this.

And that is the fear that haunts us most, whether we are aware of it or not.

Better Settle for God's Backside

After his friendship with God had blossomed on Mount Sinai, Moses asked God to show him his glory. Yet it is precisely because God favors Moses that he will not fulfill his request. Instead of his *glory*, God says, "I will make all my *goodness* pass before you and will *proclaim* before you my name, 'The LORD.' And I will be gracious to whom I will be gracious, and will show mercy on whom I will show mercy" (Exod 33:19, emphasis mine). God's glory is a manifestation of his attributes, but because his majesty can only terrify mortal creatures (and sinners even more so), God preaches the gospel of his gracious and merciful freedom to save whomever he chooses. It is not a vision of glory, but a gospel proclaimed, that Moses is capable of enduring. "But," God said, "you cannot see my face, for man shall not see me and live" (v. 20).

Of course, God is pure spirit, omnipresent; he does not have a body or a face. Yet "face" here represents his essence: God as he is in himself. God's essence cannot be penetrated by finite creatures, and even if it could, anyone beholding it would be incinerated. "And the LORD said, 'Behold, there is a place by me where you shall stand on the rock, and while my glory passes by I will put you in a cleft of the rock, and I will cover you with my hand until I have passed by. Then I will take away my hand, and you shall see my back, but my face shall not be seen'" (vv. 21–23). Just as his face represents God's hidden majesty, his backside represents the humbler revelation of himself in his goodness and grace.

The slightest brush with God's majesty fills us with dread, and this is the beginning of all wisdom. Then God condescends to reveal his favor—his gospel—and this is the consummation of all wisdom. Christ is the cleft of the rock in whom we are hidden to behold God's grace in the preaching of the gospel. Veiling his glory in the humility of our flesh, he made it possible for people to see, hear, touch, and be touched by God himself. One day this same divine Stranger, rather than send soldiers to spill their blood for his empire, would plunge the sword into his own heart for the redemption of his army, making them co-heirs of his estate. And one day in the future he will return with the sword of judgment for all the nations (Rev 19:11–16). Anyone who has trouble with the "God of the Old Testament" will have the same difficulty with Jesus—even though he is the Lamb who was slain, he is also the returning king who will destroy his enemies.

In his incarnation the eternal Son shielded us from his majesty. In fact, Isaiah prophesied of him, "he had no form or majesty that we should look at him, and no beauty that we should desire him" (Isa 53:2). What sort of divine king is this, who is "despised and rejected" (v. 3)? He could have come in majesty, but that would have been to our doom—the final judgment. Instead, in mercy he came to us for salvation, calling sinners tenderly to himself. "The Son of Man came not to be served but to serve, and to give his life as a ransom for many" (Matt 20:28).

Yet even in this descent to us, in our humanity, Jesus provoked fear: "What sort of man is this, that even winds and sea obey him?" (Matt 8:27). And when Jesus filled two boats with fish, Peter did not celebrate or ask Jesus to be his business partner, but responded, "Depart from me, for I am a sinful man, O Lord" (Luke 5:8). Upon news of his resurrection, the women ran to tell the apostles. "So they departed quickly from the tomb with fear and great joy, and ran to tell his disciples" (Matt 28:8). Notice the mixed emotions: "fear and great joy." Have you ever been so astonished at a totally overwhelming phenomenon that you were fearful and joyful at the same time?

Jesus was the anointed Messiah on whom the Holy Spirit descended. Notice the effect of the Spirit's work in Christ's ministry, as prophesied in Isaiah 11:

> There shall come forth a shoot from the stump
>   of Jesse,
>   and a branch from his roots shall bear fruit.
> And the Spirit of the LORD shall rest upon him,
>   the Spirit of wisdom and understanding,

> the Spirit of counsel and might,
> the Spirit of knowledge and the fear of the LORD.
> And his delight shall be in the fear of the LORD.
> (vv. 1–3)

Jesus is also a true and faithful human, the Last Adam, who is exactly the sort of person we were all created to be, God's faithful covenant partner. And the evidence of his Spirit-endowed wisdom was *the fear of God.*

Fear is the beginning of wisdom and knowledge. If you come to know God, the true and living God, your first response will be fear. You are astonished at how unlike anyone or anything he is. You do not have the intellectual, psychological, moral, or emotional equipment to handle, much less explain, it. You are not in charge. You realize that you have not discovered God; he has discovered you. He knows you inside and out. You now know, not just intellectually but deep in your heart, that you are a sinner in the presence of the holy God. It's disorienting because it's not what your "little voice within" would ever tell you.

And there is nowhere to flee from this disorienting encounter. This fear, though, leads us to the acknowledgement that we need a mediator—someone to intercede for us and to reconcile us to God. Christ himself *is* this "wisdom from God, righteousness and sanctification and redemption, so that, as it is written, 'Let the one who boasts, boast in the Lord'" (1 Cor 1:30–31). In his incarnation we catch a glimpse of God's "backward parts" in hearing the news of God's goodness and mercy.

If the fear of God is the beginning of wisdom, then the fear of God's righteous judgment is the beginning of the wisdom that leads to salvation. God's law, which in many ways simply echoes what we know by nature as God's image-bearers, helps us begin to realize that we are not wise. God's gospel, known only by special revelation through the prophets and apostles, reveals *Christ*—specifically, "Christ and him crucified" (1 Cor 2:2)—as *the* "wisdom from God." There is no higher wisdom than the gospel.

The Number One Reason We Reject Wisdom

It is only reasonable to pay the highest respect to the ultimate source of life and death—the one who is sovereign over us and over all things. And the strangeness of God, his absolute difference from us, overwhelms us with a sense of distance. The reality of our sinfulness also confronts us: we find his holiness threatening not merely because we are mere creatures, but because we are unholy. We're scared. The fear of the sovereign, the stranger, and the adversary all converge in our relationship to God. This mother of all fears is often buried deep beneath a mound of false securities.

This does not always seem very "reasonable." So, losing our sanity, we lessen the awareness we all have of God's holiness and arrogantly exalt ourselves. Deep down, everyone knows there is a good and righteous God *and* that we are guilty before him. This is why there is religion—of whatever sort you may prefer—with its doctrines of karma and laws and rituals for appeasement. Sacrifices must be offered, "scapegoats" must be found to deflect our sins from ourselves, and works must be done. This is why bloodthirsty Molech demanded the sacrifice of infants and Incas long ago abandoned their children atop high volcanoes to placate the lofty gods. Even today highly educated people will sacrifice unborn children and make scapegoats of either Jews and other ethnic minorities or the poor, the immigrants, the diseased, and the moral outcasts. It is why we make resolutions to do *x* if God will do *y*. We think that we can manage God's judgment.

What we have here is a proper and even natural fear of God,

but instead of this leading us to acknowledge God's analysis of our plight and the solution for it, we make up our own story that downplays the seriousness of both God's holiness and our sinfulness. We have to be the star of our own life movie. So, individually and collectively, we invent "religion" and "spirituality" as ways of avoiding reality. We're just talking ourselves into one scheme or another, seeking to build elaborate castles in the air. In contrast, God's objective testimony *is* reliable:

> Then the kings of the earth and the great ones and the generals and the rich and the powerful, and everyone, slave and free, hid themselves in the caves and among the rocks of the mountains, calling to the mountains and rocks, "Fall on us and hide us from the face of him who is seated on the throne, and from the wrath of the Lamb, for the great day of their wrath has come, and who can stand?" (Rev 6:15–17)

We know this judgment day is coming because God raised Jesus from the dead (Acts 17:30–31).

It may seem strange to say, but the main reason why people are trying desperately to scratch off any trace of God's image, living against the grain of nature, or even tumbling into insanity is simply to sleep at night. They are trying to eradicate the knowledge and fear of God in order to avoid awareness of their accountability before his inevitable judgment.

All of our fears come down to this one: we are afraid of Someone knowing our deepest secrets, cherished transgressions, and failures to fulfill our chief end. I can judge my own life to have been a success—only if there is no God. This fact comes out powerfully in Friedrich Nietzsche's description of what must have been his own character in "The Ugliest Man." In the story, "Zarathustra" (the Persian prophet Zoroaster) discovered a monster of a man. This ugliest man may have been completely destitute, unbathed, and helpless. But he loathed those who looked upon him with pity. And he claimed to have killed god—the most pitying observer of humans.

> But he—*had to* die; he looked with eyes which beheld *everything* —he beheld men's depths and dregs, all his hidden ignominy and ugliness.
>
> His pity knew no modesty; he crept into my dirtiest corners. This most prying, over-intrusive, over-pitiful one had to die.
>
> He ever beheld *me*: on such a witness I would have revenge —or not live myself.
>
> The God who beheld everything, *and also man*: that God had to die! Man cannot *endure* it that such a witness should live.
>
> Thus spake the ugliest man.[2]

Think about this for a moment. Nietzsche is not offering rational or evidential arguments against God's existence. He is saying that the sort of God described in the Bible *cannot* exist because *he will not let such a God live to judge his life.*

Robert J. Lifton, a psychologist and pioneer in brain research, observes that the source of many anxieties and indeed neuroses in society today is a nagging sense of guilt without knowledge of its source.[3] Atheists and liberals tell us that this guilt is just a neurosis, possibly requiring years of "counseling" to come out of this toxic form of religious faith. Such people are a happy sort, who can suppress the truth in unrighteousness and pretend to live in a world that has no correspondence to reality. However, the biblical law puts its finger on the true problem. And only the biblical gospel announces the good news of God's solution. It is certainly true that "perfect love casts out fear" (1 John 4:18), but only because God is the one with perfect love and he has satisfied his justice in his Son. We still fear God as sovereign and as exalted above us in transcendent majesty, but no longer as an adversary. We are not troubled that he knows our dirtiest corners. The very fact that he does—and not only pities us but imputes these sins to himself and imputes his righteousness to us—displays the depth of his merciful heart.

Angels have to assure us, "Fear not," because even in the presence of one of God's creaturely messengers a sinner can expect only bad news. We first encounter God as our Judge, with a sense of awe at his majesty *and* awareness of our guilt. This is the work of his Word *as law*, to arraign us all before God as sinners. But God then surprises us with good news: absolution of our guilt through Christ's life, death, and resurrection. On this basis, we arrive at a healthy fear of God that only increases as we come to know God and his works and experience the Spirit's work in our lives. Only when we really hear God's law in all of its seriousness can we say with Isaiah, "I am undone," and only when we hear the gospel in all of its apparently foolish too-good-to-be-true grandeur do we say, "Lord, be merciful to me, a sinner." As Jesus said, contrasting John the Baptist's mission with his own, the problem is that we don't really know how to mourn over our lost condition *or* dance when the Groom arrives for the wedding (Luke 7:31–34).

Though I've mentioned this several times already, here it may be helpful to clarify the distinction between the law and the gospel. They are both God's speech, his Word, but they do different things. Please notice this: they *do* different things. The law not only describes God's righteousness and judgment and our lost condition; it is also God's speech which actually arraigns us before his throne. We experience the law in our bones. The gospel is God's word, too, but a different one, and through it the Holy Spirit absolves us, giving us the faith to receive the gift.

The Puritans distinguished helpfully between *legal* and

evangelical repentance. Legal repentance is nothing more than being afraid of punishment: "I'd better repent so I can get out of hell." Of course hell is real and everlasting, and fear of God's judgment is part of what presses us to ask, "Then how can I be saved?" In that sense, it is a healthy facing of reality. But by itself this kind of fear is servile: it generates slaves, not sons. Only *evangelical* repentance—that is, the goodness and grace of God in the gospel—can lead us to turn not only from our state of rebellion against God but from clinging to our pretense of righteousness. When we behold the mercy of God in Christ, we melt. We see not only our sins as worthy of condemnation but our good works as a rope of sand—we need to be rescued. God must reach down to us. Faith then embraces Christ with all of his benefits as the only hope.

So, for example, we are told on the one hand, "Fear *not, for* I have redeemed you" (Isa 43:1, emphasis mine) and on the other, "But with you there is forgiveness, *that* you may be *feared*" (Ps 130:4, emphasis mine). It seems like a contradiction at first, right? But "fear" is used in different contexts with different connotations.

The context of Isaiah 43 is a courtroom scene. For forty chapters indictments have been flying around. The verdict has been rendered and Israel stands condemned, sentenced. But in chapter 40, at verse 1, the prophet-lawyer is now directed by the Judge to comfort his people with the good news of how the Judge will reverse that verdict based on *his* own actions. God's remnant who turn to him in faith have no reason to fear God anymore *as their Judge*. The verdict of the final "day of the LORD" in the future has already been rendered in the present for all who flee to the Servant who has borne the sins of his people and has been raised for their justification (Isa 53). We could summarize the "good news" half of Isaiah this way: "Don't be afraid. Beyond this exile, there is a better covenant founded on better promises and a better Mediator. There is not just long life in the land of Canaan but everlasting life: a new heart, faith, forgiveness of sins, justification, adoption, sanctification, and finally glorification. I will be your God, you will be my people, and we will camp out and feast together in peace and joy forever."

Indeed, this everlasting life in the presence of the triune God *is* fear in the *good* sense. We are redeemed *so that* we will fear God. We fail to fear God *in this sense* when we never get beyond the *servile* fear, the dread of God as a Judge. It is the gospel that makes all the difference here. As his creatures, our natural sense of God is to fear him in trepidation for his righteousness, justice, power, and majesty. Yet, based on this other word—his gospel—we have a completely different reason to fear him: for his overwhelming generosity in saving us even while we were enemies. Therefore the gospel relieves us from the fear of God's wrath so that we can fear God in joy for his amazing grace, just like the women at the tomb who responded to the risen Christ "with fear and great joy" (Matt 28:8).

In sharp contrast with other religions (which sometimes even wear the Christian label), God does not frighten us into submission. Instead, he draws us by cords of love. Godly fear, in fact, turns out to be synonymous with love, as the first fruit of faith in God's mercy and forgiveness: "But I, *through the abundance* of *your steadfast love*, will enter your house. I will bow down toward your holy temple in the *fear of you*" (Ps 5:7, emphasis mine); "but the LORD takes pleasure in those who *fear him*, in those who *hope in his steadfast love*" (Ps 147:11, emphasis mine). Through faith in Christ we no longer fear God's anger, *so that* we can begin to "fear him" for his unchangeable and merciful promises, clinging to him alone and looking for no other savior. This is true worship and, with it, true sanity.

Chapter 5

FEARS RELIEVED

Righteousness. That is a very big word in the Bible, although we do not hear it much in our society today. Perhaps this is because the word conveys moral superiority to many: *self*-righteousness. Ironically, there is indeed *so much* self-righteousness going around today. As my friend David Zahl has pointed out with great insight, we turn food, sex, friendships, work, finances—you name it—into means of self-salvation rather than gifts of God. Then our success or failure becomes a badge we wear either proudly or in humiliation before others.[1]

Some of my friends look at Christian conservatives and say, "Moral Majority? *Really*?" There's nothing worse than calling yourself righteous when it is patently obvious to everyone else that you are not. Many of us can recall Dana Carvey's *Saturday Night Live* character, Enid Strict (a.k.a. "The Church Lady"). She was judgmental and even self-righteous, but she was not a hypocrite. However, the portrait has changed significantly in recent decades. In Paul's words, "For in passing judgment on another you condemn yourself, because you, the judge, practice the very same things. . . . You who boast in the law dishonor God by breaking the law. For, as it is written, 'The name of God is blasphemed among the Gentiles because of you'" (Rom 2:1, 23–24).

Yet progressives are just as much the heirs of "The Church Lady." Dogmatic, confident that they are "on the right side of history," and eager to signal their virtue and superiority over those who just "don't get it": these vices are just as characteristic of the cultural left as the right today. (Perhaps this is not surprising, since both are offspring of a moralistic kind of American Protestantism stemming especially from the Second Great Awakening in the nineteenth century.) I have been heartbroken to see people I knew and respected who now spend their days tweeting and blogging with considerable imagination about their experiences in conservative churches that just "don't get it." There is nothing quite so self-righteous as the freshly minted progressive who displays his or her alleged moral superiority by running down others. Such people are the Truly Sanctified who stand on the right side of history, looking down on the poor "Pharisee" in their own pharisaical manner. Not content to leave, they "leave large," as they say.

We sometimes forget that Jesus ate with Pharisees, too. He loved them. He loved everybody. It was tough love, to be sure, but he did it because he really wanted Pharisees also to understand what he was doing—and he was angered when they tried to block others from coming to him. Nicodemus, after all, came secretly to learn from Jesus and Joseph of Arimathea, a member of the Jewish High Council, asked to have Jesus buried in his tomb. Pharisees can be saved, too, whether they are "fundamentalists" or "woke."

The challenge is that Pharisees rarely want to be saved. At least the Pharisees believed in the resurrection and final judgment. Sadducees, on the other hand, didn't believe in these but preferred to cozy up to the political power of the Roman empire. What stands out to me here with Jesus is that he did not care what people thought of him. Was he "woke"? Or would he side with the Pharisees? He just didn't care. What he cared about was *people.* Unfortunately, as a rule, we just don't care today. Or we care, as the clans of Jesus's day did, about "Our People," "Our Sect," and, above all, "Our Righteousness."

What is a "cancel culture"—left or right—but an ugly parading of *Our* Righteousness, measured by how much judgment we can exercise against *Them*? What does it mean, anyway, to be "on the right side of history"? Is history our judge? Rather, our concern should be whether we are on the right side of God. Do we fear the verdict of history or cherish its approval more than God's?

For Christians, "righteousness" means being in the right before God on Judgment Day. It means that we have fulfilled the law. From that perspective, "by works of the law no one will be justified," since we all "fall short of the glory of God" (Gal 2:16; Rom 3:23). The fundamentalism of the cultural left in America is suffocating. I know this. You know this too, especially if you have kids in the public schools.

In California, public education has come to the point where anyone connected to Christianity is considered an oppressor. Recently, an elementary school near where I live was stripped of the word "Mission" in its name because of the mixed legacy of Christian missions in California—even though the *city* still has "Mission" in its name. Additionally, much vexation was aroused over a local cross at a Veteran's War Memorial. The California Supreme Court ordered it to be removed, but President Obama intervened with a contrary order in 2014.

On both sides of such debates, one hears therapeutic accusations of abuse and persecution. On one hand, such memorials can be appealed to as symbols intended to celebrate a heritage that involves oppression. Many of California's main cities, streets, bays, and landmarks are named after men who were little more than villainous thugs with a royal charter and a papal blessing from Christendom. Replacing some of their names with those of their victims may serve to restore dignity to individuals who are descended from indigenous peoples. On the other hand, monuments can be occasions for learning the good and bad of history. I find it intriguing that most of the name changes in California target Franciscan missions and missionaries who opposed the whole scheme of European conquest, while leaving unmolested a host of prominent conquistadors and cruel governors.

Some figures have been honored *for* their defense of slavery by the erection of monuments during the Jim Crow period in the South. Others have been honored *in spite* of holding slaves. For example, erasing the memory of George Washington and Thomas Jefferson would not only deprive generations of appreciating their achievements but also deny them the ability to ponder those founders' failures. History is complicated; it simultaneously reminds us of God's common grace and human perversity. But the culture wars flatten history into their own simple narrative of Good Guys and Bad Guys.

Then we have Facebook, Instagram, and Twitter. There we try to find and parade our righteousness. Younger people today especially find their justification by how many followers they have or how many "likes" they get. For many, these virtual communities can be more powerful than any actual Christian community, even if it is gospel-centered. I have teenagers, so I have seen firsthand how depressed people can be when they get negative comments from individuals they don't even know. Who are these individuals? They sure seem righteous, at least in the anonymity of social media.

We all try to actualize or display our authenticity and relevance—in other words, our righteousness. We feel like we need to justify our existence. We have to be *right*. It is all about making ourselves (or appearing as) *righteous*. We do not really care about whether we are righteous before God; it's the often anonymous people out there that we are trying to please by thinking the right way, doing the right thing, voting the way we should, and repeating the right mantras. People *say* they are autonomous, expressive individualists who don't care what anybody else thinks, but we crave approval and recent generations (especially since the advent of social media) are more dependent than ever on peer evaluation.

We're all afraid of being *un*righteous. Self-justification is our default setting. And that is because we know deep down exactly what we are: the "ungodly." We know what God requires of us and what it means to be righteous, to be godly, and to be responsible, loving, and just human beings. But often we do not do what we know is right when we're up to bat. We're afraid of losing something if we do the right thing. In other words, we're selfish. We don't love God and our neighbor, and we show it not only by what we *do* but by what we *fail* to do.

What I am saying here is basically a summary of Romans 3:9–20. "None is righteous, *no not one*; no one understands; no one seeks for God" (vv. 10–11, emphasis mine). Wait a minute: *no one . . . seriously*? What about Mother Teresa or your pious grandparent? Don't *you* try do be a good person? Is Paul really saying that you *aren't* good and that you *never will be* good?

No, Paul is not saying that people do not do good things that other people can respect and benefit from. In fact, in the previous chapter he said that people who do not even have the Bible often do the right thing when people with "Judeo-Christian values" are hypocritical (2:14–24). Yes, there are good people, but compared to *whom*? Before God, no one qualifies as righteous, "no not one." Yet God requires righteousness. In fact, he says, "I will not acquit the wicked" (Exod 23:7). And after stringing together various Old Testament verses to support the point that no one is righteous, the apostle Paul says, "Now we know that whatever the law says it speaks to those who are under the law, so that every mouth may be stopped, and the whole world may be held accountable to God. For by works of the law no human being will be justified in his sight, since through the law comes knowledge of sin" (Rom 3:19–20).

Have you ever had jury duty? Then you know what it's like when the judge's entrance is announced and a hush falls on the whole chamber. Yet human judges are fallible. They know the law and they try their best to follow it in making their decisions. But God does not try: he *is* the righteousness that is demanded in his law. He judges infallibly and he knows everything about us—everything we think, desire, do, fail to do, and so on, just as Nietzsche's "ugliest man" knew.

We are all "under the law" in the sense of being responsible for our lives before God. So the law shuts all of our mouths. A hush falls (or should fall) across the globe. There is no more self-justification, spin, or blame-shifting. I am on trial. And I am guilty as charged. That is what the law is supposed to do: to arraign us before God's court and bring us to the place where we finally stop blathering on about our "righteousness."

Whether in the form of the red-faced evangelist or the smiling preacher on TV, the basic message that many hear is "try harder" or "do better." We rarely hear from the former message today. The easy-listening version of the typical message goes like this: "You're a good person deep down. You just need a little coaching. Oh, and God isn't some judge in the sky who condemns you. He's just waiting for you to take the first step, and then he'll help you follow through. Now, here are ten steps to becoming a better you!" But whether the would-be evangelist is angry or happy, these types of religion lead you to either self-righteousness or despair, and often both by turns.

No, as Paul says, the law exists to kill religion, to strip off the cloak of virtue, and to tell us the truth that ends the charade: "All of our righteous deeds are like a polluted garment" (Isaiah 64:6). You are not righteous, nor am I—in ourselves. And that is why God speaks that *other* word called the *gospel*. The reason I do not have to fearfully insulate myself from condemnation is not because God's a softy or that he exists for my happiness and so would never do anything that ended in my judgment. God is just, and he cannot violate his own character. But God is not only just; he is loving and merciful. So he found a way to do what seemed impossible: to *justify* the *unrighteous*.

This is exactly where Paul picks up in the next verses of Romans 3. Savor these words, this "good news":

> But now the righteousness of God has been manifested *apart from the law*, although the Law and the Prophets bear witness to it—the righteousness of God through faith in Jesus Christ for all who believe. For there is no distinction: for all have sinned and fall short of the glory of God, and are *justified by his grace as a gift*, through the redemption that is in Christ Jesus, whom God put forward as a propitiation by his blood, to be received by faith. This was to show God's righteousness, because in his divine forbearance he had passed over former sins. It was to show his righteousness at the present time, so that he might be *just and the justifier* of the one who has faith in Jesus." (vv. 21–26, emphasis mine)

So there is God's righteousness revealed in his law, which condemns us all. Then there is God's righteousness revealed in his gospel, which justifies all who believe in his Son. Upon hearing the gospel I give up all of my pretensions and all of my vain claims to being righteous, and I say with Augustus Toplady, "Nothing in my hand I bring, simply to Thy cross I cling" ("Rock of Ages"). The Old Testament sacrifices pointed God's people to "the Lamb of

God, who takes away the sin of the world" (John 1:29). When Paul says Christ made "propitiation by his blood," it means that Jesus—God's Son in our human nature—bore our guilt.

But Jesus did more even than this. His bearing our guilt would bring us *forgiveness*, but we still would not be *righteous*. To enter God's kingdom, we must not only be without sin (negatively) but holy (positively). Yet God provided this too. He calls it "justification," which means to declare righteous. God declares us righteous not because of anything we have done, but because of all that Christ did in his life of complete and loving obedience to his Father. Jesus did not set aside the law, but fulfilled it. He did not try harder, but actually accomplished everything he was commanded by the Father. His obedience is then credited to us. His status becomes ours, "received through faith," as Paul says. And even this faith is a gift (Eph 2:8–9). It's *all* gift!

So God did not (indeed, could not) redefine "righteousness" so that we could slip in under the gate. Nor does he just declare us righteous when we're clearly not. Instead, he credits Christ's righteousness to us so that we objectively are righteous before God because of his Son. When we try to justify ourselves, nobody wins. God is offended that we think we can do better than the gift he has offered through his Son's righteous life, sacrificial death, and glorious resurrection. So he does not get anything out of our attempts to fix things between us and him. You and I don't benefit one whit from our efforts, because apart from relying on Christ's righteousness alone we will have to be our own defense attorneys on Judgment Day. That can't go well. And my neighbors do not benefit from my efforts because I'm obsessed with my own fears and anxieties about making God think well of me instead of forgetting about myself and what I can get out of it and just giving my neighbors what they need in the moment. Later in this same letter to the Romans, Paul says, "Or who has given a gift to him that he might be repaid? For from him and through him and to him are all things. To him be glory forever. Amen" (Rom 11:35–36). God has so arranged things that he receives *all* of the glory.

If our good works cannot go up to God, as if we should expect something in return, then where do they go? Out to our neighbors who need them. Remember, God doesn't need them. And I don't need them. They won't merit me any righteousness before God. But my neighbor needs my friendship, my gifts, and my help. I go to work now because there are neighbors who need the products or services that I help provide. My nearest neighbors in my own family need me to cherish them, change their diapers, drive them to soccer, listen to them and love them, discipline them, work on projects together, and play together. This neighbor-love radiates outward in concentric circles to the wider community and world. Yet again these good works are no longer attempts to impress God or anyone else, but just to love and serve people who need me. And blessings all around—I get their gifts, too. It's a circulation of gifts.

In Every Respect Tempted as We Are

"I'm not understood."

"Nobody I know really knows what it's like to suffer with [fill in the blank]."

It would seem that the *last* person who really "gets" our fears is God, because he is holy, righteous, just, and good. Besides, he does not change in either his being or his purposes. I can neither wound nor complete him. He is self-sufficient and in no way dependent on us. What if I bring him my problems? My temptations? How can *he* understand? He is the Lord of the covenant who commands, judging right from wrong.

All this is true, but in his incarnate Son God is also the Servant of the covenant who obeyed. This is the point of Hebrews, a letter written to persuade Jewish Christians not to go back to Judaism. The first thirteen verses of Hebrews 4 have issued a dire warning not to be like the rebellious generation that never entered the earthly promised land. "For good news came to us just as to them, but the message they heard did not benefit them, because they were not united by faith with those who listened" (v. 2). Like a knife, God's word cuts us open to display our inmost desires, loves, feelings, thoughts, and actions. There is no use in prevaricating, making excuses, or hiding; God's judgment will expose everything (vv. 12–13).

But Jesus *has* entered the everlasting land of Sabbath rest, so let us follow in his train. Turning from warning to comfort, verses 14–16 are amazing relief for our fears:

> Since then we have a great high priest who has passed through the heavens, Jesus, the Son of God, let us hold fast our confession. For we do not have a high priest who is unable to sympathize with our weaknesses, but one who in every respect has been tempted as we are, yet without sin. Let us then with confidence draw near to the throne of grace, that we may receive mercy and find grace to help in time of need.

In Christ we have a better covenant, founded on better (that is, purely merciful) promises, with a mediator greater than Moses. And here we are told that in Christ we have "a great high priest" who surpasses the Levitical order. Hebrews has already used the title "High Priest" (2:17; 3:1) and the "Son" of God (1:2; 3:6), and has mentioned Jesus's temptation and suffering (2:9, 18). In describing Jesus as the "high priest of our confession" (3:1), the author is using what we can describe as a *homologias*: "same words." In other words, he is saying, "The high priest, as we confess in our creed." Consequentially; what sort of mediator do you have if you abandon Jesus and the truths about who he is and go back to the types and shadows of the old covenant?

First, Jesus is a glorious high priest because he, the Son of God, "passed through the heavens." It would be glorious if Christ had cast off his humanity on Easter morning and returned to the Father, but it would not save us. The Savior we need must be fully God but just as fully human. He assumed our humanity, not as if he was putting on a space suit, but entirely. And he raised our humanity with himself into glory at the Father's right hand. He is not only "the Son of God," but "Jesus," our victorious brother who saved the whole family by his obedience, sacrifice, resurrection, and ascension.

Under the old covenant the high priest would enter the Holy of Holies, passing through a massive curtain sixty feet high and four inches thick, made from blue, purple, and scarlet threads and "with cherubim skillfully worked into it" (Exod 26:31). Symbolically, he was passing from the earthly regions into heaven itself, carrying blood to sprinkle on the mercy seat over the ark of the covenant that housed the tablets of God's law. What could be more instructive to Israel of God's way of providing salvation in his Son? But now, Hebrews tells us, this human being, Jesus, who is also the Son of God, has passed through the true curtain and we now have one of us on the throne at the Father's right hand. When Jesus died on the cross, the temple curtain was torn from top to bottom (Matt 27:50–51). Consequentially, we are all priests in Christ our high priest and have direct access to the Father in the true Holy of Holies.

Second, Jesus our brother, the Son of God, is a *sympathetic* high priest. We're family—flesh of his flesh and bone of his bone, "brothers and sisters" (see Heb 2:11). He did not assume an angelic or celestial nature, but a fully human nature from the Virgin Mary.

> Since therefore the children share in flesh and blood, he himself likewise partook of the same things, that through death he might destroy the one who has the power of death, that is, the devil, and deliver all those who through fear of death were subject to lifelong slavery. For surely it is not angels that he helps, but he helps the offspring of Abraham. Therefore he had to be made like his brothers in every respect, so that he might become a merciful and faithful high priest in the service of God, to make propitiation for the sins of the people. For because he himself has suffered when tempted, he is able to help those who are being tempted. (Heb 2:14–18)

The apostolic writer stresses the humanity that Jesus shares in common with us by using two *kata* ("according to") phrases: "according to everything"—except for sin. Our human nature is not inherently sinful. In fact, "very good" remains God's verdict on his noblest creature. Jesus did not have to be sinful to be human. In fact, his sinlessness and perfect obedience fulfill God's original design for humanity. Jesus is *more* human than we are in this sense. Yet it does not keep him from feeling our struggles.

Actually, for the holiest man who ever lived, *his* temptations were far worse than ours. Have you ever been confronted with Lucifer in person? Even if you had been, you were not the eternally begotten Son of the Father, Light of Light, very God of very God, yet subjected to severe hunger, loneliness, and abuse. Jesus had the power to turn stones into bread or jump off the pinnacle of the temple without injury. He had the power to end his suffering, to turn aside at this fork in the road from the *Via Dolorosa* to the path of glory. Yet that would be surrendering to Satan and his plot to keep Christ's people and his world from redemption.

When I am tempted, there is something naturally attractive to me about it—even if I resist it. But Jesus was revolted by his temptations. The marvel here is not only that Jesus was tempted in every way as we are, but that we may be said to be tempted as he was! To be sure, we are talking about Jesus's humanity here. However, he was not schizophrenic. He is not a divine Dr. Jekyll and a human Mr. Hyde, but one person in two natures. "God cannot be tempted with evil," as James says (Jas 1:13). Yet because Jesus assumed our humanity, he was tempted *just as we are*. He is not naïve. His sinless holiness is not like that of a child who has not yet been exposed to vicious images. Nor is it like that of a Stoic who lives (presumably) above all passions, in detached bliss. Far from it: Jesus directed all of his passions toward his Father, in the power of the Holy Spirit. So, when evil passions assailed him it must have been horrible.

We should not speculate about Jesus's temptations. We are not told that he was tempted with every sin that every human has ever experienced, but rather "in all ways." The important takeaway here is that (a) he was *really* tempted and (b) he was *truly* "without sin." For example, Christ's loneliness is stressed on various occasions, and it must have provoked various temptations for him. We know Jesus feared death. Even though he knew he was about to raise his friend Lazarus, "Jesus wept" (John 11:35). Jesus experienced poverty and both physical and spiritual suffering. Enduring unjust abuse, mockery, and violence, he was also abandoned by his closest friends. Ultimately he also cried out with the Psalmist, "My God, my God, why have *you* forsaken me?" (Matt 27:46; cf. Ps 22:1, emphasis mine).

The report of Jesus's temptation by Satan in Matthew 4 tells us a lot, but the upshot is that Jesus responded to each one in *exactly the opposite way* that Adam and Eve, Israel, and you and I did. He was not only providing an example for us but was actually undoing the sin of Adam. He was not only "without sin" but was, positively, victorious over every temptation. Because he did this for us, we not only have our sins imputed to him but his righteous obedience imputed to us.

Look at each of the temptations here in Matthew 4. Jesus was *lonely*, facing Satan in the desert. Satan's temptations all focus on trying to persuade Jesus to prove his divine identity instead of fulfilling his human mission. Fasting forty days and nights, Jesus was *severely hungry*. "If you are the Son of God, command these stones to become loaves of bread" (v. 3). But instead of demanding the food he craved, like Adam and Israel, Jesus answered, "It is written, 'Man shall not live by bread alone, but by every word that comes from the mouth of God'" (v. 4). Having fulfilled this test, Jesus was taken by the devil to the temple in Jerusalem to be tempted by *power and glory now*, bypassing the cross. "Jump off the pinnacle," Satan pressed, since the Psalmist had prophesied that God's angels would keep him from so much as dashing a foot against the stones (vv. 5–6).

> Jesus said to him, "Again it is written, 'You shall not put the Lord your God to the test.'" Again, the devil took him to a very high mountain and showed him all the kingdoms of the world and their glory. And he said to him, "All these I will give you, if you will fall down and worship me." Then Jesus said to him, "Be gone, Satan! For it is written,
>
> "'You shall worship the Lord your God
> and him only shall you serve.'"
>
> Then the devil left him, and behold, angels came and were ministering to him. (vv. 7–11)

"One who in every respect has been tempted as we are, *yet without sin*." Jesus responded to the offer of a forbidden feast with an appeal to God's Word as his food. He answered the temptation to pride and power by embracing servanthood both to his Father and to us. He answered fear with trust, poverty and sickness by restoring life and hope to others, and loneliness by establishing a new community around himself, like a vine with its branches. And in response to abuse and shame, he showed pity, mercy, and justice. As a perfect Lamb he was without blemish, but he was also, positively, obedient in every way in which we have failed.

Third, Jesus is our faithful high priest not only in his ascension into glory and in his sympathy for our temptations but also in his constant mediation for us now. We may recall Job's lament that if he could just say to himself, "I will put off my sad face, and be of good cheer" (Job 9:27), but that does not work.

> I become afraid of all my suffering,
> for I know you will not hold me innocent.
> I shall be condemned;
> why then do I labor in vain?
> If I wash myself with snow
> and cleanse my hands with lye,
> yet you will plunge me into a pit,
> and my own clothes will abhor me.
> For he is not a man, as I am, that I might
> answer him,
> that we should come to trial together.
> There is no arbiter between us,
> who might lay his hand on us both.
> Let him take his rod away from me,
> and let not dread of him terrify me.
> Then I would speak without fear of him,
> for I am not so in myself. (Job 9:28–35)

Only later in the story does Job realize that he *does* have a mediator—an "arbiter between us":

> For I know that my Redeemer lives,
> and at the last he will stand upon the earth.
> And after my skin has been thus destroyed,
> yet in my flesh I shall see God,
> whom I shall see for myself,
> and my eyes shall behold, and not another.
> My heart faints within me! (Job 19:25–27)

In Judaism, angels are mediators. But, as Hebrews emphasizes, angels cannot save. According to Islam, Allah's greatness allows for no mediation. One cannot even pray to Muhammad for help. Hinduism teaches that Agni, just below the chief deity Indra in status, is the mediator between gods and mortals. Yet he is also the fire-god represented as having two faces, one beneficent and the other malevolent.

In Jesus Christ, however, we have the loving, holy, righteous, sovereign, and merciful God united with our suffering humanity. He is "highly exalted . . . above every name" (Phil 2:9) not only as God but also as the faithful Last Adam. "Let us then with confidence draw near to the throne of grace, that we may receive mercy and find grace to help in time of need" (Heb 4:16).

Notice how verse 14 of Hebrews chapter 4 begins: "Ἔχοντες οὖν" (since then we have). And again in verse 15: "γὰρ ἔχομεν" (for we have). Let this sink in: We *have* Christ as our high priest. He is not elusive. As eternal God, he is incomprehensible and majestic, terrifying in glory. However, by assuming our humanity he is "haveable." But this "haveability" of God in Christ is not important only by itself; the writer also makes it the indicative basis for his imperative to "hold fast our confession" in verse 14 and "with confidence draw near to the throne of grace" in verse 16. We hold fast the confession and draw near to his throne with confidence because we have this particular high priest. And what sort of person is this special high priest? He is "Jesus," who suffered just like us and was tempted as we are in every way. And he is "the Son of God." God the Father has made him high priest in order to give him to us, so that we have access to the throne of grace through him. Because he was tempted like us "but without sin," the Father finally has an obedient and faithful Son, a true human servant who has fulfilled his—and our—destiny of being human. Therefore, in him, we come with confidence.

Yet, how can we come to the holy God—even at the very moment when we are tempted with filthy lusts, violence, pride, and greed? As he has said, all of this is "laid bare" by his Law and exposed, so that we are "naked" before him. How can we come to God at all? And how can we come to him when we have actually given in to all these temptations?

Notice the writer of Hebrews doesn't say, "Come anyway. God may be a little miffed, but he's too merciful to judge." Nor does he say, "Do a little penance, clean yourself up, maybe spend a few years in purgatory, or just surrender a little more and then we'll talk." No, he says, "Come with confidence." How precious this High Priest must be that we can come with confidence and find a "throne of grace" instead of a "throne of judgment." He has expiated our sins (2:14), and even propitiated them (v. 17). The Greek term *Hina*—"In order to"—further grounds this confidence. We come with confidence "[in order to] receive mercy and find grace." Not "in the hope of" or "pleading for." We come confidently in order to receive what our high priest has objectively secured for us.

"Mercy" is love shown to the wretched. God has compassion on us right then and there, even in our misery and faithlessness. How can we come to him? With our sins. That is the only way we can come to him. And we can only do so confidently because we have a faithful high priest who guarantees that we will find a throne of grace.

The reformer John Calvin comments, "The ground of this assurance is that the throne of God is not arrayed in naked majesty to confound us, but is adorned with a new name, even that of grace, which ought ever to be remembered whenever we shun the presence of God. For the glory of God, when we contemplate it alone, can produce no other effect than to fill us with despair; so awful is his throne. So he allures us by draping 'grace' like a banner across his throne."[2] We can come to this throne of grace whenever we are afraid, in the midst of every temptation, "for timely help"—that is, "just when we need it."

Part 2

FACING OUR FEARS WITH EYES RAISED TO GOD

Christians are not taught to ignore or downplay their fears, but to bring them to the Lord and to each other. Biblical wisdom does not remove these challenges, but it guides us through them. I have broadly identified some of our fears, namely that our fears are motivated by an attempt to escape the sentence of death, to provide ourselves with security, and to deflect our own guilt and shame. We've also seen that the fear of God is the beginning of wisdom: the greater fear that drives out all lesser fears. In this second part we'll examine how to apply the fear of God from the map of God's larger story to the things that haunt us and dominate the news cycles.

Our Longing for Life

Chapter 6

THE "STING" OF DEATH REMOVED

Our advanced medical system gives us the illusion that nobody should die. Whenever there is a natural disaster or pandemic, we immediately rush to place blame on medical professionals, the government, or the media. Or, in our own daily lives, we often assume that for some reason we should be exempt from the same illnesses that more easily took down our forebears in less-developed eras. We are terrified of the fragility of life and swing impatiently to grasp any savior we can find. When these saviors inevitably fail us, we immediately clamor for them to be held responsible.

I am not suggesting that we ignore irresponsible actions by authorities or doctors. We are not called to resignedly throw in the towel when we hear a cancer or Alzheimer's diagnosis or to be reckless in dismissing health guidelines. But my point is that we inordinately fear death today, as if it should never happen in our wealthy and highly developed society. A microscopic virus can actually hold us hostage, manifesting the finitude of our would-be saviors. When a "smart bug" confronts us, our advanced technology seems nothing better than the primitive knowledge of cavemen. This terrifies us.

Death is the ultimate source of our anxieties, for it brings us to the realization that we are not autonomous and that our story—for now, at least—has a final chapter that we cannot write for ourselves. We are afraid of death—as a human condition, a global-environmental reality, and of what it means for us in terms of God's judgment. These are the prongs of the curse in Genesis 3, as we saw in the opening chapter of this book. The fear of death is what provokes us to justify ourselves before God, ourselves, and others. It is why we blame each other and try to climb over our fellow humans on our way up the ladder, futilely attempting to avoid the rising flood of divine judgment. Death, along with its eventual byproduct, despair, fuels our anxieties, depression, resentment, and self-righteousness.

At this stage in my life, I have seen a lot of death around me, including children and young people. As I write, some close friends have lost a daughter and wife to a sudden heart attack, leaving two young children. A few months ago, another good friend lost his college-age son, his only child. Goofing off with his sister and fiancée, he suddenly fell to the ground and never recovered. They don't even know the precise cause of death as of this writing. Both of my parents experienced prolonged and miserable deaths. However, we are accustomed to the death of the elderly. We have this expectation, though, that our children are going to survive and thrive, giving us grandchildren until we're eating applesauce and preparing for the end. There is nothing worse than burying a son or daughter or grandchild. I've never experienced this myself, but over the years I have known and counseled those who have, and as a father I shudder when I think about it.

As a young man I read in the dusty books of the saints that this life is "a vale of tears" and thought, "Seriously, you've never been to Six Flags." The world lay before me and I was ready for the challenge. That charged "Go For It!" attitude of youth gets us in the game. But young people die too. Despite our optimism and wishful thinking, death remains an inescapable reality of life.

Anxiety strikes different people at different places. Christians believe God's promise that upon death the soul will be present with the Lord, in anticipation of the final resurrection. But this does not mean believers face death without fear. Just recently, a very wise and godly teacher of God's Word told me, "At 85, I'm a little more nervous than I was at 80. I know that we'll be in God's presence, but will we be bodiless souls? I don't mind saying that I'm not quite sure how appealing I find that." He is not afraid of death or dying per se, and he knows that being with the Lord will be his glorious lot. But he was not sure what exactly happens on the other shore. I was comforted that someone like this could express such honest and childlike faith: confidence in the Lord but also nervous puzzlement. Curious persons sometimes try to fill in the details with purported visions in near-death or even supposedly after-death encounters. However, we truly do not know very much about what it is like between death and the final resurrection—except that we are with the Lord.

Sometimes we struggle not so much with the fear of death, but of dying—the actual experience and process of death. That's a nagging worry for me, especially after watching my parents slowly waste away after being paralyzed by a tumor and strokes. I don't want to experience that type of death, and I don't want my wife and kids to bear the burden of my prolonged agony and stress. I've put in my request to the Lord for something clean and swift—but we'll see.

A fear of dying, or even death itself, is not a sign of weakness in faith. There are many possible reasons for our fears. For example, we all have different personalities, backgrounds, and life experiences. Someone may have experienced abandonment by a trusted parent, spouse, or friend, and that betrayal shades their thinking about dying. In saying "*When* [not *If*] I am afraid, I put my trust in you" (Ps 56:3, emphasis mine), the psalmist is assuming that some fears are a normal human experience. The psalmist also begs for his life: "You overwhelm me with all your waves . . . Why do you hide your face from me? Afflicted and close to death from my youth up, I suffer your terrors; I am helpless" (Ps 88:7, 14–15). Can I really pray in this way when I'm afraid of the physical pain of suffering and death? Yes! In fact, the truth that God knows me enough to give me words that I'm feeling but can't express myself shows me the depth of his sympathy. For example, Jesus took on his own lips the cry of the Psalmist, "My God, my God, why have you forsaken me?" (Matt 27:46; Mark 15:34; cf. Ps 22:1), yet he had just assured the believing thief on the cross next to him, "Today you will be with me in paradise" (Luke 23:43). This is an astonishing paradox—the confidence of being with the Father alongside the pain of abandonment.

The fear of death can cause us to do some crazy things. An argument going back to Epicurus, three centuries before Christ, has been often heard ever since his time. Religion exists, Epicurus said, because priests exploit the fear of death to gain power over the masses. Doubtless, there are other motives, but for the most part Christians can agree with him. Very sane people will crawl on the ground until their knees bleed, cut themselves, drink poisoned Kool-Aid, serve dinner to a ceramic elephant, throw their child into a volcano, or mail in every penny they have to a preacher, all because they fear death. In contrast, the writer to the Hebrews says that Christ came to "deliver all those who *through fear of death* were *subject to lifelong slavery*" (Heb 2:15, emphasis mine). The fear of death is universal because death itself is a universal condition and human beings sense deep inside themselves that it is a divine judgment.

But being afraid of dying and death is completely normal. Death is not natural, but it is universal and is a sentence that is only removed in Christ. If fear of death were a failure to trust in God, then Jesus would be a poor example, since he wails at the death of his friend Lazarus even though he knew he was about to raise him from the dead (John 11:35). Expressing grief is a perfectly appropriate reaction to unnatural circumstances. Fear of death is not the opposite of trust in the Lord. Rather, the former is meant to lead us more and more deeply into the latter.

We may recover from an illness, but we all will die. Heart disease, cancer, injuries, chronic respiratory disease, stroke, Alzheimer's, diabetes, influenza, and pneumonia, and on the list goes. Since the moment of birth we've been dying—all of us. Today, we know that our individual cells die and are replaced many times over our lifespan. Biologists call this healthy cell death "apoptosis." This is how God keeps us in existence despite our bodily decay.[1] The ability of the brain to repair itself in stroke victims is one of the most spectacular examples of God's providence. But, eventually, the brain dies too.

Older Christian pastors once said that their main job was preparing people for death. But few pastors today want that on their resumé. We live in a "forever young" society which downplays and denies death while also minimizing the fear of God in his law and his gospel. Yet there are many things pastors can say to the dying—and to all of us—if they are ready to speak and we are ready to listen.

How We Look at Death

There are three approaches to death in our society. First, we *deny it*. Some folks will spend a lot of money on denying their own mortality—or at least the appearance of age. I had a friend who was my age but in terrific shape. He played tennis and ran, on average, ten miles a day. He took care of his body. My friend was not a believer, however, and he was sure he could keep death, or at least the effects of age, at bay. One day, with no preexisting condition that he was aware of, he dropped dead from a heart attack.

There is a general assumption that we came from nowhere special and we're going to nowhere special but we can make something special in the middle. But death is the party crasher. The problem is that we do not know how to throw a real party like God does, and it is hard to have a good time when we know that there is a 100 percent chance that we will eventually die. The process of dying is rarely sudden. For many, it involves a gradual loss of our health, wealth, and happiness. So we just deny death, embracing the notion that in the cycle of life nothing ever really dies. You just enter a different body or your cells just form some other thing—a tree or a crackling fire.

The second approach is to *downplay* death. Euphemisms creep into the frank realism of older Christian discourse. We no longer have drab *funerals* but *celebrations of life*. Our loved ones are not really gone but live on in our memories and show up at Thanksgiving and Christmas in some vague New-Agey way. We talk about an "afterlife," which is quite different from the "everlasting life" that Christ promises. Mary Baker Eddy, founder of Christian Science, introduced the phrase "passing on" or "passing away," which now seems ubiquitous even in the most conservative Christian circles. But this minimizing of death is a very *un*Christian idea.

The third view is that people actually *die*. That's why their corpses or ashes are put into the ground in the hope that they will be raised in glory at Christ's appearing. This is the third approach to death, the Christian approach: to *accept* death as real and to place our hope in a future, bodily resurrection. Jesus did not wail at Lazarus's tomb because he thought his friend had "passed on." He could appeal to a Jewish way of talking about people "falling asleep" in the hope of the resurrection, but when his disciples thought that he meant that Lazarus was taking a nap, "Jesus told them plainly, 'Lazarus has died'" (John 11:14). Christians believe that people actually die.

More than a decade ago, Lisa Miller wrote a riveting piece for *Newsweek* called "The Christian Mystery of Physical Resurrection." It was based on her book *Heaven: Our Enduring Fascination with the Afterlife*. According to Miller, "while 80 percent of Americans say they believe in heaven, few of us have the slightest clue about what we mean. Heaven, everyone agrees, is the good place you go after death, a reward for struggle and faithfulness on earth." Yet most are confused by what heaven is really like. On one hand, we talk about meeting up with loved ones and picking up where we left off on earth. On the other hand, we view heaven as an ethereal place where spirits or souls are freed from embodiment. Yet bodies seem pretty crucial to hanging out with Grandma and Uncle Ed. As Miller puts it, "If you don't have a body in heaven, then what kind of heaven are you hoping for?" That's a great question.

Miller goes on to report that 25% of those who say they're *Christians* believe in reincarnation. You just keep coming into a different body until you get it right. But then you're finally free of the cycle of karma, salvation by works, and the grand prize is . . . your spirit becomes a drop in the ocean of being. Only 26% of Americans think they'll have bodies in heaven. For her own part, Miller says she finds the resurrection hope of a new body "unbelievable."[2] Unsurprisingly, she concluded in a slightly earlier article that Americans are increasingly becoming more Hindu and less Christian.[3]

Can't Take It Seriously

Many today have also come to see the resurrection of the body as "unbelievable." But that is hardly a new problem. Jewish people did take God's promise of resurrection seriously. In Jesus's day, nothing short of bodily resurrection was expected, especially by the

Pharisees. They did not talk about "passing on" or an "afterlife," but of the "age to come" when the world would be judged, God's people vindicated, and heaven established on earth with God as King. It was not about individual souls bouncing around forever on ethereal clouds, but about eating and drinking with God and each other in a renewed world. But Gentiles were mostly shaped by the great Greek philosopher Plato. He did not like the body—it was just the prison house of the soul. So salvation for Plato basically meant dying—the release of the soul from its bodily prison. It's not really death, but liberation: the beginning of *real* life.

At the time of Christ, Philo, an influential Jewish philosopher in Alexandria, Egypt, taught Plato's doctrine under a thinly veiled Judaism. In fact, modern Judaism is closer to Philo than it is to the Hebrew prophets and the rabbis of Jesus's day. Philo interpreted Genesis 1 and 2 not as two accounts of the same creation event, but as two separate creations. The first was the creation of the spiritual world of paradigms or archetypes—models. So there was the Adam of pure spirit, the ideal Human. Then there was a second creation, this time of the physical copies. They couldn't be as good as the originals, of course, and since they were made of matter they were inherently flawed. At death your soul—the *real* you—flies off to be reunited with its heavenly model while the physical body is cast away like a shell covering.

Taking Philo's revision of the biblical hope further, some Jews and early Christians in Alexandria tried to make their message still more appealing to Greeks and Romans. They were called Gnostics. According to them, the *real* resurrection is not of the body in the future when Christ returns. (Who would want to be embodied forever?) Instead, it is merely a spiritual resurrection that happens here and now when a person is born again.

Evidently some Jews and Christians in the early church had been influenced by the Platonist idea that there is only a spiritual resurrection. This sort of Platonized Judaism was especially swirling around among the churches that had been recently planted in Greek colonies. That is why Paul warns his understudy Timothy, pastoring the church in Ephesus, that some "have swerved from the truth, saying that the resurrection has already happened" (2 Tim 2:18).

Philosophers also made fun of Christian belief in the resurrection. A good example is Celsus in the second century. First of all, he questioned, why would anyone *want* to be embodied forever? The whole point of death is that we finally escape everything physical. But, secondly, Celsus added, what nonsense it is to imagine that we'll be raised in the same body that was eaten by sharks, burned in a fire, or was lost at sea! Bodies, even those of humans, are not worthy of being raised—and even if they were, it would be against nature for a physical body to exist in heaven!

Not much has changed since Celsus's time. The idea of a bodily resurrection is still unbelievable to many people, even to many Christians.

We Must Die

So now we finally come to Paul's explanation in 1 Corinthians 15. First of all, *this body must die.*

> But someone [who denies the resurrection] will ask, "How are the dead raised? With what kind of body do they come?" You foolish person! What you sow does not come to life unless it dies. And what you sow is not the body that is to be, but a bare kernel, perhaps of wheat or of some other grain. But God gives it a body as he has chosen, and *to each kind of seed its own body.* (vv. 35–38, emphasis mine)

"You foolish person!" is someone like Celsus who mocks the gospel by saying that people cannot possibly be raised in the same body in which they had lived on earth. The philosophers should have been better logicians at this point. They committed what is called a "category mistake" by confusing the *condition* of a body with its *nature*. And that is exactly where Paul corrects those, even Christians, who are being influenced by this objection.

As a farmer knows, says the apostle, a grain of wheat or a corn seed does not exist in the same condition as the plant with its fruit. You don't plant corn seeds and expect pears—you anticipate corn to come forth. No matter the *condition* in which our body died, it will be the same body that will be raised. In other words, it is not another *body* but the same body in a different *condition*.

A good indicator of how far we will go to suppress the truth in unrighteousness is how we deny death. After all, we don't even need the Bible in order to discover the certain truth that people die. We deny death because we are afraid of it and we do not have any hope of survival beyond it. But only the Bible tells us why we die and what God has done about it.

By itself, death is bad news. As believers in Christ, we look forward to the resurrection. If people look forward to their death when they are healthy, it is justly called "morbid." But I could see in my mom and dad's eyes how much they wanted to be free of sickness, pain, and sorrow and be in the presence of their Lord. In that sense, we think of a "good death": people dying in the Lord, freed of their pain and cares.

It is true that death frees us. In fact, Paul himself says as much in other passages. However, this is not his point here in 1 Corinthians 15. His focus here is not on dying well in the Lord but on how death itself becomes reevaluated in the light of the resurrection. And here Paul thinks of death as essential to our salvation. Yes, death is a horrible *enemy*, but here he calls it the *last* enemy.

Death is not our friend or a cheerful portal to the "afterlife"; it is an enemy. And yet God works all things together for the good of his people (Rom 8:28). Death itself is not good, but God has turned something horrible into an element in our salvation. Outside of Christ, death is condemnation; in Christ, it's dusk before dawn. That is why death is actually essential for the salvation of those united to Christ. This is the part of Paul's argument I really want to focus your attention on here.

We *must* die because we are born under a death sentence. We are guilty and corrupt, from birth, as heirs of Adam (Isa 64:6; Ps 51:5; Rom 5). So, Paul says here, "in Adam all die" (1 Cor 15:22). We also are guilty of our actual sins. Taking all this together, we must die because "The sting of death is sin, and the power of sin is the law" (v. 56).

In other words, according to the law—God's righteous verdict—we are under the power of sin. That is why death has a fatal stinger in its tail. That is why it is not a sweet dream or just part of the cycle of life. We die under a far greater sentence of everlasting condemnation.

We spend a lot of money on trying to extend life. Cryonics and other sophisticated technologies are being pursued in order to put people into a deep freeze or coma-like condition so they can be revived at some point in the future. But that is not resurrection. It's just picking up where you left off. Nobody should want to live forever with a "CONDEMNED" sign hanging around his or her neck. *That* person needs to die. *That* character in the script needs to die in this episode so that he or she can be written into another story, the Christ Story instead of the Adam Story.

For believers, though, death is no longer condemnation but is essential to our salvation. Justified in Christ, believers no longer suffer death as a curse but as a welcoming party into God's presence and a precursor to resurrection. The stinger has been removed.

Then why do we still die physically? If death is the result of sin—both original sin and our actions springing from it—and the law's just sentence of condemnation has been removed, then why do we not just keep on living or at least experience bodily resurrection and glorification right when we die? Paul also gives an answer in verses 35 through 38 of 1 Corinthians 15. We must *die*—not be improved, extended, enhanced, or modified. No cosmetic touches here and there. It is for our good and the good of the world that we and it must die. There is nothing evil that God made. We were created good by a wise, loving, and sovereign God. But there is nothing in this present age, lying under the grip of sin and death, that can turn back the clock to the garden of Eden.

And this is good and necessary, because what we have up ahead is *better* than Eden! This new reality is not just a reboot after a glitch, but a condition of this world, including our humanity, that no one—including our first parents—ever knew. Even if we could go back to Eden and erase Adam's disobedience, we would still be *alive* but not *immortal*; *innocent* but not *justified* and *glorified*. Adam and Eve were created in a period of trial and testing. And, as our covenantal representative, Adam blew the trial. He did not break through the finish line and carry us, with all creation, into his victory march. We never saw what it would be like to enter God's everlasting Sabbath rest in our own power.

But the Last Adam, Jesus Christ, *has* won this race for us. He won for us the right to eat from the Tree of Life. In fact, he *is* the Tree of Life. This future reality is not a *better* you, but a new creation. God is not going to throw away your body. There is nothing intrinsically wrong with what he has made and declared "very good" (Gen 1:31). He is not going to leave your body to the worms or the urn or the sea; he is going to raise it in a completely new condition. I love the fantasy action movie *The Immortals*, based on the Homeric myth of the defeat of the Titans, but Paul is saying that we who die in Christ are the *real* "immortals." We will never be eternal, possessing life in ourselves, but we will be as much like God as it is possible for a creature to be.

But first the body has to die. It has to be absolutely, completely, 100 percent brought to an end in its present shape. Isn't that good news? Isn't it comforting to know that not a single doubt, temptation, transgression, defilement, depression, sorrow, or infirmity will come with us into the everlasting kingdom? We will not be cleaned-up versions of our current selves, but new creations, born anew for a new world. That does not mean that the new creation has nothing to do with the old creation. That was the error of Plato, Philo, and the Gnostics. The same Jesus who ate fish with his disciples after his resurrection (Luke 24:42–42; John 21:12–14) will dine with us at the Marriage Feast. And we also will be the same people, but in a wholly new condition.

Christ had to die, not because of his sin, but because of ours: "He himself bore our sins in his body on the tree, that we might die to sin and live to righteousness. By his wounds you have been healed" (1 Pet 2:24). No death, no resurrection. Not one ounce of sin and death will belong to you on that day, because you have already died. That reality, that condition—sin and death—is forever gone, buried, done and over with, in the past. Bury it. It is the clothing of the old you.

Paul does not deny that when we die our souls go immediately to be with the Lord, but this is *not* the resurrection. It's called the *intermediate* state. Although our souls are dispatched to God's safekeeping upon death, Christians confess their faith in "the resurrection of the body and the life everlasting," not just "I'll fly away." The whole creation will be renewed, not destroyed, as Paul says in Romans 8, so we wait for this final resurrection with patience. But for that resurrection to happen, our bodies in their current condition must completely die.

We Must Be Changed

Paul's next argument in 1 Corinthians 15 is that *this body must be changed.* Often I hear believers talk about "getting a new body" when they die. But this is not quite right. We do not get a new body when we die. We only have one body, and at death it is in the grave. "That's not really Grandma," we console our kids at the interment of the body. But it *is* Grandma! It's just that it is not Grandma in the resurrection. Because of the fall, the body God created *not to die* decays: "Dust to dust and ashes to ashes." Moreover, in the resurrection we do not get a new body but instead receive the same body—in a totally new condition. Death precedes change; this body has to *die* so that it can be *changed*, as Paul explains:

> So is it with the resurrection of the dead. *What is sown* is perishable; *what is raised* is imperishable. *It* is sown in dishonor; *it* is raised in glory. *It* is sown in weakness; *it* is raised in power. It is sown a natural body; it is raised a spiritual body. If there is a natural body, there is also a spiritual body. Thus it is written, "The first man Adam became a living being"; the last Adam became a life-giving spirit. But it is not the spiritual that is first but the natural, and then the spiritual. The first man was from the earth, a man of dust; the second man is from heaven. As was the man of dust, so also are those who are of the dust, and as is the man of heaven, so also are those who are of heaven. Just as we have borne the image of the man of dust, we shall also bear the image of the man of heaven.
>
> I tell you this, brothers: flesh and blood cannot inherit the kingdom of God, nor does the perishable inherit the imperishable. (vv. 42–50, emphasis mine)

Everything I italicized here is meant to underscore Paul's point that the subject of the resurrection (Mike) is the same as the subject of the death (Mike). Mike dies and is raised. There is no other Mike. Notice how Paul keeps saying, "This body . . . This body." Again, he is contrasting two *conditions*, not two *bodies*. If you read this as a typical American (like Plato), you'll think Paul is saying that we're going to get a spiritual—that is, immaterial—body. This view sees ultimate salvation as sloughing off this mortal coil. But in Paul's scheme our whole person is raised from sin and death, following in Christ's wake as we enter the Promised Land.

So when Paul says that "flesh and blood" cannot inherit the kingdom of God, he is not saying that heaven is such a spiritual place that the alarm goes off if anything physical enters. Again, in contrast with Plato, Philo, and the Gnostics, "flesh" does not mean "body" for Paul. It means all of us and all of the world *in the current condition of sin, death, condemnation, and utter impotence* to save ourselves. The flesh—that is, the fallen human being—is not capable of self-salvation. "Flesh and blood" represents the human being in Adam rather than the human being in Christ who is raised by the Spirit into the new creation. The perishable cannot *inherit* the imperishable. So we must be *changed*—not exchanged, but changed. "This mortal flesh must *put on* immortality." The body does not cease to exist, but corruption and mortality cease to exist. We become immortals by grace! But, except for those who are still living at Christ's return, we all have to die—and *everyone* has to be *changed*.

Paul draws back the curtain just enough to anticipate what lies ahead for us (vv. 50–58). Different seeds, different shoots. Instead of a dying stalk, we will be a green fresh shoot that will never grow old and die. At this point, Paul introduces a fascinating contrast.

Remember Philo's teaching that the first Adam was a completely spiritual model, pure and perfect, while the second Adam was an imperfect copy defiled by association with a material body. Paul was a highly trained rabbi who could quote the philosophers from memory at the drop of a hat, as he did in Athens (Acts 17). So it would not surprise us if Paul knew the work of a Jewish philosopher only a few decades older than him. Regardless, Paul was familiar with the idea of two creations, one spiritual and the other physical. But he completely turns this idea on its head. Quoting Genesis 2:7, he says, "'The first man Adam became a living being'; the last Adam [Christ] became a life-giving spirit. But it is not the spiritual that is first but the natural, and then the spiritual" (1 Cor 15:45–46).

In a stroke of genius, Paul reverses Philo's order. There was no creation of a perfect, spiritual model of humanity and then another inferior creation of the individual and physical Adam. Rather, human beings were physical from the beginning. But that is not a bad thing. God created all things good, and humans, in fact, were created "very good."

Moreover, the first and second Adam are not the spiritual and physical but the actual historical persons, Adam and Christ. Paul's point is that the first Adam—"The Man of Dust"—was *alive* but not *life-giving*. Being alive is good, but it is not immortality. We're all here as the children of Adam and Eve. But they don't get us any further beyond mere existence on this earth. In fact, because of Adam's fateful decision as our covenant head, we are here "in sin." We were never confirmed in righteousness and everlasting life. The first Adam is death-giving, not life-giving.

But the "Man from Heaven," Christ, is not just the genealogical source of our mere existence; he is the *life-giving* Spirit. What he achieved for us, the Holy Spirit applies to us. Their work is so integrally related that Paul can say Christ has become "the life-giving

Spirit" for us. While the first Adam was seduced by Satan's false promises, the Last Adam rebuffed his lies with God's Word and won for all of us the right to eat from the Tree of Life, which is himself! "In Adam" we are all alive for a while and then die; "in Christ" we suffer for a while and are raised forever.

The "loser" that we all are in Adam needs to die. Because Christ is a "winner" and we participate in victory through him, we need to be raised. If Christ has been raised, we *have* to be raised with him. We are members of his body. Our whole identity needs to be wrapped up in Christ, not Adam.

For Philo and probably the false teachers Paul was refuting, there was a spiritual Adam followed by a physical Adam; they believed that when we die we finally go back to being the spiritual Adam. Paul messes up this entire scheme. Instead, the contrast is between one embodied human who rejected God's law and another one who kept it, bore our curse, and rose as the "first-fruits" of the whole harvest.

Any good farmer knows that you discern how prosperous a crop of corn will be by the first ears that appear. That's why there was a "new wine" festival in Israel and other Mediterranean cultures. Is it going to be a good vintage? We'll know when we sip the first samples. Likewise, look at Adam and you know how the whole story of humanity in the power of "flesh" will turn out. But then look at Jesus, the first sample of the new creation.

Here, Paul lets us in on a "mystery." "We shall not all sleep [die], but we shall *all* be changed, *in a moment*, in the twinkling of an eye, at the last trumpet. For the trumpet will sound, and the dead will be raised imperishable, and we shall be changed" (1 Cor 15:51–52, emphasis mine). The whole harvest will be raised together when the firstfruit appears again in the flesh.

The unrighteous cannot become righteous. In justification they "put on Christ," who is "our righteousness, holiness and redemption" (1 Cor 1:30 NIV). Then, at death, the mortal cannot become immortal; it must "put on immortality." We don't have this suit in our wardrobe. We have to get it from someone else, and the good news is that we already have it in Christ. Because "there is therefore now no condemnation for those who are in Christ Jesus" (Rom 8:1), every believer is guaranteed this final clothing of his or her faded, decayed, and decomposed flesh with immortal glory (1 Cor 15:53–55).

If we conceive of the future as an escape from history, our bodies, and God's creation, we will reduce salvation to "going to heaven when we die" and see ourselves as escapees from "the late, great planet earth." But God has a plan: we will all die, but our souls will be kept in his safekeeping while our bodies and the whole creation will be raised. And this future hope orients our lives in this present age.

Paul is not yet finished. There is one more crucial point to his argument in 1 Corinthians 15.

We Must Be Raised

We must be raised. When I say "we," I mean "we." Our soul is *part of "we,"* but not the whole of it. God never has given up on his creation, and he never will. He will not throw it away and start from scratch.

The Christian hope has nothing to do with visions of a dying planet, "the late, great planet earth" that has no future except annihilation, but with the expectation that we find in the book of Revelation. In one of the visions in that book, the city of God descends from heaven to the earth. In fact, not only are all walls removed between Jew and Gentile, but even the vertical demarcations of heaven and earth are dissolved. At long last, God's dwelling will be with us forever, which Paul also emphasizes as he continues in 1 Corinthians 15:

> Behold! I tell you a mystery. We shall not all sleep, but we shall all be changed, in a moment, in the twinkling of an eye, at the last trumpet. For the trumpet will sound, and the dead will be raised imperishable, and we shall be changed. For this perishable body must put on the imperishable, and this mortal body must put on immortality. When the perishable puts on the imperishable, and the mortal puts on immortality, then shall come to pass the saying that is written:
>
> "Death is swallowed up in victory."
> "O death, where is your victory?
> O death, where is your sting?"
>
> The sting of death is sin, and the power of sin is the law. But thanks be to God, who gives us the victory through our Lord Jesus Christ. (vv. 51–57)

This body *must* rise. Why? Because *Christ* is risen bodily. Everything united to him must be raised as well. In fact, there are not two resurrections, but one. Jesus's and ours are the same event, but are separated by an intermission in which all who are brought into union with Christ are able to become part of the harvest of which he is the firstfruits. As goes the head, so go the members. If death is the penalty for condemnation, then immortality and glorification are the prize for justification. Everyone who is justified *must* be glorified (Rom 8:29–30). That is why the resurrection of all the dead did not happen on that first Easter morning. The Spirit is uniting sinners to Christ all around the world, throughout the ages, until his whole body is raised with him in glory. Do you want to see what we will be like? Look at Christ. As goes the firstfruits, so also the harvest; as goes the Vine, so the branches.

The flesh (our power) is powerless; the Spirit (God's power) is irrepressible. One of my favorite spirituals is Claude Ely's "Ain't No Grave Can Hold My Body Down." Elvis Presley and Johnny Cash both performed this song, but the latter's version is the best hands down.[4] The powers of "the flesh"—whatever you and I and the natural processes that God put in place for the *normal* working of creation (minus the fall)—cannot bring the body out of the grave or restore the world's ability to heal itself. We need a miracle. Christ, the Last Adam, *is* the Miracle.

We have two non-Christian views of the future: The first, based on atheistic materialism, is that we only have this world in its present condition, which we need to save. The second is based on Platonic, if not Gnostic, spiritualism: this world will be scrapped. Both are Gentile ways of ignoring God's saving plan. Jesus did not come to earth to make the world *better*, but to make it *new*. We need to give up *not on this world* but on any hope that *we can save it or ourselves*. We should not even want to indefinitely extend our lives nor the condition of the world under the curse. At some point, we must die. This world in its present condition must die. It does not pass away. It does not get recycled into the circle of life. It dies so that the very same body and the very same world created by God can be raised in newness. After his resurrection Jesus ate fish, but he did not experience temptation and suffering, nor did he continue to bear the sins of his people. All of that he left in the tomb.

In the third century the Christian teacher Origen of Alexandria got a little too close (actually, a lot too close) to Plato, Philo, and the Gnostics in his thinking. For Origen, the resurrection was spiritual rather than bodily. To put a fine point on it, he assured, "There are no hairdressers in heaven."[5] Now, I do not know if there will be hairdressers, but the better question is: why not? God will destroy nothing that he created good, but will certainly wipe every tear from our eyes and make sure that nothing harmful enters his beautiful land. We will be embodied—further clothed, not naked. I do not know exactly what that means, frankly. But it means that this new life will be better, not worse; a gain, not a loss; an addition, not subtraction.

Heaven and earth will become one. In the book of Revelation we notice that there is no longer any distinction between them. God's dwelling will be with humans forever. Again, it is not less than natural but supernatural, not beyond the reach of matter but beyond the reach of sin and death. Israel—all who belong to Christ—will not be raised to merely live in a sliver of the Middle East, but "the meek . . . will inherit *the earth*" (Matt 5:5 NIV, emphasis mine). The same body that was once perishable will be imperishable; it was sown (born) in the dishonor of original sin, but will be raised in the honor of Christ's everlasting glory. Short of being God, we will be all that Christ is now! By grace, we will be the true "Immortals!" Christ has just arrived ahead of us, securing our certain arrival with him.

In the meantime, this is the period of proclaiming the gospel. After all, death has a legal claim on us. "The sting of death is sin, and the power of sin is the law" (1 Cor 15:56). We are dead in Adam. Unless the guilt and curse for our sin is lifted, not even God can raise us from the dead. Why? Because it is his own righteousness and justice that has imposed the sentence. Yet "God put [Christ] forward as a propitiation by his blood, to be received by faith. . . . that he might be just and the justifier of the one who has faith in Jesus" (Rom 3:25–26).

We are now in the intermission between Christ's two advents, when we are justified through faith in Christ. "There is therefore now no condemnation for those who are in Christ Jesus" (Rom 8:1).

We will die, but not under the curse. Death can no longer hold us in its grip. It has to let us go, just as it had to let Jesus go. And the result is not repair nor resuscitation of a corpse, but resurrection. Death comes before resurrection.

Paul's argument is tight and simple (1 Cor 15:12–34). Jesus Christ "has been raised." The verb (*egēgertai*) is in the perfect tense, which connotes a past action with continuing effects. Paul uses this verb form seven times, all in reference to Christ, while he speaks of "the resurrection of the dead" more generally in the present tense: It is something that has already begun with Christ. After uniting people from every tribe to the risen and glorified Head, the Spirit will raise the whole body. Paul offers five conclusions from the denial of Christ's resurrection: (1) Christ is not raised; (2) the preaching of the gospel is useless; (3) your faith is useless; (4) Paul is bearing false witness; (5) "you are still in your sins" and believers who have already died "are lost." In summary, "If in Christ we have hope in this life only, we are of all people most to be pitied" (v. 19).

From this we learn that the gospel is not about your best life now. It is not "Come to Christ and all your troubles will be over." It is not an invitation to a better life now, marriages and families, health, wealth, or environmental and social transformation. The gospel, rather, is that God became flesh, fulfilled all righteousness, bore our curse, and rose triumphant on the third day. So, we can both physically and spiritually share with him in the likeness of his death *and* resurrection. That is already the point of life now, and it will be realized perfectly at Christ's return.

There is no consolation prize for those who placed their hope in a lie. Paul does not say, "Even if it didn't happen, haven't you lived a happier, more fulfilling life?" He didn't back up the claim with pragmatic and therapeutic benefits such as, "The family that prays together stays together." For him, especially as a Jewish rabbi, a spiritual, existential, moral, or allegorical resurrection would have been another philosophical dream. Paul does not believe in "faith." The resurrection of Christ is not a symbol of some inner peace or transformation. It does not *make* a point; it *is* the point. It happened in history, just like the Battle of Waterloo.

But how do we know Jesus was raised? Paul tells us in the beginning of 1 Corinthians 15. Writing from Ephesus between AD 53–55, Paul says that he is passing on what he had received from earlier tradition (vv. 3–7). Only twenty years after the resurrection, the empty tomb was already a settled Christian conviction. In fact, even non-Christian scholars agree that Paul must have received this brief creed when he was in Jerusalem, within one to three years of the crucifixion. And, by apostolic authority, the death and resurrection of Christ are delivered "as of first importance." Jesus appeared to Peter (Cephas) and the Twelve, then "to more than five hundred brothers at one time, most of whom are still alive. . . ." The assumption here is that the empty tomb is not a recent legend but the original claim of the eyewitnesses. If you were to interview one of these living witnesses, he or she would not merely emphasize being transformed by Jesus's life-changing work. This person would actually be able to relate what he or she saw and heard. Paul did not say, "You ask me how I know he lives? He lives within my heart." Rather, he pointed outside of himself to what occurred, which eyewitnesses, including himself, reported.

And because the resurrection entered history, it changed history forever. Our history is now literally, concretely, and even physically taken up into Christ's. Paul is not an apostle of spirituality, moral uplift, and positive thinking. If it isn't *true*, Paul says, your faith is meaningless (*kenos*) and fruitless (*mataios*) (v. 17). If Jesus is not risen, then faith isn't helpful. It's deranged. It doesn't matter how many "testimonials" we can give about improved relationships, joy, inner peace, practical guidance, and cultural benefits. *It's all for nothing.* But since Jesus Christ *is* risen, then the age to come has already dawned and this age of sin and death is fading away even now. Everyone must hear this Good News and embrace it for their salvation.

So just as Christ is our clothing of righteousness in justification, he is our garment of glorification. Having been justified, you *must* be raised bodily in glory on the last day. Resurrection and glorification are the same event. By nature we bear the image of the first Adam, but by rebirth we bear the image of the Last Adam. The new birth—spiritual resurrection—has already occurred, as the guarantee of the final resurrection not only of our bodies but of a renewed creation, as Paul highlights in Romans 8. We must die, we must be changed, and we must be raised.

The resurrection that awaits us is not just the continuation of natural existence as a "living being." It is the entrance into a new kind of existence that human beings had never experienced before until their risen Head entered the age to come. For now, as Paul says in 2 Corinthians 4:16, we are being forgiven and renewed inwardly by the Spirit. "Then comes the end . . ." (1 Cor 15:24). What is this? The end of the world? The end of time? No, it's the end of the reign of sin and death: "Then comes the end, when he delivers the kingdom to God the Father after destroying every rule and every authority and power. For he must reign until he has put all his enemies under his feet. The last enemy to be destroyed is death" (vv. 24–26).

Is That All There Is?

Utopians do not really know how to sing the Blues. There is a lot of "Blues" in the Psalms and in Ecclesiastes. In our current life "under the sun," the description of history attributed to the automaker Henry Ford makes sense: "one damn thing after another." This is literally true, if there is no resurrection and age to come. Contrary to what utopians believe, there is no hope for world peace, justice, and righteousness through the powers that already exist in nature and history. Apart from Christ we are existing for the moment, but are devoid of real life. The Spirit does not come to make the old Adam a little better, but to kill him and make him alive in Christ.

This is why young people have no reason to primarily come to church for dating tips, abstinence training, short-lived emotional summer camp experiences, or a positive circle of friends. There is no point in getting dressed every Sunday for therapeutic moralism or for hearing about how being a Christian is nice and helpful and fun, because this is not the central point of Christianity

Again Paul reiterates the point that if the resurrection isn't *true*, then there's no point in being religious, spiritual, or even moral. His fallback isn't, "Well, at least I was courageous" or "At least I lived a better life than most people." Rather, his alternative to the resurrection faith is hedonism—what we often call "nihilism" today: "Let us eat and drink, for tomorrow we die" (v. 32). Apart from this truth about the resurrection, Paul says that there is no saving knowledge of God (1 Cor 15:34). I love Peggy Lee's song, "Is That All There Is?" After recalling vividly the different stages of her life, wondering "Is that all there is?", Peggy finally comes to the last section. Instead of singing, she just starts talking to her listeners, imagining that they're thinking she might as well end it all. She reassures them that she's not ready to face that last disappointment and concludes by inviting them to drink and dance their lives away.[6]

That is exactly my outlook too, as was Paul's. If Christ is not raised, then nihilism has it right: enjoy yourself now for as long as you can.

But we know Christ was raised. And at the very end of Paul's argument in 1 Corinthians 15 he tells us how to live today:

"Therefore, my beloved brothers, be steadfast, immovable, always abounding in the work of the Lord, knowing that in the Lord your labor is not in vain" (v. 58). And Paul continues this emphasis in 2 Corinthians 4 as well:

> So we do not lose heart. Though our outer self is wasting away, our inner self is being renewed day by day. For this light momentary affliction is preparing for us an eternal weight of glory beyond all comparison, as we look not to the things that are seen but to the things that are unseen. For the things that are seen are transient, but the things that are unseen are eternal. (vv. 16–18)

Justified and renewed by the power of the Spirit, united to Christ, we struggle against indwelling sin, groaning for our release not from embodiedness but from sinfulness. Because Christ has been raised, our hope is not in vain—and neither are our labors in this age. As the gospel is proclaimed to the ends of the earth, those still dead in trespasses and sins are raised, justified, and seated with Christ in heavenly places. They are being conformed to his image, and will one day be glorified together with us. As we go about our daily callings, working in our garden or our cubicle, volunteering at a homeless shelter, falling in love, raising children, and loving and serving our neighbors, we are "steadfast, immovable, always abounding in the work of the Lord" because of the vista he has placed before us. Christ has died. Christ is risen. Christ will come again!

Chapter 7

SUFFERING ISN'T BAD KARMA

In a fascinating Pew survey, most Americans (86 percent) believe that COVID-19 had lessons to teach humanity and 35 percent say it was sent by God.[1] Jesus told us that there would be earthquakes, diseases, persecution of believers, and wars throughout history and around the world until he returns (Matt 24:1–8; cf. Luke 21:11–12). "See that you are not alarmed, for this must take place, but the end is not yet" (v. 6). Why is the end not yet? Given the state of things today, wouldn't it be great if Jesus returned today?

But just imagine your situation if Jesus had returned before you had heard the gospel. Jesus makes this point in verse 14: "And this gospel of the kingdom will be proclaimed throughout the whole world as a testimony to all nations, and then the end will come." Luke's version underscores that all of these "birth pains" are actually comforting signs to the saints: "Now when these things begin to take place, straighten up and raise your heads, because your redemption is drawing near" (Luke 21:28). Jesus did not indicate that these were direct divine judgments, but they *are* indications of a world that is *not* getting better and better, even though all that happens is under his control, fixed by the Father's timetable. So, yes, all that happens in the world is "sent by God" in the sense that he is the Lord of history and nature.

However, we should not automatically assume that every disaster is a direct judgment, as if God had sent a disease as punishment for a particular national or personal sin. In the old covenant this was often the case, where the spread of sin, like gangrene, was held vividly before Israel's eyes in epidemics of leprosy, famine, and other calamities. This was all typological, intended to show us the seriousness of original and personal sin. However, even then you couldn't always draw the specific connection between sin and disaster, as the story of Job reminds us. Sickness is just a part of a fallen, sin-cursed world. "In the day that you eat of [the tree of the knowledge of good and evil], you shall surely die" (Gen 2:17). That was God's warning to Adam and Eve. Instead, they bought Satan's lie that they could be like God—not as imitators of his goodness, righteousness, and holiness, but as autonomous sources of truth.

So, here we are. Like Job's friends, we try to make things simple. Job has been an example of piety to so many people, says Eliphaz.

> "But now it has come to you, and you are impatient;
> it touches you, and you are dismayed.
> Is not your fear of God your confidence,
> and the integrity of your ways your hope?
>
> "Remember: who that was innocent ever perished?
> Or where were the upright cut off?
> As I have seen, those who plow iniquity
> and sow trouble reap the same." (Job 4:5–8)

Talk about rubbing salt into the wounds! Eliphaz is treating Job like a godly giant who has fallen from grace, even though we know that this suffering actually has nothing to do with any particular sin on Job's part.

Bildad takes his turn with the same message: "Behold, God will not reject a blameless man, nor take the hand of evildoers. He will yet fill your mouth with laughter, and your lips with shouting" (8:20–21).

Zophar piles on,

> "If iniquity is in your hand, put it far away,
> and let not injustice dwell in your tents.
> Surely then you will lift up your face without blemish;
> you will be secure and will not fear.
> You will forget your misery;
> you will remember it as waters that have passed away.
> And your life will be brighter than the noonday;
> its darkness will be like the morning.
> And you will feel secure, because there is hope;
> you will look around and take your rest in security." (Job 11:14–18)

This is basically karma: you get what's coming to you, Job. It is also much like today's prosperity gospel: if you are suffering, it is because you've done something bad or you don't have enough faith (or perhaps have not sent in the right amount of money to the preacher). Notice how Job's friends attempt to encourage him with prospects of a bright future if he will only cough up his sin and move on. The prosperity they offer him is not a gospel at all. It is pure law, even if it is softer and gentler, with a happy smile: Do this and you will live!

Now, there is a certain truth to this in the old covenant, to which Job belonged (Ezek 14:13–14). God told Adam: Fulfill the trial, and you will win the right for you and your posterity to eat from the Tree of Life; rebel, and you and all of humanity henceforth will die. That is also how the old covenant worked: Follow the commandments and you will live long in the land that I am giving you. Rebel, and you will be evicted and carried off into captivity (Deut 28). There will be lush vineyards and fruitful fig trees, wombs, and lives if Israel will imitate her King in righteousness, love, justice, and holiness. The sad reality, however, is that "like Adam they transgressed the covenant" (Hos 6:7).

But the new covenant has better promises (grounded in God's oath, not ours) with a better mediator (Christ rather than Moses). God fulfilled his promise in sending his own Son as the Last Adam to fulfill all righteousness, which the first Adam had failed to accomplish, and to bear our curse, rising again as the beginning of the new creation. We are justified—declared righteous before God's court—solely on the basis of Christ's perfect life, sacrificial death, and glorious resurrection. Even now he is at the right hand of the Father interceding for us. We are no longer on trial. It is not our righteousness, but Christ's, that makes us accepted before the Father. Our bad "karma" fell on Jesus that afternoon two thousand years ago outside of Jerusalem. And now we are clothed in his righteousness.

Zophar promised Job that if he just found that secret sin in his life and repented, he would be healthy, wealthy, and wise again: "You will look around and take your rest in security." However, the believer does *not* take security from looking around. The more we look around, all is restless, disordered, frustrating, and ultimately challenges our hope in Christ. Instead, we must shut our eyes and *hear* the promise that God is in charge regardless of what things look like on the surface and he has taken our redemption into his own hands. This is what Abram had to realize when God first gave the promise of his gracious covenant. God promised him an offspring, but Abram could take no security from looking around—no heir, no inheritance. God's promise was pie in the sky, judging by the evidence on the ground. But God kept preaching the gospel to Abram until he found himself believing, and he was justified then and there through faith (Gen 15:6). God still does this with us.

In the old covenant God was using natural disasters to show Israel—and us, in a small-scale manner—the pervasive effects of sin and the extent to which it offends God and corrupts a good creation. However, Jesus made it clear that in the new covenant you cannot make a direct correlation between sin and suffering. For example, in John 9 the Pharisees asked whether the man Jesus healed was blind because of his sins or that of his parents. Imagine how this man, blind from birth, felt as he was told for years that it was a divine judgment for either his parents' sins or his own. "It was not that this man sinned, or his parents," Jesus answered, "but that the works of God might be displayed in him" (John 9:2–3). Just like in the story of Job, this man's blindness was part of God's purpose in glorifying his Son. Ultimately, it is not about Job or the blind man but about God and his glory. When Jesus healed the blind man, he also released him from something more serious: namely, the bondage of guilt and shame. Jesus also commented in Luke 13, "Or those eighteen on whom the tower in Siloam fell and killed them: do you think that they were worse offenders than all the others who lived in Jerusalem? No, I tell you; but unless you repent, you will all likewise perish" (vv. 4–5).

There is no place for judgmentalism when the King and Judge of all the earth has come in mercy for all who trust in him. In this age, "[the Father] makes his sun rise on the evil and on the good, and sends rain on the just and on the unjust," calling us to have the same merciful mind (Matt 5:45). Now is not the era of final judgment, as Jesus shows in rebuking James and John for wanting to call fire down on a Samaritan village that rejected their message (Luke 9:54–56). When Jesus returns in glory to judge the living and the dead, the verdict will be final and decisive forever. But his first coming ushered in this era of repentance and faith, forgiveness, justification, and conversion to God. "For God did not send his Son into the world to condemn the world, but in order that the world might be saved through him. Whoever believes in him is not condemned, but whoever does not believe is condemned already, because he has not believed in the name of the only Son of God" (John 3:17–18).

Just as unbelievers share in God's common grace, Christians suffer the common curse of a fallen world along with non-Christians. God gets our attention through suffering, and sometimes it takes something pretty big to shift our focus from ourselves to his Son. As C. S. Lewis put it, "God whispers to us in our pleasures, speaks in our conscience, but shouts in our pain; it is His megaphone to rouse a deaf world."[2]

It is one thing to say that HIV/AIDS, coronaviruses, and cancers are in God's control and that he has already determined how he will work these together for good. It is another thing to say that they are divine scourges—if they are, then there is no reason to use the ordinary means God has provided for healing. In fact, that might be getting in the way of God's judgment! However, this misunderstands—and miscommunicates to non-Christians—the character of God, the limitations of knowing his ways apart from his Word, and the fact that he expects us to make use of the good gifts he has provided through nature and his common grace to believers and unbelievers alike. Let's not call fire down upon those who reject the gospel. This is the day of salvation—and let's be glad that God does not parcel out particular diseases for the sins that we often tolerate in the church.

When a Christian leader says that a disease or pandemic is a direct judgment for a national sin, this compounds the isolation, suffering, and fears of vulnerable members of society and the church. More importantly, even, it is a serious misinterpretation of Scripture. There are two things we have to remember, based on Scripture: (1) God's providence encompasses everything that happens; (2) We can't read it. "Who has known the mind of the Lord, or who has been his counselor?" (Rom 11:34). There is a better response than judgment: the sight of suffering should automatically drive us to show mercy and not inflict further pain and ostracism upon those already laboring under the burden of their sins.

Pandemics are not the only fear we have right now. Millions of patients wait for blood transfusions, kidney transplants, matching blood types for leukemia, and antidotes to cardiovascular and respiratory failure. This affects Christians and non-Christians alike. In my grandparents' days, death was even more familiar. There was death from childbirth, the common cold and flu, polio, and on and on. These generations worked their fingers to the bone to provide us with a better life, many of them as first- and second-generation immigrants. Now those diseases have been conquered, at least in prosperous nations. But we have myriad new conditions brought upon us by obesity, poor diet, and lack of exercise. Alcohol abuse and addiction to painkillers, sometimes by overprescribing doctors, has spiked death rates in the most prosperous country on earth.

The Deeper Sickness of Our Age

We are a pretty sick nation. When you add to this the enormous growth in diagnosis and treatment of mental health disorders, the list becomes dizzying: PTSD, generalized anxiety disorder, bipolar disorder, schizophrenia, personality disorders, paranoia, depression, gender dysphoria, and so on. It is little wonder that teens are considering suicide as the answer to their problems.

These days, we are more open as a society to acknowledge the reality of mental health conditions. Slowly but surely, churches are acknowledging the seriousness of the crisis. However, there is still a long way to go. According to one study, nearly half of evangelicals think that mental illness is merely a spiritual issue.[3] Here once again we tend to fall out predictably along sociopolitical lines. On one side are those who embrace a *naturalistic* worldview. Secularists assume that we are just a bundle of organs, neurons, and chemicals. There is no such thing as nature, personal identity, or the soul. We are accidents, and therefore have no particular goal that transcends happiness here and now. In short, we are not created; we create ourselves, inventing our identities. Scientific explanations are the only relevant data.

On the other side of the aisle we have a *hyper-supernatural* worldview. It is not surprising that many who are most skeptical of medical science in general and psychiatry in particular are in the "health-and-wealth" camp. But even in more conservative churches there is a tendency to reduce mental illness to a spiritual problem. Like Job's counselors, many sufferers are told that if they just repented, read their Bible, and prayed more, their pain would go away. But when it doesn't, these brothers and sisters are often made to feel as if they just don't have enough faith or obedience. And, once more, unscriptural theology compounds this fear, loneliness, and isolation.

A more biblical orientation reveals that we are complex creatures who are simultaneously spiritual and physical. "I praise you," says the psalmist, "for I am fearfully and wonderfully made. Wonderful are your works; my soul knows it very well" (Ps 139:14).

We are not just meat in a chemical soup. We intuitively know that we have a center of consciousness which cannot be reduced to a physical-chemical explanation or observation. But we are also not souls temporarily housed in a body. God made us as body-soul creatures, so spiritual issues are intertwined with physical ones and vice versa. Chronic back pain makes me more irritable and impatient, and sometimes it makes it easier to take my focus off of Christ and wallow in self-pity.

Only because of the fall do we die and experience the separation of our souls from our bodies. Yet believers die in the hope that just as Christ was raised and glorified in the union of body and soul, so too will they. The fact that our bodies will be included in this ultimate healing should help us appreciate the importance of caring for them even now.

The problem is that many Christians today seem to forget that the brain is part of the body—an organ just like the lungs, kidneys, or liver. I have seen firsthand in many cases how rebalancing the brain chemistry of a person can bring remarkable relief. Most of us as Christians acknowledge that when someone breaks a leg or has cancer, it is not because of a secret sin or a lack of faith. We don't say, "Just pray more or read your Bible more; it's a spiritual issue." There is no reason why brain health should be any different.

But the spiritual component is also key. A lot of depression these days is caused by social isolation, as Ben Sasse points out.[4] "Among epidemiologists, psychiatrists, public-health officials, and social scientists," he documents,

> there is a growing consensus that the number one health crisis in America right now is not cancer, not obesity, and not heart disease—it's loneliness. And with our nation's aging population, it's only going to get worse. . . . Loneliness is surely part of

> the reason Americans consume almost all the world's hydrocodone (99%) and most of its oxycodone (81%).[5]

Among Sasse's recommendations is to set tech limits, since the hours we spend in the echo chamber of our own tribe only fuels the isolation and loneliness.[6]

This is also where regular involvement in the life of a local church is essential. There is no one-size-fits-all biblical rule here. But God has given us one day in seven for resting in body and soul from the labors and anxieties of the week. So why not liberate ourselves from the news of this passing age along with the flurry of emails and texts, and recalibrate our hearts to the age to come? It is the day when Christ the King works for us, stooping to wrap a towel around his waist and wash his disciples' feet. On this day he proclaims himself as an all-sufficient redeemer even through the lips of another sinner. He who bathed us in baptism also comes around to our table to serve us with his own body and blood as our food and drink to eternal life.

Through the work that Christ does by his Spirit on this special day for us, we "who have once been enlightened" (which was early-church-speak for baptism) also "have tasted the heavenly gift, and have shared in the Holy Spirit, and have tasted the goodness of the word of God and the powers of the age to come" (Heb 6:4–5). Having heard the news of this fading age for a week, we are refreshed with the news of the Lamb. Having been catechized in the dogmas of an anxious world, we become realigned to the "kingdom that cannot be shaken" (Heb 12:28). Instead of being alone with our Facebook "friends," we are gathered with our brothers and sisters, along with the angels and archangels, in festive assembly. Together we confess our sins and our faith and join our hearts in praise, lament, sorrow, joy, confession, and thanksgiving.

John Newton, author of "Amazing Grace," writes in another hymn, "The Lord's Day,"

How welcome to the saints when press'd
    With six days' noise and care and toil,
Is the returning day of rest,
    Which hides them from the world a while.

Now from the throng withdrawn away,
    They seem to breathe a diff'rent air;
Compos'd and soften'd be the day,
    All things another aspect wear.

How happy if their lot is cast,
    Where the stately gospel sounds!
The word is honey to their taste,
    Renews their strength, and heals their wounds!

Tho' pinch'd with poverty at home
    With sharp affliction daily fed;
It makes amends if they can come
    To God's own house for heav'nly bread:

With joy they hasten to the place,
    Where they their Saviour oft had met;
And while they feast upon his grace,
    Their burdens and their griefs forget.

This favour'd lot, my friends, is ours,
    May we the privilege improve;
And find these consecrated hours,
    Sweet earnests of the joys above!

We thank thee for thy day, O Lord,
Here we thy promis'd presence seek;
Open thine hand with blessings stor'd,
And give us manna for the week.[7]

Cherishing God's Ordinary Care

The Bible reorients us to avoid naturalism on one side and hyper-supernaturalism on the other. Maybe you know someone who has had a stroke. It is amazing how the circuits in the brain rewire themselves. One part of the brain goes to work doing the job that an injured part of the brain once did. We are indeed "fearfully and wonderfully made" (Ps 139:14). This is the work of God's providence. Sometimes God works miraculously. After my daughter had a brain bleed in the NICU, a team of doctors explained that the X-ray showed *not* that it had resolved but that *there had never been* a brain bleed in the first place. "You must have a friend upstairs," the main doctor said, "because this is what you might call a miracle."

As a Christian, I believe in miracles, pray for miracles, and rejoice in miracles. But most of the time God loves and serves us through providence. God gives us doctors with knowledge and skill, and also provides us technology and medicines. In a successful surgery God is the healer, but he performs his work through the ministry of doctors and nurses. Just think of how your finger heals itself after a cut. That isn't a miracle, but an amazing example of providence. People will often say at the birth of a child, "What a miracle!" And in that moment I would agree—this is not a good time for a theology lesson. But childbirth is not a miracle at all. It is one of the greatest demonstrations of God's *ordinary* operations. Miracles are—by definition—out of the ordinary. The slogan on the coffee mug, "Expect a Miracle!" overlooks the fact that although we may pray for a miracle, we cannot *expect* one.

So those who embrace a naturalistic worldview and those who assume a hyper-supernatural worldview agree in their presupposition that the only place where we can identify God at work is in extraordinary, miraculous signs and wonders. Since these are rare, the secularist concludes that if there is a God he is not involved in our lives, while the hyper-supernaturalist counters by saying that miracles happen all the time. What gets lost in both perspectives is the grandeur of God's providence. In the case of a successful surgery, the naturalist says, "The doctor did it." The hyper-supernaturalist says, "No, God did it!" But the truth is that God did it *through* the medical team. God gave the team its knowledge and skill. Through his marvelous plan, he gave people gifts for inventing the instruments. He even planted the raw materials from which the medicines were made and his Spirit enlightened the chemists who extracted them.

So we have to get beyond this false choice between natural explanations and supernatural explanations. God can operate directly in miracles, but most of the time he works through means that he created and oversees. Science is one of the chief blessings that God has given humanity, to both believers and unbelievers. If we want to see God at work, we need to recognize that he ordinarily operates through natural causes. For the most part, it is these means that we actually see. Martin Luther called them the "masks" that God wears to serve us. Most of the time we do not see God's hands, but only the creaturely gloves he wears. But on the basis of his Word we exclaim, "You open your hand; you satisfy the desire of every living thing" (Ps 145:16). Even when we cannot *see* God's involvement in our lives every moment, we can *hear* him assure us of it.

Whenever we are sick, we need to know that God has not

taken a break, nor does he just not care. He is not punishing us and driving us away from all hope and mercy. It *is* a spiritual issue, as all suffering is, and that is why we need to soak ourselves in the truth of God's Word, both corporately with his saints and in private counseling. We need to cry out to him in lament, trust, sadness, and joy. We need his promises, confirmed to us in baptism and the Lord's Supper. We need to be surrounded not with Job's comforters but with informed believers who can encourage us when everything seems hopeless. And we also need good doctors and perhaps therapists.

Scripture reminds us that sin is a condition, not just actions or things we do. This means that we are both sinners and sinned-against. Suffering, in body and soul, is part of this fallen condition, and that means this condition is not only individual but social. There is real clinical depression, often with genetic roots. Nobody chooses depression; it is part of the universal human curse. No one chooses gender dysphoria or schizophrenia any more than one chooses cancer.

There is no recipe for a single medical prescription in the Bible, because there is never any single cause. We are complex creatures: "fearfully and wonderfully made" while still fallen in all of that complexity. Yet God in his common grace to a fallen world has equipped his creation with medicinal substances that heal the very humans who, collectively in Adam, are responsible for its bondage to corruption (Rom 8:20). And in this age he sends rain and sunshine—and medicinal healing—on the just and the unjust alike (Matt 5:45).

As we seek the means that God has provided for physical healing, we do not forget the spiritual healing that we need at God's hands, especially through his servants of the Word, in public and in private, and the care of elders and deacons. We fix our eyes not on our successes or our failures, nor on our dignity or our diagnoses, but on "Jesus, the founder and perfecter of our faith" (Heb 12:2). We are all pilgrims together as we look for a "better country" (Heb 11:16). God's "Yes" trumps all the "No's" we get from our doctors, creditors, judges, and news outlets. It is a "Yes" that we may have to wait for with patience (Rom 8:25), but we will enjoy it together with the whole creation (Rom 8:22–25). It is not a return to Eden but a forward march into the everlasting Sabbath that Adam forfeited, something unimaginable—"What no eye has seen, nor ear heard, nor the heart of man imagined, what God has prepared for those who love him" (1 Cor 2:9).

Our Daily Bread

Chapter 8

A SECURE FUTURE

Some of us remember the one-hit-wonder '80s band Loverboy, with its song, "Working for the Weekend." We put in our five days or forty hours of drudgery and toil to enjoy two days of freedom. Isn't that how most of society thinks about the meaning of work? Does the Bible have anything to say about this? Does God really care about what we do and how we do it? How does the message that we hear on Sunday and discover in our times of prayer and Bible reading affect our lives on Monday morning?

The whole idea of "securing our future" is actually insane. Why? Because we only exist in the first place as a *gift*. And we only have our being as God's "analogies"—in his image, receiving and then reflecting and relaying his goodness to others.

As Paul told the philosophers in Athens, God isn't an idol they feed, dress, or placate to keep him in his place; "nor is he served by human hands, as though he needed anything, since he himself gives to all mankind life and breath and everything" (Acts 17:25). We often talk about "serving the Lord," but actually *he* serves us. "The Son of Man came not to be served but to serve," said Jesus, "and to give his life as a ransom for many" (Matthew 20:28). Jesus went on to tell his disciples that they were to imitate his service to others. See, that's the point: God serves us and then wants to serve others through us.

But we forget even as disciples that we're on the receiving end of everything good in life. God doesn't need us to serve him. "Or who has given a gift to him that he might be repaid? For from him and through him and to him are all things. To him be glory forever. Amen" (Rom 11:35–36). Sure, God gives us salvation, we think (although we try to place even that in our hands, too), but "all things"? God may get all the credit for my salvation, but he gives me my breath—and breathable air? My job, relationships, and "daily bread"? Yes, *all* of these. We don't first exist and then have occasional gifts from God—our very being is a generous donation. Any happiness or security we experience, any common joy or aptitude, any excellence or cleverness in life—all these are gifts. And then our salvation is secured by God's gift, giving us the hope of feasting together with our triune God as glorified immortals!

Sanity starts with raising our eyes to the Giver. Knowing that he has everything—and us—in his hands, we are free to embrace our callings, our responsibilities, and each other because these aren't really ours either, but are more of God's gifts. With those gifts, looking up to God in faith, we look out to neighbors and the wider creation for opportunities to be his means of loving and serving others.

When we raise our eyes to heaven and catch a glimpse of God's glory and grace, even the most menial task takes on a new and lustrous meaning. Part of our experience in a fallen world is the sense that our work lacks meaning. "So I hated life," said the Preacher in Ecclesiastes, "because what is done under the sun was grievous to me, for all is vanity and a striving after wind" (2:17). These words are a pretty dim view of our daily labors, but they are in the Bible because God understands how we feel "under the sun"—that is, in this present age that is fading away. There is no promise in the Bible that believers will not experience this "vanity" in their work. It is only when we catch a glimpse of things from God's perspective—"above the sun"—that we begin to discern how our work is actually part of God's big plan.

Jobs and Callings

We often speak about having a job or going to work, but a job is something you do. God, however, gives us more than just a task to accomplish. He gives us a calling, and that calling informs what and how we work. A calling is something that, by definition, comes *to* you from *outside of yourself.* The Father calls us to himself in his Son and by his Spirit, uniting us to Christ through the gospel. But there are also callings that all human beings receive from God for the circulation of gifts in secular society. Unlike effectual calling into union with Christ, God's calling to posts in the world is grounded in creation, not redemption, and is sustained by his providential common grace. We cannot save the world by our works, but we can be people through whom God serves the world through our works.

At the same time, we work on this side of the fall. Remember, the multipronged curse in Genesis 3 is neither removed nor the last word over the common life of Christians and non-Christians in a fallen world. Our work cannot therefore be regarded as somehow fulfilling the cultural mandate and ushering in God's kingdom, but it is also not useless because God preserves creation and our own meaningful labors in it. Our callings cannot save, but they can serve.

Let's take the fear of losing our job. Especially if you are a younger person, you will lose not just one but likely multiple jobs. So instead of focusing on *our job,* we need to first focus on *God's calling*. There is a story about a man who passed a construction site, engaging various workers to discover what was being built in his neighborhood. One worker replied, "I'm hauling stones"; another, "I'm mixing concrete." But the third worker said, "I'm building a cathedral." "Under the sun," his job was no less menial and repetitive than that of his crewmates. Yet to him it was not a job, but a calling, because he saw the larger goal. He was doing his part to build a cathedral.

Christians and non-Christians alike, simply by virtue of being created in God's image, are given a calling by God. This comes with his providential gifts, both of natural talents and of education, training, and skills acquired for a specific vocation. A calling is not just our thing, a pursuit of our own identity and self-worth, much less is it the accumulation of money and toys. God calls each human being to "build a cathedral" together—to share in a common project. It is the project of a particular culture, with its art, science, technology, customs, languages, business, and so on. And there is not just one calling, but many. I am not only a father and husband, but a minister, professor, neighbor, citizen, and so forth.

Our common grace callings to various posts in the world are distinct from God's calling of his sheep, drawing and uniting them to the Good Shepherd. For this, Christ has given ministers to build up the body in the faith (Eph 4:11–16). However, the calling of pastors, teachers, evangelists, and missionaries to spread the gospel, planting and watering the saints, is limited. These fruitful saints are also sent out into the world alongside non-Christians with callings for the common good.

Our goal should not be just a good living but a good life. And what is a good life? It is to fulfill our *telos*, the reason for our existence. And what is that, exactly? The first question of the Westminster Shorter Catechism asks, "What is the chief end of man?" The answer is, "to glorify God and to enjoy him forever."

This is hardwired into us as human beings, which is why everyone worships someone or something. We know that we cannot ultimately find happiness in our work or in anything else, but only in God. Unfortunately, this does not keep us from trying to find fulfillment apart from God.

A good watch is one that keeps time. A good house is one that keeps out the rain. And a good human life is one that glorifies and enjoys God. Isn't that a rich purpose for life? Not only to glorify God, but to enjoy him, and not only now but forever. Do you enjoy God in your work? Some of us recall the movie *Chariots of Fire*, where the Olympic runner Eric Liddell tells his missionary sister (who expects her brother to join her overseas), "But God made me fast and when I run, I feel his pleasure." That is not always what you hear on the street when people are talking about their work, is it?

The problem is, once again, the fallen condition in which we find ourselves. Created to glorify and enjoy God, we instead focus on glorifying and enjoying ourselves. Even as Christians we often find that we work not to feel God's pleasure and to love and serve our neighbors as much as to use them by climbing the ladder, making a lot of money, and perhaps leaving our mark. Obviously, that's not going to be fulfilling. Why? How much money does it take to make you happy? "Just a little bit more," supposedly quipped John D. Rockefeller.

So what if you work your way from the mail room to the board room: Does it really matter? A lot of people who have made it to the pinnacle of the skyscraper ask with the author of Ecclesiastes, "Is this all there is?" Many conclude that they've neglected their inner spirit, so they try yoga, Eastern meditation, and the occult. "Spiritual but not religious," they know that there is more to life, but they do not want to acknowledge a God above and outside of them who is their creator, judge, and savior. They want to create themselves, judge themselves, and finally save themselves. But that doesn't fix their emptiness, because they are living against the grain of reality. We *are* created, we *are* judged, and we can only *be* saved by another—namely, by the God who made us. This is what distinguishes our jobs from callings.

Made in God's image, we are given many different callings at the same time. Foremostly, I have been called out of darkness into God's marvelous light (1 Pet 2:9). By his Word and Spirit, the Father has called me to Christ, united me to Christ, and is conforming me to Christ. This is the "high calling" that Paul refers to in Philippians 3:14: "I press on toward the goal for the prize of the upward call of God in Christ Jesus." As I mentioned earlier, I am also simultaneously a husband and parent, brother in Christ, neighbor, professor, and friend. Each of these callings is important. Changing diapers or teaching a class are jobs. Yet like the cathedral builder above, these tasks take on greater significance when I see them as part of a calling. My greatest calling to my neighbors, whether the ones living in my house or the ones living on the street, is to love and serve them with the particular gifts that God has given me.

Of course I want to excel in my vocations, but *why*? Recognition, money, power? No, but because when I glorify and enjoy God and love and serve my neighbors in the way God has specifically equipped me, I feel God's pleasure. Of course, we need to also work for our daily bread—and house and car payments. But when I focus on these things, I'm held hostage to the things that are *most* susceptible to change. By contrast, when my focus is on glorifying and enjoying God and loving and serving my neighbor, then I can apply this in all sorts of ways, whether in this job or another one.

I think this is what Jesus meant when he said in Matthew 6 that we cannot have two masters. A master, by definition, is the one who calls the shots. Money, beauty, security, success, and power make a tyrannical master. "You cannot serve God and money," Jesus says (v. 24). By contrast, Jesus is the master who actually serves us:

> "Therefore I tell you, do not be anxious about your life, what you will eat or what you will drink, nor about your body, what you will put on. Is not life more than food, and the body more than clothing? Look at the birds of the air: they neither sow nor reap nor gather into barns, and yet your heavenly Father feeds them. Are you not of more value than they? And which of you by being anxious can add a single hour to his span of life? And why are you anxious about clothing? Consider the lilies of the field, how they grow: they neither toil nor spin, yet I tell you, even Solomon in all his glory was not arrayed like one of these. But if God so clothes the grass of the field, which today is alive and tomorrow is thrown into the oven, will he not much more clothe you, O you of little faith? Therefore do not be anxious, saying, 'What shall we eat?' or 'What shall we drink?' or 'What shall we wear?' For the Gentiles seek after all these things, and your heavenly Father knows that you need them all. But seek first the kingdom of God and his righteousness, and all these things will be added to you." (vv. 25–33)

Jesus takes care of us. He *really* does. By putting Christ and his kingdom first, we are tempted to think, we give up satisfaction in this life. No, Jesus says: Chase God and his priorities—gain the big picture of things. And then everything else—the job, the income, clothes, and food and drink—will follow. Why? Not because of our efforts, or because good guys finish first, or because if you follow the rules God will bless you, but because God takes care of everyone and everything that he has made. In short, if you make the world or your job your master, you will never enter the joys of God's everlasting kingdom; acknowledge Christ as Lord instead, and you'll not only have heavenly joys but also receive earthly joys thanks to God's providence.

Here is the irony: "Money" pretends to make us gods while in truth it makes us slaves; by contrast, Christ, who is God, became a servant in order to liberate us from slavery and to make us coheirs with him of the everlasting inheritance. Bondage to health, wealth, and happiness steals our life from us. But in letting go of our life here and now, we not only receive joy hereafter but "abundant life" right now, whether we live in a penthouse or an outhouse. "Therefore," Jesus concludes, "do not be anxious about tomorrow, for tomorrow will be anxious for itself. Sufficient for the day is its own trouble" (v. 34). Looking outside of myself, beyond my own self-interest, I am given a sense that there is something larger than me and my happiness. Now I can be joyful even when I am not happy, satisfied even when I'm not prosperous, and confident even when I've lost my job.

For some Christians a calling is just a job calculated to help them accumulate more stuff. Others downgrade their callings by seeing their work as a necessary evil with no spiritual significance. As the story goes, after abandoning the monastic life a brother asked Martin Luther, "What now?" Well, Luther asked him, what were you doing in the monastery? "Making shoes." He was a cobbler. "Then make a good shoe and sell it at a fair price," Luther told him.

God does not need our good works (Rom 11:35–36). His Son has fulfilled all righteousness for us. When we try to leave the world to find good works we can perform to please God, nobody wins. God is not served, and instead is offended that we would presume to deserve his grace, as if Christ's righteousness were somehow deficient. I am also not served by pursuing good works, since I am only adding self-justification to my list of sins. And my neighbor is not served by my good works, because I am so busy trying to climb the spiritual ladder that I don't actually give them what they need. So, it's not quite right to say that I go to work in order to serve the Lord.

Rather, God serves me. I'm always on the receiving end of *God's* service. He gives me everything I need—breath, food, drink, romance, and employment. Most importantly, he serves me his Son, especially through the means of grace on the Lord's Day. I cannot serve him, so I serve my neighbors in his name. And to whatever extent I am able to be used in that way, I feel God's pleasure—not his acceptance, which I have only in Christ, but his pleasure in working through finite and even sinful creatures to keep his gifts circulating.

Cultivating a Secure Future

The original calling given to Adam and Eve was to tend the garden and to work the soil, making it fruitful—all for the glory of God. And though that calling was frustrated and disrupted by human rebellion and sin, it remains God's good intention for us to do good in our work, for the sake of our neighbor and for God's pleasure. Our first parents' callings were positive ("ruling")—extending God's reign—and negative ("subduing")—casting out everything that defiled and beguiled, especially the serpent. They failed in this mandate, and we are not continuing it. Thankfully, Jesus picked up where they failed. He is the Last Adam; we are not. This means that our present callings are not extending God's saving kingdom, but are under God's common grace as well as common curse alongside non-Christians. The delay of Christ's return is not for the improvement of this "passing age" (1 Cor 7:31) but for the success of the Great Commission.

So our work cannot be *ultimately* meaningful, but it can be *penultimately* meaningful. This frees us up to pursue ordinary vocations without thinking that somehow we have to use them as culture transforming and sacred, even saving, enterprises. Our calling is not just a job, but it is also not the "ruling and subduing" that could only come from Jesus.

Today, there is an acute anxiety about the state of our world, and much of that anxiety centers around global climate change. That anxiety has grown considerably in recent years and for understandable reasons. Yet we seem caught between two unbiblical worldviews—two extremes. On the one hand, many who are committed to a sort of ideological environmentalism today are more pantheistic than atheistic. Pantheists believe that all is god and god is all. Panentheists acknowledge a god who may be *more* than the world, but depends on the world for his own fulfillment. That is, instead of rejecting divinity entirely, they attribute divinity to nature itself. For them, the planet must be saved because it is the divine body, so when we wound creation we are wounding God in his very being. The distinction between the Creator and creation thus becomes practically illegible.

On the other side of the spectrum, many evangelicals default to what we might call a Gnostic creation theology. The ancient Gnostics believed that the body and this world (in its materiality as opposed to the spirituality of the divine realm) cannot be saved. On the contrary, the goal is to be saved *from* creation, not *with* it. The classic example of this view is Hal Lindsey's *The Late, Great Planet Earth* (1970), which was the national bestseller of the entire decade.

Some Christians react against their conservative background by simply gravitating toward the secularist outlook: It's our world and we have to save it. Consequently, the tendency is to trust the government to solve all the problems facing the planet. Without confidence in a sovereign God who created, preserves, and redeems *his* world, the fate of our planet rests solely in our hands. Still, there *is* a place for collective action through governments.

God commanded Adam and Eve to "work . . . and keep" his creation before they fell (Gen 2:15). God has given us government and commands us to pray for and obey our secular leaders as his own ministers (Matt 22:21; Rom 13; 1 Tim 2:2; 1 Peter 2:13). But while policies and programs may help stem the effects of climate change, they cannot bring about a renovated creation.

Younger people especially feel this burden of saving the world, particularly when their parents, teachers, and social media bombard them with the suggestion that this generation must finally solve ecological disaster, racism, and economic inequities. And they will do all of this, evidently, while being saddled with a $3 trillion deficit that continues to grow. It is inevitable that this perpetual state of crisis will lead to burnout and apathy for our youth. Like other fears, this inflated view of ourselves and deflated view of God tends to paralyze rather than empower. Saving the world turns out to be more than we can handle, so by the time we reach middle age we tend to shrug off any sense of personal responsibility for creation stewardship.

Happily, as Christians we are freed from bondage to worldviews based on purely secular coordinates. So let us focus simply on the facts. When it comes to care for God's creation, what has almost every generation of Christians considered enormously significant, at least until recently?

Don't Blame God

It is common today to blame environmental degradation on the Judeo-Christian ethic. Some of this is likely due to the strong current of neo-pagan spirituality in the modern environmental movement. "Divinity," identified with nature, replaces a personal God who created the world by his own free act and causes it to exist every moment by his loving will and command. Obviously, this qualitative distinction between God and his creation runs counter to the belief that environmental violence wounds God. But it is good news that God does not need the world. Because he is *not* wounded by human disobedience, he can *save* the world that he freely loves.

A second frequent criticism is that, according to the Bible, God put man in charge of the planet so he could do whatever he chose with it. This hierarchical and human-centered view of the environment has given its blessing to centuries of wanton abuse, we are told. How should we respond to this common characterization?

The first thing we should say as Christians is to agree that there are plenty of examples in modern history that seem to support this narrative. Many Christians in more recent times have assumed an adversarial view between humans and the rest of creation. If nature replaces God in the neo-pagan outlook, in this one humans replace God. This view is based on a grave misunderstanding of the biblical mandate. Ever since Francis Bacon (1561–1626), people have tended to view science and technology as instruments that reduce nature to a lifeless thing to be manipulated, harnessed, and exploited for the sole benefit of human beings. Yet this view of the relationship of humans to creation was largely fostered by modern science rather than by religion. Many in Bacon's day (especially the Puritans) and since that time have countered this worldview with a more robust, biblical one.[1] Secularists cannot take credit for the role of modern science and technology in contributing to human progress and then blame Christianity for the negative impact of human progress on the environment.

We should acknowledge that we *have* failed to fulfill the office that God gave us in creation. Sadly, this has been true ever since the fall, but there is a lot of evidence to support the biblical command that we should be stewards, not exploiters, of the earth.

We should not defend ourselves by misinterpreting God's commission. For example, as some Christians reply, did God not say, "Be fruitful and multiply and fill the earth and subdue it, and have dominion over the fish of the sea and over the birds of the heavens and over every living thing that moves on the earth" (Gen 1:28)? Yes, God did give Adam and Eve this mandate, but they failed to carry it out. Instead, they rejected God's claim, ensnaring the whole creation in their sentence. So it is true that creation suffers because of human sin—first, against God, provoking his just curse; second, against each other and all of our fellow creatures (Rom 8:20). Moreover, in that original mandate the dominion that humanity was to exercise under God was "to work it and keep it" (Gen 2:15), not to exploit it as if it were our personal possession. The dominion was for protection of creation, not its abuse.

Since the law and the prophets condemn the kings of Israel and Judah for behaving tyrannically and oppressively rather than leading and protecting, it is impossible that God had in mind such a vicious job description for the king and queen that he made in his own image. Furthermore, this original mandate became obsolete once it had been violated. This means that humans have forfeited their right to rule under God, which is why God himself, the eternal Son, assumed our nature in order to be the victorious Last Adam who fulfilled that commission on our behalf. The human race is now under the Noahic covenant of common grace, not the special covenant that Adam broke.[2] In that covenant with Noah, God made a promise not only to humans but to the whole creation to extend his common grace in spite of human sin.

Even if humanity still had the dominion mandate, the "ruling and subduing" chiefly has to do with guarding Paradise from Satan and his minions who had been cast down to earth. This becomes clearer when Adam fails to do this and not only allows entrance of the serpent but sits idly by while the serpent seduces

Eve with false promises that they might become gods themselves. On the contrary, Adam's job was to keep God's garden free of anything that defiles. To have dominion over "every living thing" is thus to be a good shepherd, not a cruel despot.

We catch a broader glimpse of this fact when we read specific laws in the Torah about caring for the land and animals. There is a time for working the land and enjoying its fruit, "but in the seventh year there shall be a Sabbath of solemn rest for the land, a Sabbath to the LORD. You shall not sow your field or prune your vineyard" (Lev 25:4).

The fourth of the Ten Commandments says of the Sabbath, "On it you shall not do any work, you, or your son, or your daughter, your male servant, or your female servant, or your livestock, or the sojourner who is within your gates" (Exod 20:10). Even aliens are to be given this release from toil and rest in the Lord. Adding to the basis of the Sabbath in God's resting from creation (v. 11), the rationale is supplemented in Deuteronomy 5:15: "You shall remember that you were a slave in the land of Egypt, and the LORD your God brought you out from there with a mighty hand and an outstretched arm. Therefore the LORD your God commanded you to keep the Sabbath day." The biblical redefinition of ruling as *serving* is seen especially in Jesus, the Good Shepherd in the flesh, who scolded his disciples for jockeying for position in his kingdom. Gentiles "lord it over" others, but "It shall not be so among you," for service will prevail over domination (Matt 20:25–28).

We have to answer to the Creator and Judge of all the earth for how we steward his world and its creatures. From a biblical perspective the world is not an abstract *environment*, but is *creation*—God's creation. Ironically, many on both the left and the right share a similar premise: That this is *our* world either to be saved or exploited.

What pantheists fail to realize is that all of the commandments are really unpacking the first: "You shall have no other gods before me" (Exod 20:3). God is the King, and it is his land—in fact, his world. The human viceroy, Israel, must act righteously and justly, "lest the land vomit you out when you make it unclean, as it vomited out the nation that was before you" (Lev 18:28). It is not Israel's land, but God's land. In fact, God tells the nation, "The land shall not be sold in perpetuity, *for the land is mine*. For you are strangers and sojourners with me" (Lev 25:23, emphasis mine). The Israelites are thus tenants in God's land—the complete opposite of a secularist worldview, in which there is no overlord above humanity. On the other hand, Christians have every reason to repent to their Creator and trust in God's future plan to redeem creation.

As in Eden, the land is clean first and foremost when there is no idolatry, when God is Israel's only ultimate King. Then there is peace, fruitfulness, and rest—not just for human beings, but for the whole environment that they inhabit. From this flows love and respect for all of God's creation. One problem with monarchies in history is that you can have cynical and self-serving autocratic rulers. But when God is on the throne, and his viceroy imitates him, there is goodness, righteousness, freedom, and flourishing—not just for human beings but for the land and everything that lives on it. It is filled with fruitful vines and fig trees—a land flowing with milk and honey. Pantheism and other forms of idolatry actually contribute to the undoing of God's good creation by thinking that humans can run the world better than its Creator, Lord, and Redeemer. But that is exactly how we landed in this mess in the first place.

Chapter 9

STEWARDS, NOT SAVIORS

When we raise our eyes to heaven, something strange happens to us. Fears of our circumstances, including life, vocations, and the condition of the environment, are so moderated that we are able to engage in stewardship with hopeful responsibility instead of utopianism or despair. Our fears really can be relieved by the one fear that matters most. We no longer feel that a secure job or a secure planet rests in our hands.

The kingship of Yahweh is exactly what we need in order to put the rulers of this age in their place. Again and again in the prophetical books, God indicts priests, prophets, and kings for imagining that God is a pet they can put on a leash and manipulate. We see this clearly in Psalm 2. It is in some ways a strange song, but as we look more closely at it we clearly see how God turns the tables on his rebels. Instead of the rulers not taking God seriously, it is he who does not take them seriously at all. In fact, he laughs at them:

> Why do the nations rage
>   and the peoples plot in vain?
> The kings of the earth set themselves,

and the rulers take counsel together,
against the LORD and against his Anointed,
saying,
"Let us burst their bonds apart
and cast away their cords from us."

He who sits in the heavens laughs;
the Lord holds them in derision.
Then he will speak to them in his wrath,
and terrify them in his fury, saying,
"As for me, I have set my King
on Zion, my holy hill."

I will tell of the decree:
The LORD said to me, "You are my Son;
today I have begotten you.
Ask of me, and I will make the nations your heritage,
and the ends of the earth your possession.
You shall break them with a rod of iron
and dash them in pieces like a potter's vessel."

Now therefore, O kings, be wise;
be warned, O rulers of the earth.
Serve the LORD with fear,
and rejoice with trembling.
Kiss the Son,
lest he be angry, and you perish in the way,
for his wrath is quickly kindled.
Blessed are all who take refuge in him.

In America, *everyone* is a "king of the earth." We can be whoever or whatever we choose. We can pursue whatever job or career we desire. Follow your dreams. Listen to your heart. Of course, that only works if you are wealthy enough to do it. And we can do whatever we want to the earth as long as we rightly calculate how it advances our national and personal wealth.

There are several problems with this declaration of independence, though. For one, if everyone is an autonomous and sovereign individual, then other people besides myself cannot be. I *have* to dominate, bully, push, and shove, even if I have a smile and a firm assurance that I am on the right side of history. More importantly, as we have seen, we are *not* independent little kings and queens. Rather, we are dependent yet deluded and treasonous viceroys of the Great King. Transgressing God's boundaries does not authenticate our existence but does just the opposite. It drains our existence of all meaning and significance. *Sin does not exercise power, but impotence.* In the Book of Common Prayer there is a "general confession" for "what I have done and what I have *left undone.*" The Westminster Shorter Catechism, question 14, defines sin not only as "transgression of the law of God" but as "lack of conformity thereto," and in covering the Ten Commandments Lutheran and Reformed catechisms explain not only what is forbidden but what is required. To paraphrase, "Thou shalt not kill" means "Thou shalt do everything you can to preserve the life of your neighbor and his or her reputation."

Some time ago, I was intrigued when I read theologian Karl Barth's description of sin as, more than anything else, *sloth*. Most of our sins are in the "left undone" category I just mentioned. We're lazy. Apart from God's grace, we are not inclined to care about God or our neighbor. We don't even really care about ourselves—at least not about our most important needs. We just want to have fun, make a splash, let a few people know we were here, and . . . whatever. Most of us are not even brave enough to be truly awful; mostly, we're just indolent. In Psalm 2, the rulers of the nations seek to break the bonds of the King of kings: a sin of *commission*, to be sure. Yet their ultimate crime is sloth: a sin of *omission*. They refuse to acknowledge the Son as the rightful heir and as sovereign over the kingdoms of the earth, including their own. This filters down to us. I often find that I have to have a Vocation (capital V), to leave my mark. Well, actually, I don't. I have lots of vocations: husband, father, minister, neighbor, citizen, and so forth. And I have different callings at different points in my life. My wife has needed me to be there for her in various stages of her life, just as I have needed her. Things change. Same with the kids. When my triplets were born, my new major calling was to change diapers. I pride myself on the assembly line, timing myself to get everything done more efficiently than the last round. I also had a calling to take care of my parents. And I preach and teach seminarians. There's a lot going on. So, we can easily see that we have a variety of callings and priorities at different stages of life. This should caution against the search for a "Calling" that is more about me than it is about neighbors who need what I have to offer to them right then and there. That's what vocations are about: serving people exactly when and where it's needed. They really aren't about finding personal meaning in life. Rather, the meaning is found in Christ, who wants to love and serve my neighbors through me.

Failing to give the Son his homage is the worst example of sloth, however. It is not so much an active insurrection as a failure of nerve. When the Son appeared, robed in our flesh, he took his authority not from worldly powers but from heaven (John 18:36). When a new British monarch is crowned in Westminster Abbey, long-established custom has traditionally been to ask the nobles and other prominent attendees, "This is your lawful sovereign. Will you do him homage?" (The answer is yes, by the way.) Similarly, in the ancient world the nobles lined up to offer this fealty with a kiss. Jesus Christ is the royal Son in Psalm 2. He is gathering his empire of grace from every nation. In the meantime, he patiently allows Caesar to collect taxes (Mark 12:17), but Caesar's realm is a petty fiefdom compared to Christ's universal and everlasting reign. Caesar happily accommodated native religions in the Roman Empire; the more the merrier, in fact. As long as they surrendered their bodies to Caesar, his subjects could give their hearts to any god they liked. The gods could have the heavens, as long as people recognized that the earth belonged to Caesar. Yet Jesus says in his Great Commission, "All authority in heaven *and on earth* has been given to me. *Go therefore* and make disciples of all nations . . ." (Matt 28:18–19, emphasis mine). The rulers of this age may persecute the church, but they cannot authorize, legitimize, protect, or advance the church and its mission. Even Christian rulers must acknowledge that their jurisdiction is limited to the common good of the people.

In Psalm 2, then, God laughs at the pretension of the would-be autonomous self. The powerful ones of this age are not living with the grain of reality. Insanity has gripped them. It just does not make sense that they would not acknowledge the Messiah as their lawful sovereign. It may seem a little off-putting that God's response to all of this vaunted show of autonomy is to *laugh*. Once more we meet a God who is not necessarily the familiar one in our culture today. Yet his response makes perfect sense. Here are rebels God created in his image and still loves, running around on the ground like ants and spoiling their realms and natural resources. They think that they're free and can make their own choices, but they don't realize that only God's fetters can liberate them.

However, unlike the ants, our ordered processions are not determined by nature and common welfare, nor even by a pretended power of choice. The social media silos, marketing demographics, seasonal fashions, political movements, and parties actually shape our desires, determine our range of choices, and then curate and sell them for further exploitation. Not just our carbon footprint but our pretensions to technological mastery are laughable. It's silly. Like our first parents, we quickly realize that our prized autonomy is just a dream—a nightmare, in fact. It is not consistent with reality. We can declare our independence, but that does not mean that we have succeeded in gaining it. We may cry out in elation, "I am free!", but we are actually in bondage to lords which cannot liberate but merely seek to pull us deeper into their deathly depths.

God's laughing is not the sardonic cackle of a tyrant, but the head-shaking amazement of a liberating King at just how deluded we are as we seek to "burst [*his*] bonds apart." We cannot actually do this, because we cannot choose or unchoose to be God's creatures. But we try, however feebly, to resist anyone or anything that exposes our charade of autonomy. This is not power, but impotence; not freedom, but bondage; not authenticity, but vanity; not intelligence, but foolishness. Why would anyone want to cast off the bonds of *this* king, who said, "Come to me, all who labor and are heavy laden, and I will give you rest. Take my yoke upon you, and learn from me, for I am gentle and lowly in heart, and you will find rest for your souls. For my yoke is easy, and my burden is light" (Matt 11:28–30)?

It is certainly true that monotheism is essential to the Judeo-Christian outlook and that God is represented by the analogy of a king. However, the biblical narrative is the antithesis of tyrannical domination; the adopted prince and princess treasonably rebelled against the holy and just Great King. And yet "God so loved the world, that he gave his only Son" (John 3:16). The Son, who is of the same essence as the Father, assumed our nature to redeem us "while we were enemies" (Rom 5:10) and included the rest of nature along with us. While the rulers of this world typically demand the blood of their subjects for the spread of their empires, the King of kings lays down his life to make his subjects sons and daughters of God. He also crushed the serpent's head and one day will remove from the earth—indeed, the whole cosmos—anything that defiles. Thanks to Christ, the eternally begotten Son who lovingly sacrificed himself for us, humanity has at last been restored to the place of dominion as guardian and protector of creation. The writer to the Hebrews elaborates,

> For it was not to angels that God subjected the world to come, of which we are speaking. It has been testified somewhere,
>
> "What is man, that you are mindful of him,
> or the son of man, that you care for him?
> You made him for a little while lower than the angels;
> you have crowned him with glory and honor,
> putting everything in subjection under his feet."
>
> Now in putting everything in subjection to him, he left nothing outside his control. At present, we do not yet see everything in subjection to him. But we see him who for a little while was made lower than the angels, namely Jesus, crowned with glory and honor because of the suffering of death, so that by the grace of God he might taste death for everyone.
>
> For it was fitting that he, for whom and by whom all things exist, in bringing many sons to glory, should make the founder of their salvation perfect through suffering. For he who sanctifies and those who are sanctified all have one source. That is why he is not ashamed to call them brothers. (Heb 2:5–11)

Creation at last has a restored human viceroy, but it is not the would-be autonomous human; it is the faithful Son who obeyed every word from his Father. With the first Adam the whole creation was subjected to futility, but with the Last Adam the whole creation will at last share in the freedom of the children of God (Rom 8:21–22). I don't think we often appreciate the extent to which the Son, equal in every way to the Father, subjected himself to the Father in his incarnation and carried out his vocation. He is exactly what "Adam" was supposed to look like. Christ wholeheartedly and faithfully followed the Father's perfect plan to save humanity.

Jesus did not come to redeem us *from* creation or our callings. Just as our own bodies will be raised, so too will the rest of creation be completely regenerated. Dietrich Bonhoeffer expressed this beautifully: "Only he who loves the earth and God in the same breath can believe in the kingdom of God."[1]

The only alternative to this biblical narrative is to embrace the myth of a world that is intrinsically evil and essentially born in conflict. Such a world is the exact opposite of the original product of the Creator, whose goodness was marred by *human* rebellion but will be restored beyond even its first beauty. The "survival of the fittest" was the creation story of Israel's neighbors, and it continues up to our day in Marxism along with many forms of capitalism. By the way, I have no idea why anyone faithful to this dogma would have the slightest fear of environmental destruction. In a dog-eat-dog world, the war of humans against each other is part of a larger struggle of humans against nature. Rooted in ancient paganism, it is the belief that this evil is natural, rather than a perversion of God's good creation.

The Restoring of All Things

As Christians, we can say that God did *not* create our world the way it is now. Rather, this present world displays our fallen condition.

Given their worldview, secularists can only shrug and say, "Well, that's just the way things are." If there is a Creator, he has done a pretty bad job. So we shift the blame to God and then announce that "God is dead." Whoever is best prepared by nature and nurture to cross the finish line and grasp the crown of life is to be celebrated, but whatever or whomever gets in the way—especially the dependent, weak, or sick—is trampled. Such thinning out is just the way of the world. The world is too populated. It is a world of scarcity, not abundance. Like prisoners with a limited water supply, we have to kill off the weak to keep ourselves alive and to save the planet.

Even though the members of the Godhead needed nothing but each other, they created the world as an expression of free love. Those who deny God's existence and lordship must accept that this world was not created from the Father, in the Son, and by the Spirit. Rather, it is an "environment," a frail lifeboat limited in its occupational capacity and prone to sinking. There are too many human beings (the bane of the "environment"). The world itself is not intrinsically good from the beginning, so why should we feel any responsibility to preserve it? Hobbes, Marx, and Darwin see nature and history as nothing more than a war of all against all. Shouldn't we try to just push the weak members who can't survive out of the lifeboat?

Why shouldn't COVID-19 be seen, like abortion, as a natural way of thinning the herd, ensuring that the healthiest animals carry their genes on to the next generation? Maybe the cyborgs will rule humans; is that so bad? It's just the way of evolution. Why would anyone want to "save" such a world? It seems like one would just want to survive it and try to make it to the top during our brief time on earth. So, actually, those who adopt a purely naturalistic story should be least concerned about this world. If humans are expendable, then why should one care about owls, forests, and rivers?

Here again we see similarities between a secularist outlook and the assumption of many conservative Christians. The former may be described as *nihilism*: there is no reason we're here except to party and try to get ahead. A lot of conservative Christians sound perilously close to something like this Gnostic idea that "it's all gonna burn anyway," so God will replace this world with something else instead of redeeming it. So the irony is that so many secular nihilists actually behave like Christians in taking an active interest in this world, while many Christians behave like secular nihilists.

I was raised in churches which taught that this world will be destroyed rather than redeemed. Our only business on earth, therefore, is "saving souls." This is probably not entirely fair to my teachers, but I imagined that the climax of this story is souls going to another world—a nonmaterial place. This is the myth of the Gnostics, not the Christians. The Gnostic error has a long heritage; the third century theologian Origen, whom I mentioned earlier, was too influenced by the Platonic philosophy of the Gnostics to believe that Jesus ascended bodily and that, in him, our bodies will be restored. The orthodox church eventually condemned his teachings as heresy, but these errors have continued to persist, infiltrating many of our churches and traditions.

God is ashamed of nothing he has made. Rocks, rivers, seas and mountains, cities and towns—along with their myriad inhabitants—are objects of God's delight, not detestation. The human body, fearfully and wonderfully made by God's art and skill, is not going to be scrapped for a new model but raised in a glorified condition. If the *Late, Great Planet Earth* were the end game, then Christ's costly work was a waste. In that case, the triune God would merely need to destroy the whole physical world, including human bodies, to release all souls from their prisons.

The incarnation, life, death, resurrection, ascension, and

return of Christ seem like the wrong solution for salvation *from* this world. But, happily, the Gnostic heresy is the antithesis of the biblical hope. Resurrection, not annihilation, is God's plan: redemption, not rejection, of creation. Jesus has ascended in our flesh, "whom heaven must receive until the time for restoring all the things about which God spoke by the mouth of his holy prophets long ago" (Acts 3:21). The phrase *apokatastaseôs pantôn*—the restoring of all things—is the antithesis of the annihilation of all things. Jesus said to his disciples, "Truly I tell you, at the renewal of all things, when the Son of Man sits on his glorious throne, you who have followed me will also sit on twelve thrones, judging the twelve tribes of Israel" (Matt 19:28 NIV). The NIV rendering is better than the ESV ("new world") since *palingenesia* means "regeneration" or "restoration," referring to circumstances such as the nation of Israel returning from exile. It is also the same word used of spiritual regeneration in Titus 3:5. We do not receive a new soul or any other faculty in the new birth, but are *made new* within. That inward renewal by the Spirit will finally culminate in the outward renewal of all things when Christ returns.

One of my favorite verses is Luke 24:41, where Jesus appears to the disciples after the resurrection. "And while they still disbelieved for joy and were marveling, he said to them, 'Have you anything here to eat?'" Feasting with God, without fear of serpents and the specter of sin and death, was the goal held out to Adam and Eve and to Israel. Now we have a covenant head and mediator who has secured this right for us. When he returns, the prophecy of Isaiah 25 will be fulfilled:

> On this mountain the LORD of hosts will make for
>   all peoples
>   a feast of rich food, a feast of well-aged wine,

of rich food full of marrow, of aged wine
well refined.
And he will swallow up on this mountain
the covering that is cast over all peoples,
the veil that is spread over all nations.
He will swallow up death forever;
and the Lord GOD will wipe away tears from all faces,
and the reproach of his people he will take away
from all the earth,
for the LORD has spoken. (vv. 6–8)

The new creation will not be an *alternative* to this world any more than Christ's risen body was an alternative to the body he assumed in the incarnation. He now rules in heaven, with hair and hands and feet, and in that same body he will return to this earth to judge, cleanse, and renovate the world (Acts 1:11). The *only* thing from this world that *won't* enter into the age to come is anything "unclean" (Rev 21:27). At last, the garden will be cleansed. The serpent will be judged and cast into the lake of fire. The world that God made will finally be redeemed, not by the petty prince who made himself to be god and then built Babylon, the City of Man, but by the Son who is God and by whom all things were made, who became flesh to redeem all of creation to make it the City of God forever.

So, the biblical story from the "tick" of Genesis to the "tock" of Revelation is pro-creation in a way that secularist nihilism, neo-pagan spirituality, and Gnostic heresy can never be. If, in spite of inconsistence with their worldview, non-Christians have stepped into a vacuum created by apathetic Christians with nihilistic assumptions, then it is essential to recover a biblical outlook on creation and redemption. There is no philosophy or religion on earth that has as high a view of creation as we find in the Bible.

Christian Concern for Environmental Stewardship

We have no examples in history of a pantheistic or polytheistic society that sowed the seeds of environmental stewardship in a civilization. Even in Plato's dialogues, where the cosmos is treated as a god, the material world is the source and habitat of evil. Factories, not natural resources, were on Marx's mind, and environmental stewardship has never been a concern of communist regimes. Nietzsche offers no plea for environmental responsibility; on the contrary, in his view a new race of pitiless Supermen will soon emerge to dominate the weak.

All of the environmental movements before the twentieth century have originated in Jewish and Christian circles. In the biblical outlook of Francis of Assisi, we are fellow creatures with birds and beasts. Neither divine nor demonic, creation is the work of God's hands; we see his signature on everything he made. The Puritans were successful in the banning of cockfighting and other forms of animal mistreatment. During the Industrial Revolution, evangelicals were a nuisance to unscrupulous barons because they fought for—and occasionally won—legislation against cruelty to animals as well as children and women. Besides his key role in abolishing British slavery, William Wilberforce, an evangelical member of Parliament, succeeded in the banning of bullfighting and founded the Society for the Protection of Animals (SPCA) in 1824. The Humane Society of the United States website includes a fascinating tour of past evangelical support and now shows, after a period of decline, a resurgence of concern for the treatment of animals.[2]

Some conservative Christians are, in fact, waking up to the need to look out for other creatures that not only feed and entertain but depend on us. Matthew Scully, senior speechwriter for former president George W. Bush, provides a good overview of the Christian legacy, theological underpinnings, and defense of animals today.[3] The conservative Roman Catholic senator Rick Santorum supported legislation against puppy mills and horse slaughter. Richard Land, former head of the Religious Liberty Commission of the Southern Baptist Convention, successfully championed the abolition of cockfighting in the South.[4] All of these concerns have roots in earlier historical movements by conscientious Christians.

"Pro-life" has become a banner for a single issue—abortion. This issue is of paramount ethical concern, and Christians are not simply foisting their religious views on others but are loving their neighbors when they defend this cause. In fact, we may have gained more support in defense of the unborn if we had been more consistently pro-life across the board. It is difficult to imagine how Francis Schaeffer would be received today in some conservative evangelical circles. His crusade against abortion and euthanasia would be welcomed, but what about his published warnings against racism and the lack of concern for creation stewardship in churches? Today these ethical concerns have nothing to do with each other in the minds of many Christians. In fact, they are bullet points in progressive policy agenda items. However, these issues are intertwined in a Christian perspective: "The earth is the LORD's and the fullness thereof" (Ps 24:1). And the whole creation will share in the liberty of the children of God (Rom 8:22–23).

Hope: Beyond Utopianism and Despair

Utopianism and despair are two types of fear-driven ideology. The Christian alternative is hope. Utopianism requires a plan with us (especially me) as the agent. However, it is never fulfilled because we (and I) are part of the problem. If everything depends on us and we are ourselves corrupt, that is a problem. Utopians assume that "we"—those of us who "get it"—are already on target and we just need to enlighten enough dull, insensitive, and perhaps even evil people so that they join the cause. "If we just . . . , then. . . ." Fill in the blanks. Such statements, whether in our personal character, attitudes, choices, and actions or in broader causes, often presuppose a baseline view of human beings as good people who could be a lot better if they just did what we say. We become really angry at them when they don't, because they are obviously just refusing to be as virtuous as we. Some conservatives may be drawn to an individualistic utopianism, while liberals tend toward a more social and global vision. That is in part why their political agendas differ. But either type of utopianism is bound to lead by turns from self-righteousness to despair because human beings are not perfect or even perfectible in this present age of sin and death. Utopianism eventually paralyzes us because it's impossible. The perfect becomes the enemy of the everyday good we can do, which is so small it's hard to measure. (Disillusioned utopians are among the most unpleasant dinner guests, by the way.)

Despair is another common response to the problems we see either in ourselves or in the world. Some of us assume that although *I* am a relatively good person, there are too many people who are *not*—and there's no way that I can change them. Again, this is fed by hours spent in our preferred silo of so-called "news" and social media instead of actually rubbing shoulders with neighbors.

But self-righteousness is not the only way despair manifests itself. Many believers are heartily willing to agree that they are in the same boat with everyone else, born in sin and still sinners although forgiven. As the bumper sticker from a while back had it, "Not Perfect, Just Forgiven." Or, as one wag described rather cynically, "I like to sin, God likes to forgive—what a great relationship!" Whether as individuals or as societies, we cannot expect any changes for the better until we die or Jesus returns. Despairers are often former utopians.

Hope is different from these alternatives. On the one hand, it eschews utopianism by acknowledging that sin is a pervasive and ineradicable condition that expresses itself in sinful desires and actions by both individuals and societies. There is no perfection until Christ returns. Even Christians remain simultaneously justified and sinful. If the holiest believer in this life still falls short of God's glory and stands in constant need of God's forgiveness, then even if the citizens of entire nations were converted to Christ there would still be greed, strife, disease, war, and injustice. The history of Christendom offers sufficient needles to pop the balloon of Christian nationalism.

On the other hand, hope clings to a promise anchored in the fact that right in the middle of this sordid history God planted a cross where Satan, sin, and death were objectively vanquished. The good news gets even better: Christ has been raised in our humanity as the beginning of the new creation, seated at the Father's right hand to intercede for us. The one who will sit in judgment on all people one day is already our defense attorney in God's court. We thus rejoice that when we die our soul will enjoy God's presence, but that is not our final salvation. Our ultimate hope is in our bodily resurrection and the sharing of the whole creation—this world—in that final liberation.

The apostle Paul unpacks this hope in a powerful summary:

> For I consider that the sufferings of this present time are not worth comparing with the glory that is to be revealed to us. For the creation waits with eager longing for the revealing of the sons of God. For the creation was subjected to futility, not willingly, but because of him who subjected it, in hope that the creation itself will be set free from its bondage to corruption

> and obtain the freedom of the glory of the children of God. For we know that the whole creation has been groaning together in the pains of childbirth until now. And not only the creation, but we ourselves, who have the firstfruits of the Spirit, groan inwardly as we wait eagerly for adoption as sons, the redemption of our bodies. For in this hope we were saved. Now hope that is seen is not hope. For who hopes for what he sees? But if we hope for what we do not see, we wait for it with patience. (Rom 8:18–25)

A few points are worth highlighting.

First, "the present time" is marked by "sufferings." Just as Jesus the head of the church suffered and *then* entered his glory, we as his members follow the same path. The church does not look very spectacular right now. In fact, to the world it looks pretty weak and even sometimes hypocritical. It is a flawed institution because it's made up of sinful people. We sometimes suffer because of our ongoing sinfulness and at other times because of the rebellion of humanity against Christ and his kingdom. The common division of history among Jewish leaders at the time of Jesus was between "this present age," dominated by sin, suffering, and death, and "the age to come" marked by the Messiah's reign. Jesus and his apostles repeatedly invoked this distinction in the New Testament. So in "the present time," as Paul says, we can expect suffering, not glory.

Notice how Paul emphasizes the wide scope of the curse, extending it beyond the believer's suffering to the bondage of the whole creation due to human rebellion. Ever since Adam's fall, the whole creation has been "subjected to futility." The powerful gifts which God bestowed upon nature in creation are often out of whack. The amazing potential of ecosystems to rejuvenate themselves after natural or human-caused disasters has been slowed, twisted, and thwarted.

The whole creation suffers and is subjected to "vanity," but not because of its own fault. It is because the humans called by God to guard and keep it failed that task. This present age has no power to revive itself. Like our bodies, it is dying, fading. We still care for our bodies, sustaining them through food and drink. We still go to doctors and try to extend our lives. Of course, such concerns are not only responsible but also godly. But we're falling apart. When things are going well (especially for the preacher who is purveying health, wealth, and happiness), we may try to avoid the somber evaluation of this situation with a lot of upbeat chatter. But when we're tossed on the waves of suffering, we discover a wiser evaluation in Scripture:

> "Man who is born of a woman
> is few of days and full of trouble.
> He comes out like a flower and withers;
> he flees like a shadow and continues not.
> And do you open your eyes on such a one
> and bring me into judgment with you?
> Who can bring a clean thing out of an unclean?
> There is not one." (Job 14:1–4)

> "O Lord, make me know my end
> and what is the measure of my days;
> let me know how fleeting I am!" (Ps 39:4)

> Remember how short my time is!
> For what vanity you have created all the
> children of man! (Ps 89:47)

> Man is like a breath;
> his days are like a passing shadow. (Ps 144:4)

"Under the sun"—that is, in this present age under the curse—even "youth and the dawn of life are vanity" (Eccles 11:10). All of this is true of the wider creation. We cannot stop decay, vanity, and death in ourselves and in our world.

Second, Paul directs our attention to the hope of Christ's imminent return. The age to come has already pierced the membrane of this present evil age. The Spirit even now brings us fragrances and sounds of the wedding feast up ahead. Christ's kingdom is here in suffering, but is not yet consummated in glory. Christ "gave himself for our sins to deliver us from the present evil age, according to the will of our God and Father" (Gal 1:4). This world as we know it "is passing away along with its desires," John says, "but whoever does the will of God abides forever" (1 John 2:17). Peter also encourages us with these words:

> Blessed be the God and Father of our Lord Jesus Christ! According to his great mercy, he has caused us to be born again to a living hope through the resurrection of Jesus Christ from the dead, to *an inheritance that is imperishable, undefiled, and unfading*, kept in heaven for you, who by God's power are being guarded through faith for a salvation ready to be revealed in the last time. In this you rejoice, though now for a little while, if necessary, you have been grieved by various trials . . . (1 Pet 1:3–6, emphasis mine)

If Paul had gone no further than "the present time" in Romans 8, we might have reason for despair. The whole creation is falling apart. While this is offensive to utopians, it gives no quarter to despair in God's scheme. Just as we look after our own bodily needs, we should extend care to all that God has made. But if we're looking for *salvation* for ourselves and for the rest of creation, deliverance is out of our hands. It will take a miracle.

And, thirdly, Romans 8 describes just that miracle to which Paul directs our attention.

Just as the whole creation is subjected to bondage and futility because of the fall, the whole creation will share in salvation. We rejoice that when we die our souls will enjoy God's presence. But this is called the "intermediate state" for a reason. Our ultimate hope is not going to heaven when we die but rather "the redemption of our bodies," and the entire creation will rejoice with us at that time. Paul thus concludes that the proper attitude right now is *hope*. "For in this hope we were saved. Now hope that is seen is not hope. For who hopes for what he sees? But if we hope for what we do not see, we wait for it with patience" (Rom 8:24–25).

Utopians are impatient. Full salvation has to come now, and if God won't intervene then we will. But even if we could gather a global consensus on climate change and act quickly to reverse human-caused violence against God's creation, we could not bring *resurrection*, which is what God promises and has secured by Christ's resurrection from the dead. That upcoming new age is not an *extension* of this present age, a world in a state of decay, but a completely new era . . . forever. Nor is it even "Paradise Restored," which is simply a return to pre-fall existence. Rather, it is entrance into the everlasting Sabbath that the first Adam forfeited but the Last Adam has secured for us by his ascension. We can no more raise this world from physical death than we can raise our own souls or bodies. We know, because of Christ's resurrection, that the realization of this hope is just a matter of time.

But here is the paradoxical thing about hope, or at least the specific hope Paul has in mind in this passage. Instead of demotivating us, this hope fills us with patient longing that actually fuels our attitudes and actions here and now. We are not acting out of fear, as if the fate of the world were in our hands. Instead, we take a deep breath, relax, and now act out of the certain conviction that *this* body that is decaying and *this* world that is subjected to vanity *has been* redeemed and *will be* released from the grip of sin and death. As "far as the curse is found," as we sing in "Joy to the World," "And heaven and nature sing."

> Joy to the world! the Savior reigns;
> Let men their songs employ;
> While fields and floods, rocks, hills and plains,
> Repeat the sounding joy.
>
> No more let sin and sorrow grow,
> Nor thorns infest the ground:
> He comes to make his blessings flow,
> Far as the curse is found.[5]

So What Now?

A non-Christian who embraces despair has an easy excuse for negligence. With no God above us, and no creation with a noble origin and glorious future, all that matters is my own existence here and now. Besides, scientists tell us that the cosmos is gradually moving toward entropy and collapse. Whether that happens in a century or millions of years from now, I'll be long gone. Ironically, a despairing Christian assumes something close to this perspective with the idea of a "late, great planet earth."

A properly Christian approach, however, takes its coordinates from creation, providence, redemption, and the final consummation at Christ's return. We are called neither to save the world nor run from our responsibilities. The fear of God compels us: He is the sovereign Creator who holds us accountable for the world that *he* has made, but the fall has proved that he cannot trust us. So he has sent his own Son, clothed in our humanity, as the Last Adam. This world is not an abstract and anonymous "environment" that we can either abuse or save, but is God's *creation*. To ignore our responsibilities as stewards is to imitate the selfish individualism of our first parents. Moreover, God never for one moment turns away from caring for his creation. "The LORD is good to all, and his mercy is over all that he has made. . . . The eyes of all look to you, and you give them their food in due season. You open your hand; you satisfy the desire of every living thing. The LORD is righteous in all his ways and kind in all his works" (Ps 145:9, 15–17). We are neither saviors nor spectators but servants of God as guardians and keepers. Just as we are responsible to take care of our own bodies which we cannot save, we are called to take care of God's creation.

We have failed in this office, which is why we need a Redeemer. In his Son, and by his Spirit, the Father has taken matters into his own hands, saving us and our world from the guilt and dominion of our own wicked ways. Forgiven, justified, and being renewed according to Christ's image, we groan together with creation in the hope of final salvation. And then we act in the present in light of the future. Yes, this age is fading. But it will be wholly liberated! How can I look away from my human neighbors and nonhuman fellow creatures when Christ literally gave his life for the world?

The same Spirit who hovered over the matter which the Father called into being through his Son—"cherishing the confused mass," as John Calvin put it—hovered over Jesus in his baptism as the head of the new creation. And this same Spirit indwells us, making us new creatures in Christ, so that we look up to cry, "Abba, Father!" and look out in love to our neighbors, the birds, the mountains and streams, the cities and plains, and the antelopes and lions. This same Spirit brings the powers of the age to come into this present age, like Noah's dove returning with evidence in its beak of a new world of life beyond death. The specific hope that

Scripture holds out to us leads to patient yet active responsibility, as opposed to either anxiety or apathy.

"The earth is the LORD's and the fullness thereof" (Ps 24:1). Nothing belongs to us; there is nothing we can acquire, either for our earthly or heavenly welfare, but we can only gratefully receive and share with others.

We need not "redeem" the culture or the environment in order to love and serve our neighbor and be good stewards. Christ has already taken care of the salvation of the creation. Even before the cross and resurrection, "the earth is the LORD's and the fullness thereof." As Leif Grane explains:

> The world is neither mine nor the government's, nor is it merely the result of the working together of its different laws. But it is God's, which includes these laws and institutions and me and whatever may be the decisive person, or thing, in our world and time. . . . As to the features of reality, one may put it sloppily this way: Because God is the proprietor of our reality, its immeasurability and inconsistency are God's problem and not ours; and if there is anybody at all able to solve it, then it is God alone. Therefore we leave it to him. *We are free to realize our tasks.*"[6]

Thus, God remains Lord over creation and redemption, culture as well as cult, and society as well as the church, but in different ways. Through the mask of ministers in their office of proclamation and sacrament, and the witness of all believers to God's saving action in Christ, as well as through the vocations of believers and unbelievers alike, God still cares for his world through both saving grace and common grace. Even though he draws us into the parade of thanksgiving, using us as his means of loving and serving creation, "the earth is the LORD's," not ours.

We need not wallow in our unworthiness, but instead we can

join the thanksgiving parade that is already in progress, until one day we join our voices with the rest of redeemed creation. The vision of the heavenly kingdom in Revelation is a restored liturgy, with every part of creation performing its ordained role. It is a universal city without manmade walls or a manmade temple, for the Lord surrounds it in safety and the Lamb is its temple. At last, the symphony resounds throughout the empire: "Praise him, sun and moon, praise him, all you shining stars! . . . Young men and maidens together, old men and children! Let them praise the name of the LORD" (Ps 148:3, 12–13).

Confronting Our Fear of Each Other

Chapter 10

WHY WE FEAR EACH OTHER

It is striking that in the courtroom trial of Genesis 3, Adam charged God with negligence in giving him Eve, as though he would have fulfilled God's mandate without her. The final prong of the curse is the blame game that continues to the present day. Nobody can take responsibility, it seems; we are all just victims of someone else's sin.

While impoverished nations suffer from dictatorships, religious strife, famine, and disease, developed nations face rising deaths from drug addiction and suicide. In an age of advanced technologies, we are jarred when these innovations don't work, when they don't fulfill their promises, and especially when they reveal their dark side. Ironically, the new gods—like the old ones—promise liberation and autonomy, but we only find ourselves more enslaved and powerless than ever before. They promise to unite us, but instead divide us into splintering sects of mutual distrust and acrimony.

As we have seen, loneliness is a fear-driven epidemic with plenty of health risks. And it stokes our fear of Each Other. In the social media era, people tend to drift away from actual communities with people who might differ from them in all sorts of ways and attach themselves to a virtual community that mirrors their own cultural demographic and political ideology. Then the political right and left, with their vast machinery of cynical fear-mongering, spring into action blaring focus-group-tested alarms, ensuring that a divided nation will react as predicted. The rhetoric is apocalyptic on both sides and even among Christians, as if the options were Jesus and Satan.

According to a recent poll, a vast majority of Trump and Biden voters agree that curtailing freedom of speech and having "a powerful" leader are necessary "in order to destroy the radical and immoral currents prevailing in society today." "Overall," on both sides, "more than two thirds support—and one third *strongly*—emboldening and empowering strong leaders and taking the law into their own hands when it comes to dealing with people or groups they view as dangerous." Furthermore, ". . . more than 31 million Americans . . . *strongly* agree it would be better if 'a President could take needed actions without being constricted by Congress or courts.'" In short, 52% of Trump's voters and 41% of Biden's say "it's time to split the country."[1] Like a drug, the hyperbole of disdain loses its high and must be continually adjusted upward. And our preferred surrogates/entertainers are paid a lot of money to make us fearful, resentful, and angry while they continue to sell the illusion that we think for ourselves.

Both sides virtually anathematize professing believers who fail to vote the way they feel certain Jesus would. Watching the world through the distorted lens of our own preferred media sources and blogs, we hunker down in our silos and prepare for Armageddon. So the neighbor one might have been close friends with despite the way she votes is now the Other. The more we live and move and have our being in these virtual echo chambers, the lonelier and meaner we become. "Jesus" has become a mascot or symbol for Us, like the cross on the shield of the crusader as he cleaved the skull of an infidel while crying, *Christus est Dominus!* ("Christ is Lord!"). This deep division in the church between Us and Them spills over into society, and indeed has even shaped the wider discord in it. Both sides invoke Jesus and biblical allusions, but they are usually little more than rhetorical window dressing for secular ideologies.

One of the most unsettling scenes I can recall was from the January 2021 storming of the U.S. Capitol: members of the mob had erected a wooden cross and a faux gallows (the latter intended for Vice President Mike Pence) on the Capitol grounds. The verse that came to my mind is Romans 2:24: "For, as it is written [Isa 50:5; Ezek 20:27; 36:20], 'The name of God is blasphemed among the Gentiles because of you.'" Peter similarly warns, "And many will follow their sensuality, and because of them the way of truth will be blasphemed" (2 Pet 2:2).

The culture wars did not begin with the Trump presidency. Along with many others, I addressed the phenomenon in my 1994 book, *Beyond Culture Wars: Is America a Mission Field or a Battlefield?* However, deliberate and elaborate lies on both the left and the right have become so routine that there is almost nothing sinister that one side will not believe about the other side. Everyone is trigger-happy. Even masks have become weapons. We do not think there is even one thing the Others say which might be true or even worth listening to. Bob Woodward documented one side of this in *Fear: Trump in the White House.*[2] However, an uncritical embrace of the Democratic agenda is just as sycophantic as following the right-wing agenda many conservative Christians embrace. Such people on the left also simply assume that they are following the inexorable "arc of history that bends toward justice," which apparently excludes the unborn and the elderly. During the same week that I received a hysterical mass email calling upon me to support Mr. Trump, I received the same type of message from a progressive evangelical group promising that if we elected Mr. Biden we would save the church from disgrace and the world from bigotry. Mangling Jesus's promise in John 14:12 in a move that sounds eerily similar to Joel Osteen's exegetical magic, one such leader's *Outdoing Jesus: Seven Ways to Live Out the Promise of "Greater Than"*[3] merely substitutes the miracles of the Social Gospel for those of the Prosperity Gospel. So now we can outperform Jesus by our works!

In an equally blameworthy way, many on the extreme right lauded Donald Trump not just because they preferred his policies (personal character aside) but also because they saw him as a quasi-messiah.

Consequently, the rhetoric of both the left and the right has become recklessly blasphemous. Idols abound, exposing what we fear the most. Mr. Trump himself knows how to wield fear as a driver of his base, telling evangelical Christians that they have "everything to lose" if they do not support him. Almost in a cultic way, rallying around any national "savior" perpetuates quasi-eschatological conspiracy theories and an aura of secrecy. You need to show unwavering fidelity to the leader to belong. For example, on March 29, 2021 the National Republican Congressional Committee sent out a tweet: "FINAL NOTICE: 1 hr to tell Trump you're joining his social media site. If you don't reply he will think you abandoned him . . . link expires SOON."[4]

Nothing is complicated in this Manichean world of Good and Evil. No reflection, deliberation, or conversation is required. Just choose your side—and your savior. Jonathan Haidt calls this syndrome "the righteous mind."[5] Ironically, given that "we see in a mirror dimly" on heavenly matters in Scripture (1 Cor 13:12), why should we as Christians think that we have an absolutely transparent blueprint for American domestic and foreign policy? God's invitation to Israel, "Come now, let us reason together" (Isa 1:18), is about the last thing that one would expect from current public discourse. But this is a terrific opportunity for Christians to shine their light instead of turning up the heat.

God on Our Side?

We need the wisdom that flows from the fear of God instead of the fear of a demonized Other. For example, James and John were nicknamed "Sons of Thunder" (Mark 3:17). Luke records the argument that broke out among the disciples "as to which of them was the greatest." Just after this report, he tells us that Jesus took James and John with him to preach the gospel among the Samaritans. Looked down upon as neither truly Jewish nor Greek, the Samaritans in a certain village stoutly refused the good news. "And when his disciples James and John saw it, they said, 'Lord, do you want us to tell fire to come down from heaven and consume them?' But he turned and rebuked them. And they went on to another village" (Luke 9:46–56).

Wouldn't you like to know what Jesus said when he sharply rebuked his disciples' presumption? Judging by what we know from the rest of the story, he may have said, "I will exercise the final judgment myself, but this mission is for salvation, not condemnation, and you should be glad for that yourselves." In any case, Luke connects these two episodes: the disciples jockeying for dominance reveals the ugliness of selfishness within the church, which it then displays to the outside world. Would you want fellow sinners to have a final say on whether you should be destroyed? But that's just it. James and John did not think of themselves as sinners, but as the righteous. They were comparing themselves to others, and not to God's standard.

People on the left think it is credulous to believe in a God who would not bring immediate judgment to those who abuse our planet, embrace capitalism, and perpetuate racism, homophobia, and so forth. They are the Righteous. God, if he exists, is unrighteous for not exercising his judgment right now on Them, so We will just have to take matters into our own hands. We find exactly the same self-righteousness in people on the right. Like the sons of thunder, we would feel much better about ourselves if God would just zap *Them* here and now. And then there would only be decent folks like *Us*.

I recall a sermon in my teen years in which my pastor said, "If God doesn't rain fire and brimstone on San Francisco, he owes Sodom and Gomorrah an apology." Many felt during that time that God had heard this complaint by sending HIV/AIDS upon the gay community. It's certainly self-righteous, as if straight people deserved his stay of execution. And it is ungenerous, as if we are saying that since we're already in the ark, the flood may as well start rising. So what if Jesus returned before his kindness would have led *you* to repentance?

The real tragedy is the quasi-apocalyptic and eschatological claims which churches on both the left and the right hurl forth, creating a cycle of false hopes and false fears. Yes, there really is a judgment coming. However, our calling is not to pretend to invoke this wrath, but to do normal work with our hands "and to wait for his Son from heaven, whom he raised from the dead, Jesus who delivers us from the wrath to come" (1 Thess 1:10). There is a legitimate fear—and genuine way of salvation—to which Christians are called to testify. But when we invoke the biblical language of the singular event of Judgment Day for our own apocalyptic fearmongering, the *real* fear loses its salience.

A good example of this transfer of biblical eschatology to contemporary political events is "The Battle Hymn of the Republic" by abolitionist Julia Ward Howe, first published in *The Atlantic*

Monthly in 1862. "Mine eyes have seen the glory of the coming of the Lord," the hymn begins, followed by a vivid and, dare I say, blasphemous confusion of Christ's return in judgment with the Union triumph in the Civil War.

The official name for this is *idolatry*. Who is Lord, Christ or Caesar? Churches and Christian leaders often send mixed signals on this question. As we look to powerful leaders for security, we often seem to be telling our neighbors that we don't really trust the one who said, "Fear not, little flock, for it is your Father's good pleasure to give you the kingdom" (Luke 12:32). We imagine that we are building this kingdom ourselves. We forget that Jesus told us it would not be a glorious and powerful movement or worldly institution that we can point to and say, "Look, here it is!" (Luke 17:21). We have trouble accepting that the kingdom of Christ expands in depth and breadth by his "little flock's" witness to him even as it seems threatened on all sides. When Jesus warns of coming persecution, he did not mean that his disciples should fear but that they should hope in him alone, based on his victory: "I have said these things to you, that in me you may have peace. In the world you will have tribulation. But take heart; I have overcome the world" (John 16:33).

It is marvelous for God to be on our side in mercy, but it is dangerously foolhardy to imagine that he is on our side because we are better than others. That is a key theme of the parables of the Pharisee and the tax collector (Luke 18:10–13) and of the elder brother and his sibling who squandered his inheritance on debauchery (Luke 15:11–32). One major way of avoiding the seriousness of God's character and judgment is to futilely imagine that any of us can appear before him in our own righteousness. More than anything else, that religious supposition keeps people from realizing that *They* and *We* are in the same boat. Instead of repenting and fleeing to Christ from the coming wrath, we are angry that God has not yet judged *Them*. That is the most obnoxious stench of worldliness, ungodliness, and sin in God's nostrils.

Yet when we are really in the presence of God, we consciously tremble in great fear. Now I can only confess with Isaiah, "Woe is me! For I am lost; for *I* am a man of unclean lips, and I dwell in the midst of a people of unclean lips; for my eyes have seen the King, the LORD of hosts" (Isa 6:5, emphasis mine)! As a Californian, I've experienced my share of earthquakes and fires. People who don't even know each other and do not share a common religious, political, or cultural background suddenly come together during such calamitous events. They surround each other, check on each other, and weep with each other. There is a sense that "we're all in this together," which contrasts sharply with the normal acrimony of the daily news. The magnitude of our fear is much greater when we all experience the holy God in his terrifying majesty. But it is only then that we can receive his forgiveness, as Isaiah did, and reply, "Here I am! Send me" (Isa 6:8).

Typically, it is easy as individuals and churches to start out with an appreciation of God's grace. God did all of the saving in Christ alone. We merited death, but Christ merited life. As we sing in "Rock of Ages," "Nothing in my hand I bring, simply to Thy cross I cling." But before long we tend to get cocky. This also happened in Israel's history. God knew it would happen even after his people had seen him single-handedly cleanse the land and bestow it upon them. When the people of Israel enter the land, Moses warns, they are not to say in their hearts that they gained it because of their righteousness. God was fulfilling his promise to Abraham, not crowning their good works with brotherhood from the Euphrates to the Red Sea. After reminding Israel of the sins of the wilderness generation, Moses says, "Know, therefore, that the LORD your God is not giving you this good land to possess because of your righteousness, for you are a stubborn people" (Deut 9:6).

Not long afterward, Joshua was having a good day. After the fathers who had rebelled died in the wilderness, the new generation had been brought into the promised land. They had been circumcised. The manna ceased because they were now able to eat the bountiful produce of the land of Canaan. So imagine Joshua's surprise:

> When Joshua was by Jericho, he lifted up his eyes and looked, and behold, a man was standing before him with his drawn sword in his hand. And Joshua went to him and said to him, "Are you for us, or for our adversaries?" And he said, "No; but I am the commander of the army of the LORD. Now I have come." And Joshua fell on his face to the earth and worshiped and said to him, "What does my lord say to his servant?" And the commander of the LORD's army said to Joshua, "Take off your sandals from your feet, for the place where you are standing is holy." And Joshua did so. (Josh 5:13–15)

The last time the Lord commanded someone to take off his shoes, his voice was calling to Moses from the burning bush, "Do not come near; take your sandals off your feet, for the place on which you are standing is holy ground" (Exod 3:5). Moses then hid his face from the glory of God and listened only to his voice (v. 6).

And now Joshua, Moses's successor as the prophet and leader of the Lord's people, is faced with a fearsome figure who will not reveal whose side he is on: Us or Them. Every nation and army wants God on their side, but not even Israel can take God for granted. He is on his own side, and if the Israelites pollute the land then the same thing that is happening to the pagan nations will also happen to Israel. God is above and beyond all sides. He is the Holy One.

It is significant that this event happened after the circumcision of the new generation. Joshua and his lieutenants had just spent a long day performing the covenant rite with swords drawn. Circumcision is a visible cutting: one comes under the sword of divine judgment, but he is not completely "cut off"; only his foreskin is cut away. Symbolizing the sin that passes from generation to generation since Adam, this circumcision separates believers and their offspring from the nations that God has cut off from the land.

The stranger approaches, with his own sword drawn, and announces that *he* is the true "commander of the army of the LORD." The book of Joshua recounts God's victory over the idolatrous, violent, and immoral peoples who occupied his land. We are repeatedly told that the Lord triumphed over his enemies. Psalm 68 recalls it all in a beautiful song: "The LORD gives the word; the women who announce the news are a great host: 'The kings of the armies—they flee, they flee!'" That God alone gained victory is emphasized: "The women at home divide the spoil—though you men lie among the sheepfolds . . . When the Almighty scatters kings there, let snow fall on Zalmon" (vv. 11–14). The whole story finds its best summary in Joshua's name, which means "Yahweh Saves!"—a name that he shared with Jesus. God repeatedly emphasizes that he is *giving* Israel the land, *delivering* his enemies *into* Israel's hands, and *causing them to inherit* their allotted territories. All that Israel has to do is to divide the spoils according to his command. "I gave you a land on which you had not labored and cities that you had not built, and you dwell in them. You eat the fruit of vineyards and olive orchards that you did not plant" (Josh 24:13).

Few generals have ever faced the relentless and bloody conflict that Joshua experienced. Fear must have gripped him as he saw the enemy's armies flooding the battlefield from city to city throughout the land. Yet he had seen the mighty arm of the Lord. And now, immediately convinced that the Lord himself stood before him, he surrendered his sword to the true commander, falling on his face in worship. I see no good reason to doubt the traditional Christian interpretation of this as an appearance of the preincarnate Son of God. There are several theophanies that identify "the Angel of the LORD" as a mysterious appearance of none other than Yahweh (Gen 16:7–14; 22:11–19; Num 22:22; Zech 3).[6]

God strictly forbids the worship of creatures, including angels, and we have examples of similar formula to the one used here by Joshua when Yahweh appears: "Then Abram fell on his face. And God said to him, 'Behold, my covenant is with you, and you will be the father of a multitude of nations'" (Gen 17:3–4). God also says in Exodus 23:20–21, "Behold, I send an angel before you to guard you on the way and to bring you to the place that I have prepared. Pay careful attention to him and obey his voice; do not rebel against him, for he will not pardon your transgression, for my name is in him."

So the mysterious Commander is the one who *will become incarnate*, a man like us yet without sin (Heb 4:15). In Joshua's period of biblical history, he is the Angel of the LORD who is himself the LORD. We hear something similar in Psalm 24:10: The King of glory ascends in victory to the throne of Yahweh, and yet he is Yahweh: "The King of Glory, Yahweh Mighty in Battle"—Commander of the LORD's Army.

From then on, Joshua's fear was turned to absolute confidence. Not he, but God himself, was the conqueror. And yet the sinful tendency of the Israelites, like all people, made their tenure in the land precarious. The book of Joshua opens with a promising new day, with God leading his people to conquest, but ends with Joshua pleading for redoubled commitment to the law. It is almost as if he feels that he is alone in this commitment by the final chapter: "Choose this day whom you will serve . . . But as for me and my house, we will serve the LORD" (Josh 24:15).

God is not a plaything. After enduring the speeches of Job's friends—and Job himself—God steps in to take his proper role as the central character. In Job 41 God points out that humans can't even kill Leviathan (a large sea creature, probably a whale). Can they catch him on a hook or "fill his skin with harpoons"? "Behold, the hope of a man is false; he is laid low even at the sight of him." If that is how terrified people are at the sight of an animal that they cannot seize or control, "Who then is he who can stand before me? Who has first given to me, that I should repay him? Whatever is under the whole heaven is mine" (vv. 1–11).

Finally, Hebrews 2:5–15 testifies that the "world to come" is subjected to the incarnate Commander. That would be awful news were it not for the fact that he has finally assumed our common humanity, calling us "brothers and sisters." He took the sword meant for us into his own breast and is now risen and exalted, announcing, "Behold, I and the children God has given me." The writer of Hebrews continues, "Since therefore the children share in flesh and blood, he himself likewise partook of the same things, that through death he might destroy the one who has the power of death, that is, the devil, and deliver all those who through fear of death were subject to lifelong slavery."

This narrative should challenge our categories of Us and Them. Early in the fifth century, the church father Augustine wrote *The City of God*. He was responding to the pagan critics who said that the sacking of Rome by the Visigoths in AD 410 was because of the resentment of the old gods against the Christians. In short, Augustine's thesis is that the City of God is heavenly, based on God's eternal election of his people from every nation, and the City of Man is earthly, based on common creation and God's common grace. A perfect commonwealth cannot be found in this age, but that does not mean that Christians cannot contribute to genuine vestiges of common life and government for now.

Jerome responded quite differently than Augustine because he had not distinguished clearly between Christ's kingdom and the kingdoms of this age. Jerome was gripped by fear: "What will become of the church now that Rome has fallen?" However, Augustine saw more clearly that the City of God is not the Roman Empire or any temporal kingdom. Instead, the City of God is where Christ spreads his realm in all places and times through the gospel. In Augustine's view, God had brought the mission field to the missionaries. Indeed, he added, the Visigoths had behaved more virtuously in their conquest than Romans in their own victories; many of them, in fact, had been converted to Arian Christianity in the preceding decades. Precisely through becoming the new rulers of Rome, the leaders of these Germanic tribes came into contact with orthodox Christian teaching and were eventually baptized. Jerome was a remarkable biblical scholar, but he simply could not separate the Roman Empire from "Us," while Augustine defined "Us" as believers. What if we thought with Augustine, Why not consider our identity to be more than just Romans, tied to a physical city or empire? As Christians, shouldn't we accept not only "Us" Romans into brotherhood in Christ but also "Them" from outside, wherever they may come from?

The Christian's Threefold Enemy

The call to embrace rather than fear our neighbors, especially fellow Christians, coincides in Scripture with a call to stand against the world, for the world. It is common among Christians to refer to the "threefold enemy": the world, the flesh, and the devil. The *world* is our context, the ambient culture in which we are conditioned toward particular sins against God and each other. The *devil* gets up in the morning with sinister alacrity to tempt us to see reality with ourselves rather than God at the center. But we have only *ourselves* to blame for our thoughts, desires, and actions. The Bible calls this "the flesh"—not the body itself, but the whole person in the grip of sin and death. It is contrasted with "the Spirit"—not our spirit, but the Holy Spirit. The flesh is powerless to save, but through the living and powerful word of God the Spirit raises us from spiritual death and indwells us with his life-giving power (Eph 2:1–5).

Generally, I believe that we need God's wisdom more than ever on all three fronts. First, by demonizing the Others we have missed the devil's real ambitions. The best-known passage for spiritual warfare is Ephesians 6: "Finally, be strong in the Lord and in the strength of *his* might. Put on the whole armor of God, that you may be able to stand against the schemes of the devil" (vv. 10–11, emphasis mine). But notice the very next verse: "For we do not wrestle against flesh and blood, but against the rulers, against the authorities, against the cosmic powers over this present darkness, against the spiritual forces of evil in the heavenly places" (v. 12).

Frankly, I do not think that Satan spends much time worrying about who is in the White House. And he probably laughs at preachers whose "deliverance ministry" antics and cleansing the Rose Garden of evil spirits seem more like a Marvel movie. Satan probably spends more time at church than I do, as he plots to undermine and overthrow the progress of faith in Christ. And he goes home with the saints, hiding in the back seat of the car. That is the focus of this entire passage. Paul was familiar with the formidable appearance of Roman soldiers, but notice here that all of the pieces in the armor coalesce around a spiritual battle in which Satan targets the believer's faith in Christ.

First, there is the "*belt of truth*"—that is, the objective truth of the gospel (Eph 6:14a). If Christians do not know what they believe and why they believe it, they will eventually succumb to worldly assumptions. Satan is not put off by my appeals to my experience or feelings, but "by every word that comes from the mouth of God," as Jesus replied in his temptation (Matt 4:4). If we do not know that we are saved because God chose us, redeemed us, called us by his regenerating grace, justified us, and adopted us, and that he alone sanctifies us and will one day glorify us, then Satan's crafty theologizing will gain a foothold.

Then there is the "*breastplate of righteousness*" (Eph 6:14b). That is not *our* righteousness. If, in the face of temptation to fear that I am not really saved, I appealed to *my* righteousness, Satan would have a field day. He curates a library of sins that I have committed in thought, word, and deed: what wrongs I have done and what rights I have failed to do. So, as Paul says also in Romans 13:14, "Put on the Lord Jesus Christ." The breastplate is the most important piece because it covers the heart. When Christ is my breastplate of righteousness, Satan has no success. Whenever he tempts me to doubt God's favor, I tell him, "Christ is my righteousness."

Our feet are even shod with "gospel shoes" to run with the good news (see Eph 6:15). "In all circumstances take up the *shield of faith*, with which you can extinguish all the flaming darts of the evil one; and take the *helmet of salvation*, and the sword of the Spirit, which is the *word of God* . . ." (vv. 16–17, emphasis mine). We do indeed feel these wonderful realities. These truths fill us with experiential joy and thanksgiving, motivating our good works. But the truths themselves, not their effects, must be our only armor when God's most intelligent enemy takes note of us. We have an enemy, to be sure, but he is not our neighbor.

We also need to recognize that the world is *Us*—all of us—and not *Them*. For many today, "the world" has become either the Democrats or the Republicans, or maybe even wholly identified with the devil. Scripture, however, refers to the world (*kosmos*) in different ways. Even in the same author, the apostle John, we find diverse uses of the term. "World" can refer to the good creation the Father made through his Son (John 1:2–3), which he loves so much "that he gave his only Son . . ." (John 3:16). But it can also mean humanity in its hostility to God (John 1:10), a world system that believers are not to love (1 John 2:15). It is easy for us who sport "NOT OF THIS WORLD" bumper stickers to imagine that we don't belong to the world in either sense. But this is not true. We are part of the world that God created and for which Jesus died, and we are also part of the worldly opposition to God until he calls us out of darkness into his marvelous light.

But "the world" in the second sense (a system of rebellion) encompasses Democratic and Republican parties, capitalism and socialism, democratic and autocratic regimes, and FOX and CNN. These are all just districts of the same city called "Babylon" in Scripture. There may be more justice, virtue, and peace in one district than in another. America might be more just than Iran, Russia, or China. But all of it is still Babylon—and it will never be Zion.

As citizens of Zion, we are called to love people whose lifestyles run counter to our deepest convictions about what God's Word teaches. Paul explains,

> If I speak in the tongues of men and of angels, but have not love, I am a noisy gong or a clanging cymbal. And if I have prophetic powers, and understand all mysteries and all knowledge, and if I have all faith, so as to remove mountains, but have not love, I am nothing. If I give away all I have, and if I deliver up my body to be burned, but have not love, I gain nothing.
>
> Love is patient and kind; love does not envy or boast; it is not arrogant or rude. It does not insist on its own way; it is not irritable or resentful; it does not rejoice at wrongdoing, but rejoices with the truth. Love bears all things, believes all things, hopes all things, endures all things. (1 Cor 13:1–7)

The clause I am inclined to highlight is that love "does not rejoice at wrongdoing, but rejoices with the truth." Love is not a sentimental blanket that covers over sin. "Don't judge, just love" can actually be a way of silencing the testimony to righteousness, truth, and justice. And I see a lot of wrongdoing on both sides in the culture wars, even instances of people rejoicing in sin or at least ignoring it. But why am I supposed to rejoice in the truth rather than in wrongdoing? Love is the answer. After all, who am I to put myself in the Judge's seat when I have been, am being, and will always be forgiven of so many debts against love?

Our first response to LGBTQ+ neighbors and relatives—*or* to those who take QAnon seriously—should not be moral indignation, rejection, scolding, or even instruction, but love. Zacchaeus, a tax-collecting thief, had no doubt heard about this Jesus who ate and drank with sinners and tax collectors. So he climbed into a tree to catch a glimpse of Jesus instructing a crowd. "And when Jesus came to the place, he looked up and said to him, 'Zacchaeus, hurry and come down, for I must stay at your house today'" (Luke 19:5). He does not say, "Now, I'm open to talking to you if you listen to my views on tax law and theft." Nor does he affirm Zacchaeus's corrupt lifestyle. Rather, he lets the scene unfold from love. "Zacchaeus, hurry and come down," not ". . . so I can scold you" or "offer you my terms for joining me" but ". . . for I must stay at your house today." This "must" that impels him to go to the cross also drives him to be Zacchaeus's guest. This reveals the loving heart of God. It is not as if Zacchaeus lacks a conscience and doesn't know stealing from his neighbors is wrong. Only after being received, forgiven, and embraced by the Savior does a repentant Zacchaeus determine on his own to pay back his victims and give the rest of his money to the poor. Jesus also loved Pharisees, eating and drinking with them. And a few received him: he was even buried in the tomb of a member of the Sanhedrin. He wanted a meal with everybody.

For some, nothing short of endorsing a sinful lifestyle will count as love. However, we cannot do this precisely because of love. Additionally, Paul reminds us in 1 Corinthians 13 that because of love we also cannot be noisy, obnoxious, boasting, arrogant, rude, irritable, or resentful. Jesus sees the Other not as *Them* but as friends with whom he eats and drinks, whether they become disciples or not. He showed his grace toward us even "while we were enemies" (Rom 5:10). The "we" here is you and I. And since we don't know if today's most ardent persecutor will be tomorrow's evangelist, like Paul, it's best to love people and stay out of God's business.

Yet there is indeed a world system in rebellion against God. And sometimes Christians—and even churches—become part of that system. When Jesus warned in John 15 of the world hating the church, he had in mind his own fellow Jews who rejected him and would evict believers in Jesus from the synagogues. That is why the exhortations we find in the New Testament letters are so relevant in every age, including our own:

> I appeal to you therefore, brothers, by the mercies of God, to present your bodies as a living sacrifice, holy and acceptable to God, which is your spiritual worship. Do not be conformed to this world, but be transformed by the renewal of your mind, that by testing you may discern what is the will of God, what is good and acceptable and perfect. (Rom 12:1–2)

But there are different ways of being "conformed to this world" instead of being "transformed by the renewal of your mind" through God's Word. Paul had his hands full with the church in Corinth, which imitated the world's immorality, greed, pride, power struggles, and self-indulgence. That hardly sounds like the *Others*. That is you, I, and all of us together.

We *were* part of this world system. We still find it alluring, and at times we act like we belong to this city of destruction. The world has often seen and delightfully publicized the hypocrisy of Christian leaders who fulminate against worldliness while practicing some of its worst sins. It is bad enough that the elder brother in Jesus's parable looks self-righteously down on his younger brother. But when he does so while simultaneously living a prodigal life himself, perhaps secretly, then love is doubly assaulted. However much we act like Babylon, we need to remember that we are citizens of Zion and act accordingly.

For the Christian every nation is Babylon, with better and worse districts. Although Babylon can never become Zion, tribes of Zion may become Babylon. Lampstands—that is, particular churches—can be removed from the house of Israel if they do not repent of their evil (Rev 2:5). The danger to the true church comes not from the persecution of the Gentiles but from the apostasy of professing churches that become absorbed into the bloodstream of this fading age. And worldly churches are always the worst enemies of the true church.

Chapter 11

"CHRISTIAN AMERICA" VERSUS THE BODY OF CHRIST

Today, many Christians seem to feel that the American empire is being invaded by strange, foreign Visigoths. Often, these "others" are people of color who are professing, Bible-believing Christians. In other cases, they are opposed to traditional Christianity. Our outlook is very different, though, if we switch our vision from a *nationalist* ideal to the New Testament's *missionary* vision.

Christ is the head of a new creation, and wherever he is heralded in the world a patch of desert becomes a lush vineyard. It's all about him, as he delivers himself to sinners through preaching and teaching, baptism and Communion. That's the Great Commission (Matt 28:18–20). But any particular church that loses interest in Jesus in his saving office fades away until it's just part of the desert again. To give an analogy: A chess club wouldn't exist for long if it lost interest in chess and started playing poker. It would now be a poker club. The sweatshirts might still say "Chess Club," and the club members might still talk about chess and how great it is, but they've now organized around something else. Likewise, liberal Protestantism still wears the Christian sweatshirt but is playing a different game. And now evangelicalism seems precariously close behind. The only difference between these two groups is which game they want to play instead. For example, many feel that they are playing the "Christian Nation" game in a heated tournament with the "Progressive Agenda" team. As Christians take sides, churches that are just wearing the sweatshirt become part of the political right and left. Something other than "that word above all earthly powers," as Luther's hymn "A Mighty Fortress Is Our God" put it, creates something which is no longer a church of Christ.

At both political extremes one discerns a deeply religious vision which even employs Christian symbols and slogans, but it is not Christian. Its object of worship is not the triune God but "America," however defined. In the most important demographic study of Christian nationalism to date, Andrew L. Whitehead and Samuel L. Perry examine this phenomenon by outlining a spectrum ranging from Ambassadors and Accommodators to Resisters and Rejecters. Surprisingly, it turns out that "Christian nationalism" is not merely a white evangelical phenomenon: "Sixty-five percent of African Americans are supportive of Christian nationalism, which is the largest proportion of any racial group." However, African Americans are appealing to the Christian nation narrative which calls for greater social justice rather than the narrative which defends white privilege.[1] Hispanics are split evenly, as are whites overall. "Most evangelical Protestants are Ambassadors (40 percent) or Accommodators (38 percent)." "Yet," happily, "nearly a quarter (23 percent) of evangelicals are Resisters or Rejecters."[2]

So we have two metanarratives that practically yield violent opposition. For white Christian nationalists, the narrative is that America's "Christian" culture is under attack. Meanwhile, secularists quote Thomas Jefferson, for instance, about a "wall of separation" between church and state. Both sides hurriedly manufacture one-sided quips and propaganda quotes to boil down their viewpoint for each army in the culture war. So let us reason together. I begin with a scriptural evaluation of this concept of a Christian America and then give a brief historical argument.

Is Christian Nationalism Biblical?

First, there is biblical opposition to any notion of a Christian nation apart from the worldwide body of Christ. There was a time, in Old Testament Israel, when the church was the state and vice versa. God was the head of state and the whole nation and land were holy—that is, set apart to the Lord. Like Abraham, individual Israelites looked to the coming Savior and were justified even as we are by grace alone, through faith alone, in Christ alone. But there was another covenant that *the people* rather than God swore at Mount Sinai, promising, "All that the LORD has spoken we will do" (Exod 19:8; 24:3). If they broke it, then God would drive them out of the land just as he had their enemies (Deut 28). (It is like the covenant that Adam swore to keep, which he instead transgressed and was driven out of the garden.) Unlike God's unilateral promise in the Abrahamic covenant of grace, the national covenant's promises of blessings and curses were based on Israel's faithfulness. However, "like Adam they transgressed the covenant" (Hos 6:7). In the fullness of time, God sent his Son, the Messiah, to fulfill the law and to bear the sin of the world. Having done this, he has rendered the national covenant with Israel obsolete (Heb 8:13).

The new covenant is far greater in its promises, blessings, and mediator. The exclusive designation "a chosen race, a royal priesthood, a holy nation, a people for his own possession" originally belonged to the geopolitical nation of Israel (Exod 19:6) and is then applied in the New Testament to the worldwide body of Christ (1 Pet 2:9). The new covenant covers not physical descendants but all who trust in Christ from every people (John 8:39–59; Rom 9:8; Gal 3:10–29). The first major controversy in the church was over Gentile inclusion, which was settled at the council of Jerusalem (Acts 15). If regarding ethnic Israel as a "chosen nation" in the new covenant would violate a decision included in inspired Scripture, how much more offensive to God would it be to give that same status to Americans, particularly those of a certain ethnicity, some of whom are completely unrelated to Abraham?

So the problem is not that some Christians are taking a biblical idea too seriously, but that they are confusing America with Israel under the old covenant. From a biblical perspective, this is heretical, confusing the law with the gospel. Christian nationalism violates the doctrine of "one holy, catholic, and apostolic church." Despite what we hear in the oratory of the left and the right alike, there is no "national soul." Salvation does not come to nations that, like Israel of old, rededicate themselves to the law (2 Chron 7:14). And, besides, even if it did, we have broken it, even while we sing about God having "crowned our good with brotherhood from sea to shining sea." This unbiblical ideology of an American covenant not only coincided with but helped to provide the spiritual justification for slavery, Manifest Destiny, and ethnic segregation. And, ironically, as we have seen, it was also embraced by a majority of African Americans in their struggle for freedom from slavery and racism. Scripture addresses both justice in the civil sphere and Christian unity in the body of Christ, but we need to settle these issues on something other than this unscriptural myth.[3]

The Massachusetts Bay Colony, which its governor John Winthrop called "a shining city upon a hill" (cf. Matt 5:14), consisted of Independent Puritans who had fled England to set up a Christian community. However, Jesus's use of this phrase in the Sermon on the Mount was directed to his own flock gathered from the world, not to another geopolitical entity of the world. This misuse of Scripture for civil religion has plagued churches across the political spectrum. The worldwide church is actually Christ's kingdom, his beloved community, the shining city upon a hill, and a chosen nation. And Christ, not America, is the best, last hope for mankind.

Is Christian Nationalism Historical?

Second, history does not support the idea of Christian nationalism. This was the mistake of "Christendom" and the fabricated "Holy Roman Empire." Especially in the Romantic movement of the nineteenth century, there was much talk of "Holy Russia," a sacred Germanic "Fatherland," and God's kingdom being established in "England's green and pleasant land." It was just this sort of Christian nationalism that many—especially persecuted Christians from these countries—sought in the New World.

Secularists often quote Thomas Jefferson's "wall of separation" between church and state without actually reading the "Letter to the Danbury Baptist Association." Jefferson's presidency was opposed by many, including his predecessor John Adams, who had accused him of being an atheist during the virulent election campaign between them. In his first term Jefferson did not proclaim thanksgivings and days of prayer, so in 1802, as he prepared to seek a second term, the Baptists in Danbury, Connecticut might have had reason to fear that he did not respect religion at all. After all, Congregationalism was still the established church in Connecticut (until 1818), as Anglicanism had been in Virginia until 1786. However, the reaction the Danbury Baptists received from Jefferson was encouraging:

> Believing with you that religion is a matter which lies solely between Man & his God, that he owes account to none other for his faith or his worship, that the legitimate powers of government reach actions only, & not opinions, I contemplate with sovereign reverence that act of the whole American people which declared that their legislature should "make no law respecting an establishment of religion, or prohibiting the free exercise thereof," thus building a wall of separation between Church & State.[4]

That was all that Baptist preacher, abolitionist, and defender of religious liberty John Leland needed to hear. Leland is best known for vehemently arguing that a "Christian commonwealth" is exactly not what Christians should desire. Instead, they should rather give liberty to "Popish, Jewish and Turk" to reject or freely embrace the gospel.

It is important to situate this question in its historical context, one in which the tendencies of two revolutions—the English and the French—contributed to the American. I do not presume to offer a history lesson here, but merely to highlight the complexity that still plays such a large part in our political negotiations.

The English Civil War (1642–51) laid the groundwork for greater civil liberties based on the view that God gave dignity, rights, and responsibilities which constitutions recognized and laws protected. The "Glorious (also called Bloodless) Revolution" of 1688 brought to the thrones the Dutch king William and his wife Mary, the princess of England. Only with the return to absolutist policies under the Hanoverian George III did American colonists begin to rebel.

The French Revolution was more radical in both religious and political terms. English political writers like John Locke had argued for religious toleration *of* various religious sects. This had been the Dutch policy as well. But the seventeenth-century philosopher Benedict Spinoza had encouraged a republicanism that sought freedom *from* religion—or at least create a new civil religion controlled by the state. The most radical French revolutionaries eagerly grasped at these suggestions, having endured a long period of oppressive absolutism under both church and king. They instigated a fiercely *secularist* revolution, setting up the goddess Reason in place of all Christian symbols in the Notre-Dame cathedral. Spinoza, not Locke, was the dominant influence.

America's founders were a mixed bag, some drawn to the English and others to the French styles of revolution. And, in many respects, we still encounter that enduring legacy today. Some of America's founders, especially Jefferson, Adams, Paine, and Franklin, frequented the salons of Parisian atheists like Baron d'Holbach. Jefferson and Adams, disdaining orthodox Christianity, seem to have believed in the usual supreme "Architect" of deists and Freemasons, who created the world and gave human beings certain rights. In their correspondence, both founders ridiculed "Athanasian divines" who defended the Trinity, the divinity of Christ, and miracles. Jefferson famously created his own Bible, editing out such references. Furthermore, after reading Lucretius's *On the Nature of Things*, Jefferson announced, "I too am an Epicurian [*sic*]."[5] We may feel like America is overrun by "secular humanists," but it is still difficult to imagine someone being elected president today who could publicly criticize Christian beliefs so brazenly.

Ben Franklin was a "freethinker" who did not attach himself to any form of Christianity, so was suspected of atheism by many. Thomas Paine's enormously popular *The Age of Reason* ridiculed Christianity, provoking considerable controversy in Europe and America. A baptized Episcopalian and dedicated Freemason, George Washington was not a regular churchgoer and would leave just before the Eucharist. But there were also orthodox Christians like John Jay, Patrick Henry, and many others. Overall, the setting of the Founders seems quite similar to our own day, with a variety of beliefs and perspectives.

Secularists are historically wide of the mark when they imagine that opposition to orthodox tenets and practices meant antipathy toward religion. However, just as Christian nationalism distorts the biblical meaning of Christ's body, it also requires a broadening of Christianity into a generic religious moralism. George Washington firmly believed that a self-governing people could not last long without generic religion, but for him—as with the likes of Franklin and Jefferson—this could be best preserved by a competition of sects rather than privileging one.

In terms of policy, though, America's Treaty with Tripoli (1796) during George Washington's administration importantly needed to point out that the relationship was not between two state religions—Christianity and Islam: "As the government of the United States of America is not in any sense founded on the Christian Religion," it said, ". . . it is declared by the parties that no pretext arising from religious opinions shall ever produce an interruption of the harmony existing between the two countries" (Art. 11).[6] Washington was not unaware that most Americans were Christians of various sorts, as in some sense he even considered himself. Nor did he want to sideline religion from public life. However, the genius of the American experiment showed that the government has no business interfering with the conscience or the exercise of religion. Jefferson did not identify a "wall of separation" because he thought that religion was dangerous, but that state churches were wrong. That is precisely why he had been such an encouragement to non-Anglicans in Virginia, where half of Baptist preachers had been jailed between 1768–74. Jefferson and Madison, along with other Christians, put their weight behind the movement for disestablishment of the Virginia state church in 1786.

Madison, Witherspoon, and the American Constitution

Some will be surprised to know that James Madison by intention did not write Christianity or Christ into the U.S. Constitution. Madison's personal faith is ambiguous. Although he was raised Anglican and later became a member of the Presbyterian Church, Madison seems to have gradually moved in a more nominal direction. Yet he remained a product of his education, much of which he apparently still found intellectually persuasive. A Virginian, Madison nevertheless chose to study at Princeton over William and Mary, particularly because John Witherspoon was president there. He was a Scottish Presbyterian minister and a signer of the Declaration of Independence; many of the nation's founders learned moral philosophy and theology from him. Madison also drew from Montesquieu's *The Spirit of the Laws* (1748), whose key principle is that "the government must be such that one citizen cannot fear another citizen."[7] However, Witherspoon was his dominant influence at crucial points.

Witherspoon shared the Augustinian view of Luther and Calvin that although humanity is created in God's image, it is fallen. Children of Adam are not capable of attaining justification before God or renewal of their fallen nature by their own efforts. And yet the image of God is only corrupted, not destroyed. Even the unregenerate are capable of civic righteousness (i.e., virtuous acts before other human beings). Yet there must be checks on power because of moral depravity. "It is an invaluable gift if God allows a people to elect its own government and magistrates," Calvin stated.[8] In addition, there should be several political institutions or branches, with checks preventing one from gaining inordinate power over the others. As Lee Ward explains,

> Calvin's republican sympathies derived from his view of human nature as deeply flawed. Compound or mixed governments reflect the reality that human frailty justifies and necessitates institutional checks and balances to the magistrate's presumed propensity to abuse power. It was this commitment to checks and balances that became the basis of Calvin's resistance theory, according to which inferior magistrates have a duty to resist or restrain a tyrannical sovereign.[9]

Calvin did not believe that one form of government is universal; it all depends on the particular history and culture of a people. However, checks on human power are essential.

Similarly, Witherspoon preached in a sermon, "Man is every where considered as in a fallen and sinful state. Everything that is prescribed to him, and everything that is done for him, goes upon that supposition." However, civil virtue sufficient to curb the passions of self-love still remains because of God's providence and the creation of human beings in his image.[10] Government cannot heal the wound of original sin and its effects, but it can restrain injustice, violence, and vice. This thinking was totally counter to that of the French Revolution, which was based on the moral perfectibility of humanity.

Witherspoon's influence dominates in Madison's very non-Enlightenment reflections on human nature. He argues that a good constitution must protect against the pooling of power in any department of government, explaining,

> It may be a reflection on human nature, that such devices should be necessary to control the abuses of government. But what is government itself but the greatest of all reflections on human nature? *If men were angels, no government would*

> *be necessary. If angels were to govern men, neither external nor internal controls on government would be necessary.* In framing a government which is to be administered by men over men, the great difficulty lies in this: You must first enable the government to control the governed; and in the next place, oblige it to control itself. A dependence on the people is no doubt the primary control on the government; but experience has taught mankind the necessity of auxiliary precautions.[11]

Not to be left to the realm of general theory, Madison's Federalist No. 51 offers detailed prescriptions for practical checks and balances on government and people alike.

Unlike Aristotle and many today, Madison did not believe any more than Luther or Calvin that good laws make good people. "[Since] the *causes* of factions cannot be removed . . . relief is only to be sought in the means of controlling its *effects*."[12] The heart is beyond the reach of government and laws. Since it cannot reform human nature, the state must at least supply "opposite and rival interests . . . that each [office] may be a check on the other." If these "inventions of prudence" are important among individuals, they "cannot be less requisite in the distribution of the supreme powers of the state."[13] We do not have a great Constitution because Madison thought the American people possessed superior virtue or capacity for moral improvement, but for the opposite reason: because he was convinced that they share in the common corruption of the human race.

If we were to follow the logical arguments undergirding key elements of the U.S. Constitution, not only theological liberals but evangelicals would have to recover the doctrine of original sin. However, that ship has sailed for the former. The only time we hear the phrase "original sin" from liberals refers to slavery. But, tragically, evangelicals seem just as optimistic about the human condition. Between 2016 and 2020, about half of evangelicals said that humans are basically good.[14] Many conservatives today seem to think *individuals* are good but government is evil; this is one reason for the rise in radical democratic populism. To them, Madison replies, "If men were angels, no government would be necessary." Calvin had made the same point in a sermon on Galatians 3:19–20 in 1558: "If we were like angels, blameless and freely able to exercise perfect self-control, we would not need rules or regulations."[15] But to those who think that *government* is good, Madison adds, "If angels were to govern men, neither external nor internal controls on government would be necessary." Because of moral depravity, there must be checks on private *and* public power.

Madison was also convinced of another Augustinian idea that was key in Witherspoon's instruction. Adopted by the Protestant reformers, it is the doctrine of "two kingdoms."[16] This view states that Christ is Lord of all but he rules the temporal nations through his moral law and common grace, while he exercises his saving grace in the church through the Word and the sacraments of baptism and the Lord's Supper.[17]

None of the Protestant reformers went so far as to think that a Christian state would tolerate open preaching against the Trinity or the resurrection. They were not early representatives of the First Amendment to the U.S. Constitution, but their teaching did contribute to greater liberty. According to Luther, the gospel cannot be enforced and the church must never take up arms to defend the Word of God.[18] Calvin said, "It is impossible to resist the magistrate without, at the same time, resisting God himself."[19] Ironically, Calvin did believe that a legitimate authority —a parliament—could depose a despot, but he also insisted that the church can never inspire social or political revolution for its faith. If a ruler failed to uphold the true religion, he would have to answer to God alone. As Carlos Eire observes, Calvin cautions that the believer has one of two options when facing a tyrannical ruler: "to flee or face persecution."[20] In short, the church does not assume responsibilities of the state and vice versa. It is striking how far this doctrine reached across the religious spectrum. Even Jefferson frequently appealed to it.

Madison actually used the "two kingdoms" doctrine to oppose Patrick Henry's proposal of giving tax-exempt status to churches in Virginia. However, he did not do this on secularist grounds. Rather, he was even more concerned about how tax exemption would corrupt the church. What competence and authority does the state have to determine what churches are true and therefore entitled to tax exemption? A citizen pays taxes to support common welfare and defense, but his or her involvement in civil society is always conditional, "with a saving of his allegiance to the Universal Sovereign." According to Madison, because its adherents have this higher allegiance, "Religion is wholly exempt" from the authority of "Civil Society." Madison also recounts the history of the church's alliances with the state to display how these tended to corrupt the church.

> Who does not see that the same authority which can establish Christianity, in exclusion of all other Religions, may establish with the same ease any particular sect of Christians, in exclusion of all other Sects? [T]hat the same authority which can force a citizen to contribute three pence only of his property for the support of any one establishment, may force him to conform to any other establishment in all cases whatsoever?[21]

Such a tax to support instruction in Christian doctrine would make the teachers employees of a lesser kingdom. When it seemed that the bill would pass in the Virginia legislature, the Hanover Presbytery declared, "Religion as a spiritual system is not to be considered an object of legislation," but asserted its claim for funding teachers if the bill passed.[22] Such are the inconsistencies in the church that contribute to a compromised witness.

Madison's take on this matter is instructive for us right now. A time may come when faithful churches lose their tax-exempt status. This benefit (it is, after all, a long-standing benefit, not a right) may very well be withdrawn by a hostile government. It may even be necessary for churches to refuse tax exemption rather than risk gradual and deadly concessions in exchange for financial support. The faithful have always and will always support the Lord's work with or without any respect to tax write-offs.

Madison had many influences, but he was in Witherspoon's camp in thinking about checks and balances in the light of human nature. In a *Harper's Magazine* article, historian Scott Horton observed, "A number of historians, pointing to the overlap between pockets of Calvinism and democracy, convincingly argue that Calvinist thought propelled Enlightenment values including respect for the dignity of humankind and democracy."[23] Consequently, James Madison, John Jay, Alexander Hamilton, and Patrick Henry emphasized the freedom *of* religion from state interference. So did Baptists, Quakers, Lutherans, and Presbyterians. Thomas Jefferson, John Adams, and Ben Franklin may have wanted freedom from orthodox Christianity, too, but the ultra-partisan of the French Revolution, Thomas Paine, was widely snubbed by all parties for his attacks on religion. It is very clear, then, that the majority of America's Founders were not antagonistic toward religion, but toward the state or federal government playing any role in privileging any creed or confession.

Applying These Lessons Today

I have included this brief historical digression because it seems to speak directly to our current social and political crisis. We have two very different oceans converging at our nation's founding: Reformation-influenced British republicanism and secularist republicanism of French inspiration. Yet today there is very little of the former; it has been replaced by an infusion of the radical eschatology and Manichean outlook of the early Anabaptist revolutionaries in Germany, who sought to immediately set up the kingdom of God on earth. The same black and white revolutionary outlook characterizes the extreme left today. Today's radicals may be found at both extremes of the political spectrum, whether shouting down speakers and looting shops or violently storming the Capitol. This common vision is neither progressive nor conservative but is an unambiguous divide between Good and Evil, perilous to civil liberty *and* the cause of Christ.

If we examine political speeches from George Washington to Barack Obama, they are laced with biblical allusions, often taken out of context and woven into the narrative of America rather than old covenant Israel as a sacred nation. Nevertheless, importantly, many American politicians still assumed that there is a God (however conceived) above all rulers and peoples and a Law above the laws of nations. For example, President Dwight Eisenhower said, "In other words, our form of government has no sense unless it is founded in a deeply felt religious faith, and I don't care what it is. With us of course it is the Judeo-Christian concept, but it must be a religion in which all men are created equal."[24]

On the plus side, the recognition that neither individuals nor governments are ultimate authorities has tempered populism and tyranny. It allowed abolitionists and civil rights leaders to appeal to the Law above the laws of nations, just as many today do in defense of the unborn. On the negative side, this vague civil religion, regardless of its usefulness to the republic, has corrupted Christianity in America in the same way similar combinations of religion and civil society have done so elsewhere in history.

Yet even this shared consensus has evaporated now. In fact, in comparison with Barack Obama, an active member of a liberal Protestant church, Donald Trump's speeches were practically devoid of familiar biblical references. Trump even preferred to use the Bible as a symbolic prop for his base during a Black Lives Matter protest. In the media, even among otherwise well-informed journalists, there is little knowledge of the beliefs of particular religions nor an adequate comprehension of how these religions might play a significant role in people's lives. And, most tragically of all, most Christians—including evangelicals—have little comprehension of what *they* believe. For the first time since polling on the issue began, participation in any religion has fallen below half of the U.S. population.

Whatever advantages they may point to in terms of policy and appointments, conservative Christians need to confront the fact that President Trump made anti-Constitutional statements privileging his white evangelical base. This pandering is red meat for many supporters but poison to the witness of Christ. Yet Trump is hardly the first to exploit the fears of white Protestants. Opposing John F. Kennedy's presidential run in 1960, Protestant leaders declared that a Roman Catholic could not serve as president. Mitt Romney, the Republican nominee in 2012, lacked support from vocal evangelical leaders because he is a Mormon. Yet evangelicals elected a president who is not a professing, communicant Christian because he vowed to protect them. My point is not about whether Christians should have cast their vote for Mr. Trump. Many did so in good conscience and without any sympathy for quasi-messianic claims. However, the fear of losing cultural, social, and political power often drives a large number of evangelicals to "put their trust in princes." Looking for leaders who will privilege and protect "Christian America" is toxic to the faith and crippling to the church's missionary mandate.

Serving or Consuming Each Other

The church in Galatia provides an excellent example of how Christian witness can be compromised when the church does not make the gospel its main focus. This particular church had turned the gospel into the law and made ethnic distinctives an entry requirement. Yet, ironically, the church was not purer or holier but was filled with self-righteous gossips and slanderers. Paul thus tells them that if love is the summary of the law, the Galatian church was lawless. "But if you bite and devour one another, watch out that you are not consumed by one another" (Gal 5:15). In contrast, only faith rooted in the gospel bears the fruit of the Spirit, which is "love, joy, peace, patience, kindness, goodness, faithfulness, gentleness, self-control; against such things there is no law" (vv. 22–23). Ironically, legalism and license foster their own distinct sins which are tolerated and even celebrated as righteousness by adherents of both camps.

We should take note of the fact that gossip and slander make it into every one of Paul's "Top Ten," right alongside sexual immorality, idolatry, and murder. Liberals and conservatives like to pick out the *real* sins in this list, but Scripture treats them as a package. And gossip is one of the "works of the flesh" Paul warns us about, along with "enmity, strife, jealousy, fits of anger, rivalries, dissensions, divisions, envy." This cluster of sins is placed right in the middle of "sexual immorality, impurity, sensuality, idolatry, sorcery... drunkenness, orgies, *and things like these*" (vv. 19–21, emphasis mine).

Gossip and slander are deadly sins that have become increasingly comfortable to us in a digital age. During just the last couple of years reputations have been ruined, relationships fractured, and tempers fanned into a collective flame of mutual acrimony. Terrible harm has come from reckless social media posts. Sheep have slandered shepherds, and shepherds have been verbally abusing sheep and other shepherds. This is a serious problem, and it is heightened by our fear-driven social and political tribalism. No one gets a fair hearing, much less a fair trial, on social media. There are many things which we'd never say to someone—or about someone—in a personal setting that we somehow feel free to broadcast just by pressing "send."

Today, it is acceptable to *gossip* about others so long as it is about those *other* sins in the list. We deflect sin to Them to confirm Us in our "righteousness." Yes, you might be telling the truth, but a conceited heart is revealed in the relishing of other people's failures—in doctrine or life. Social media is like the Wild West, with self-appointed (and often self-righteous) vigilantes ruining reputations and families, pushing people away from the church, and rejoicing in wrongdoing. This behavior is flagrantly tolerated even in the name of defending the truth, but in reality it is an "appearance of godliness, but denying its power" (2 Tim 3:5).

The remedy is love grounded in the forgiveness of sins, even of those committed by others as well as by us.

"Above all, keep loving one another earnestly," Peter exhorts, "since love covers a multitude of sins" (1 Pet 4:8). Peter must have had Proverbs in mind in writing this: "Whoever covers an offense seeks love, but he who repeats a matter separates close friends" (Prov 17:9; cf. 10:12). "Whoever goes about slandering reveals secrets, but he who is trustworthy in spirit keeps a thing covered" (11:13). "Good sense makes one slow to anger, and it is his glory to overlook an offense" (19:11). Especially in view of the dawn of the new creation in Christ, who is Love Incarnate, such wisdom takes on a new luster: "Love is patient and kind; *love does not envy or boast*; it is *not arrogant or rude*. It *does not insist on its own way*; it is *not irritable or resentful*; it *does not rejoice at wrongdoing*, but rejoices with the truth. Love bears all things, believes all things, hopes all things, endures all things" (1 Cor 13:4–7, emphasis mine).

This doesn't mean we ignore violence, vice, or false teaching. "Take no part in the unfruitful works of darkness, but instead expose them" (Eph 5:11). Notice that "expose them" refers back to the sinful "works," not to people. Gossip always aims at exposing the weaknesses of others so that we appear stronger and more righteous. By contrast, properly exercised church discipline always aims at repentance and restoration, no matter what the sin is (Gal 6:1). Public reproof does need to happen sometimes when public stands are taken that are "contrary to sound doctrine" (1 Tim 1:10). Additionally, when crimes have been committed police involvement may be needed. Otherwise, when we have suspicions or a problem with what someone has said or done, we follow Jesus's instruction in Matthew 18. An offense is initially treated one-on-one between parties. If this does not work out, a third party is brought in. If there is still no resolution, Jesus instructs, "tell it to the church"—that is, take it to the elders. "For where two or three are gathered in my name, there am I among them" (vv. 17–20).

We aren't to judge the world, Paul says, but to mind our own business and ensure that there is proper discipline in the church (1 Cor 5:12–13). When faithfully executed, such instruction, rebuke, and exhortation not only recovers a brother or sister and upholds God's commands, but it also tells an understandably suspicious and increasingly cynical world, "We can 'police' ourselves, thank you very much." But the practice of gossip not only requires church discipline but is the unholy alternative to it, ignoring the due process, privacy, reputation, and restoration of offended parties. If we fling this kind of mud at each other, we should not be surprised when the world scoffs at us. And we fall into the sin of gossip more easily when we seek to uphold Christian nationalism rather than the body of Christ.

To restate the main theme of this chapter, Christians are called not only into union with Christ through the gospel, but are also called to citizenship in their temporary country. There is nothing wrong with Christians as citizens participating in non-religious and nonviolent protests or in advocating for particular candidates and policies. However, this must not be done in the name of Christ or his church. Ministers and churches not only may but must proclaim God's law and gospel to all people and nations, including rulers. However, they have no authority beyond God's Word. The church as an institution does not have a president or legislative body to appeal to, but a King who has given it a specific commission: "Go therefore and make disciples of all nations, baptizing them in the name of the Father and of the Son and of the Holy Spirit, teaching them to observe all that I have commanded you" (Matt 28:19–20).

Chapter 12

RELIGIOUS LIBERTY

Cancel Culture and Persecution

The hatred of the world for God and his Messiah is becoming increasingly explicit and virulent. Christians, for whom Scripture is the final authority, are understandably fearful that much of American society, particularly many leaders in education, the media, politics, and culture, are self-consciously determined to eliminate religion in general and Christianity in particular from public discourse. Both sides are on full alert.

Increasingly, it does seem that religious freedom is heading into choppier waters. It is always perilous to drop the "Nazi" bomb willy-nilly on targets, but we regularly read of universities firing professors because they refuse to parrot the party line. An assistant professor with the most radical views becomes tenured, while a mild-mannered conservative with an endowed chair is fired, especially if he or she is openly Christian. Cases like this happen regularly now. Universities may well be the least truly liberal spaces in America. Happily, the courts mostly overturn these denials of free speech, but who knows how long this will last? According to Pew Research, 40 percent of millennials think free speech should be limited.[1] Fifty-three percent of university students said that students should be punished for making undefined "racially offensive statements."[2] Indeed, campuses have become ground zero in the culture wars and are now incubators of tomorrow's Manichean sects of the elect determined to wipe out the reprobate.

Cancel Culture

Ironically, the majority of students today say that the university environment is not conducive to them expressing their true beliefs, but they nevertheless support restricting freedom of speech for others. LGBTQ+ students significantly affirm limiting free speech, which is an odd position to be held by beneficiaries of the American doctrine. On most secular college or university campuses, more than anywhere else, "liberal education" is a thing of the past. Instead of inculcating democratic values, these institutions are fostering generations of fragile egos that cannot withstand the slightest attempt at careful reflection, self-criticism, and nuanced argument.

Can a speaker be shouted down by people who disagree, so that he or she cannot go on with the talk? Students break almost evenly on that question.[3] In fact, 19% of students in a survey thought that violence against a speaker was acceptable.[4] Several Supreme Court cases have ruled that "hate speech"—threats leading to lawless actions as well as obscenity—is not protected. Ironically, on many campuses today free speech guidelines are being threatened by some of the same groups that they were meant to protect.

This trend is discouraging to anyone who values the Bill of Rights. These first freedoms are the DNA of the American experiment. Christians and Enlightenment deists together crafted and defended these documents, even though they fundamentally disagreed in their religious views. Both agreed that these freedoms come from God and are not granted by the government. Nor are they just for Americans, but for all human beings. Though a deist, Thomas Jefferson could write in the Declaration of Independence that these rights are grounded in the "Law of Nature" and "Nature's God."[5] These fundamental, God-given freedoms are under threat at a time when especially younger generations today have no sense of their being grounded in God's universal gift to his image-bearers.

Progressives were heroic in defending free speech in the 1940s and 1950s against McCarthyism and again in the 1970s. In fact, one might suggest that "cancel culture" emerged during the witch hunts of that era and continued into the 1990s with boycotts of products and parks that affirmed gay rights. It is strange, then, that today—under the umbrella of "progressive"—a chilling suppression of free expression has fallen like a fog upon college and university campuses.[6] A new fascism of the far left is matched by the alt-right extremists. And as these largely social media-driven sects gain adherents, they threaten the American experiment. In spite of the deep divisions that led to the Civil War, both sides back then shared a common worldview. In fact, they appealed to that shared horizon (including appeals to the Bible) to judge each other's actions. These common convictions are gone now.

The divide between Us and Them has never been wider. "Cancel culture" is not a privileged weapon of one side; both sides wield it to end the conversation. In a recent poll, four in ten Republicans said that violence against the Other may be necessary.[7] In recent years, prominent conservative evangelicals have been "canceled" at Liberty University and their chapel talks removed from the website, simply because they had made public statements critical of Donald Trump. The decision was made by the school's president and vocal Trump ally Jerry Falwell Jr., whose scandals have been widely reported.[8]

Christianity is a religion that thrives in an environment of freedom of thought, speech, and conscience. There are doctrines inherent to the faith that favor such liberties, as we have seen. But whenever the church seeks to shut down conversation in its own ranks, power corrupts and silences truth. And when the church tries to defend *its* voice by marginalizing alternative and even opposing voices, then it is understandably regarded as a danger to civil discourse and democracy. When Christians join with fellow citizens in defending *human* rights, everyone benefits. Yet when Christian churches and organizations use their institutional might to defend *Christian*-specific protection, they engage in the zero-sum game of identity politics. Everyone loses. And everyone *is* losing. For me as a minister, the worst loss is to the honor and advance of Christ's name.

Isn't Persecution Normal?

The church, both as a collective body and as individual believers within it, is forbidden by Christ to react to religious persecution with violence. Jesus proclaims this new order in his Sermon on the Mount (Matthew 5). Since there is no longer any earthly theocracy and all nations are common, there is no earthly arms—including legislatures, presidents, or courts—that the church can appeal to for aid. The church can only employ the weapons of faithful witness to the gospel and prayer for persecutors. After all, Paul was a former persecutor of the church. Today's enemy may become, by God's grace, tomorrow's brother or sister in Christ.

So does all of this mean that we just sit back and watch the radical-progressive agenda achieve its aims? Not at all. Remember,

Christians are citizens of both kingdoms. Christians participate alongside non-Christians in the political process, especially in democratic nations. They do this not in the name or in defense of Christ's kingdom of grace, but as common citizens. All citizens are shaped by particular worldviews, and Christians cannot be expected to ignore theirs in forming social and political views. Yet the realm of public policy is not meant to be a power struggle where one side wins and the other loses. Rather, it is a space of negotiation and compromise. There are no demons or angels. Non-Christians are still God's image-bearers and are, like us, blessed with his common grace. Sometimes a non-Christian is better informed and more morally just than a Christian on a particular civil issue. As Christians in the world, we are called not to run the world but to serve the common good alongside non-Christian neighbors in this fading age.

When we take this approach, we are able to work together with non-Christians who respect human life. When Christians defend the life of the unborn (or even the born, as in post-birth abortion) or the elderly, they are not merely following distinctively Christian convictions, much less trying to legislate a distinctively Christian morality. Rather, they are calling the government to do its most important job: namely, to protect human life. "The Law of Nature" and "Nature's God," to quote the Declaration of Independence again, is sufficient justification. General revelation, including the conscience, sophisticated ultrasound imaging, and philosophical arguments, also offers persuasive evidence. And when Christians stand firm on defining marriage as between one man and one woman, they are not only following God's revelation in Scripture but also the law of nature that all people know in their conscience (Rom 1:18–32). The testimony of peoples in all times and places attests to this truth about marriage. And now that same-sex marriage is legal, the church must do what it did all the way back in the second century: keep to biblical standards of marriage in the church regardless of the state's approval or societal norms. This is not just a retreat of the church into private obedience, but is a public testimony to the world that America is our temporary residence and we submit to the laws of a greater commonwealth.

The world—that is, the system of this passing age—has always opposed Christ and his church. If the world hates us because we are racist, homophobic, and self-righteous, then it is merely one part of the world hating another part of the world. That is not the church of Christ, but just another district of Babylon fighting to defend its shrinking territory. But our Lord prepared his disciples for the world's hostility:

> "If the world hates you, know that it has hated me before it hated you. If you were of the world, the world would love you as its own; but because you are not of the world, but I chose you out of the world, therefore the world hates you. Remember the word that I said to you: 'A servant is not greater than his master.' If they persecuted me, they will also persecute you. If they kept my word, they will also keep yours." (John 15:18–20)

Importantly, as noted earlier, Jesus was not thinking of the Roman Empire but of his fellow Jews when he spoke of "the world" in this passage. Of course, that designation would have infuriated the religious leaders, whose whole regime was focused on separating Israelites from the world—i.e., Gentile impurity. Tragically, "the world" that persecutes the church can be and often has been leaders of the false church. This includes any Christian church or organization today that is opposed to the gospel of Christ.

The prophets were either ignored, laughed at, or even killed. As he was about to be stoned, Stephen recounted to the crowd the history of Israel's rebellion: "Which of the prophets did your fathers not persecute? And they killed those who announced beforehand the coming of the Righteous One, whom you have now betrayed and murdered, you who received the law as delivered by angels and did not keep it" (Acts 7:52–53). Jewish Christians were cast out of the synagogues and therefore were beyond the special provisions the Roman Empire made for Jewish practice. As I noted before, Paul started out as an unusually dedicated persecutor of Christians until the Lord appeared to him. Arian rulers persecuted those who proclaimed the Trinity. The Protestant Reformers were excommunicated, tortured, and burned by the papal church, and Protestants persecuted other Protestants.

Theological Liberalism and Progressive Politics

When orthodox theologians and preachers challenged the growth of anti-supernatural religion in mainline Protestantism during the 1920s, they were defrocked and deprived of their livings and pensions. There is no persecutor so ferocious as a denomination that has turned its back on God. For about a century now, these denominations have been replacing the authority of Scripture and the gospel ministry with the authority of the secular academy and political liberation. In fact, the progressive political agenda is to a very large extent the creation of liberal Protestant theologians, preachers, and activists.

Politics aside, I agree with J. Gresham Machen's provocative argument in the 1920s that *theological* liberalism is not the left end of the radio dial; it is simply another religion.[9] Its anti-supernaturalism placed salvation in the hands of enlightened humanity. Yale theologian H. Richard Niebuhr described its message well: "A God without wrath brought men without sin into a kingdom without judgment through the ministrations of a Christ without a cross."[10] This whole worldview is human-centered. Lacking the vertical connection to God (as in Psalm 51:4, "Against you, you only, have I sinned"), sin becomes redefined in purely horizontal (sociopolitical and economic) terms ("The Others who are oppressors"). Jesus becomes a model of resistance, redemption now means salvation by our collective works, we are justified by our allegiance to the righteous cause, the church is a society of social reformers, and the eschaton is the kingdom of love and justice that we have built.

Throughout the nineteenth century, evangelicals were known for their concern for the plight of the poor, women and children, and workers. Many were at the forefront of the movement to abolish slavery. Evangelicals—especially Baptists and Methodists—mainly created the Labour Party in Britain and advocated similar policies in the United States. However, as the *effects* of the gospel became confused with *the gospel itself* and drifted into a sort of moralistic social gospel, orthodox Protestants tended to defend the status quo.

This crack in Protestantism widened into a gulf in the early twentieth century when theological modernists pressed their Pelagianism (faith in human moral improvement) into a denial of central doctrines. Convinced that they were called to be the great transformers of society, they had more interest in social experiments than in the truth of the Christian faith. In reaction, fundamentalists generally embraced a pessimistic view of the end of history and of the world. While defending the "fundamentals," the movement eventually altered their meaning, narrowed their scope, and focused on making rules to keep young people in check. Both factions became more beholden to a segment of American culture than to the ecumenical creeds and Protestant confessions. Thus, in radically different ways, they jointly contributed to the marginalization of what was left of traditional Reformation

Christianity. To a large extent, the present culture wars are the ripened fruit of the modernist-fundamentalist battles in American Protestantism.

Christians are commanded to love all people, including persecutors; this is a higher priority than seeking justice for themselves. In the Sermon on the Mount Jesus establishes a new regime—a new covenant, to be sure. It isn't the gospel, but an ethic founded on the gospel, "for [God] is kind to the *ungrateful* and the *evil*" (Luke 6:35, emphasis mine). Isn't that astounding? After all, we are all in that boat, as were the disciples who first heard it. Therefore, the new ethic is: "Be merciful, even as your Father is merciful. Judge not, and you will not be judged" (vv. 36–37). This is not a call to greater civility and public virtue among Romans, as Seneca and Cicero offered. Only those who embrace, feed on, and live from this peculiar gospel, reborn by the Spirit, are given this peculiar ethic. It is not a constitution for any secular nation. Against the Anabaptist radicals, Luther explained that the Sermon on the Mount does not provide the blueprint for a political state:

> Christ is preaching for his Christians alone . . . in contrast with the carnal notions and thoughts which then were still cleaving to the apostles, who supposed that he would establish a new government and empire, and give them places in it, so that they might rule as lords, and bring into subjection to them their enemies and the evil world . . . after this, too, the pope has hankered . . . So we now see, too, that all the world is seeking its own in the gospel . . . as Münzer began with his peasants.[11]

Actually, Thomas Müntzer's violent insurrection of the "pure Christians" against church and state was about as far from the Sermon on the Mount as one could imagine. In contrast, Paul explained,

> Bless those who persecute you; bless and do not curse them. Rejoice with those who rejoice, weep with those who weep. Live in harmony with one another. Do not be haughty, but associate with the lowly. Never be wise in your own sight. Repay no one evil for evil, but give thought to do what is honorable in the sight of all. If possible, so far as it depends on you, live peaceably with all. Beloved, never avenge yourselves, but leave it to the wrath of God, for it is written, "Vengeance is mine, I will repay, says the Lord." To the contrary, "if your enemy is hungry, feed him; if he is thirsty, give him something to drink; for by so doing you will heap burning coals on his head." Do not be overcome by evil, but overcome evil with good. (Rom 12:14–21)

Peter also reminds us that suffering will come for the church. "But let none of you suffer as a murderer or a thief or an evildoer or as a meddler. Yet if anyone suffers as a Christian, let him not be ashamed, but let him glorify God in that name. For it is time for judgment to begin at the household of God; and if it begins with us, what will be the outcome for those who do not obey the gospel of God?" (1 Peter 4:15–17). When non-Christians object to Christians imposing the church's constitution on the body politic ("meddling"), they are actually closer to the New Testament than many Christians. When the church even modestly reflects Christ's will for his covenant people to be a fellowship of love, it becomes a parable of the age to come even in this passing evil age.

The Problem with the Martyr Complex

We had a martyr complex when I was growing up. We were nourished with the fears of Armageddon and the possibility that we might be left behind by the rapture. God's creation was "the late, great planet earth." Hopefully, I would be among those raptured before the final apocalypse, but until then we could expect things to get worse and worse. Persecution is coming—no, it's *here*. I used to read the newsletters documenting the waning of religious liberty with great interest. Thankfully I remain a concerned advocate of religious liberty, but the hyperbole surrounding the martyr complex certainly contributes to a culture of fear and resentment.

Having briefly taught and preached in China's underground church and in other places where persecution is something faithful Christians face every day, I've found it ironic and personally challenging to me that these brothers and sisters are more filled with joy in the gospel than with the fear of man. While I was still asleep, they were an hour into their morning prayers—seeking the Lord, reading Scripture, and singing together. Sure, they could tell me stories about persecution, but they would rather talk about God and his saving grace in Christ—and tell others.

This memory sharply contrasts with a meeting President Trump had with evangelical leaders at the White House, in which he reportedly warned of violence against conservative Christians if he lost the election for his second term. Evangelicals, Trump said, were "one election away from losing everything that you've got."[12] That sort of fear-based rhetoric is evident across the evangelical landscape. Losing *everything*? Then what is it exactly that we have in the first place? The church is not a voting bloc in the dangerous game of identity politics. What at least some evangelical leaders apparently don't recognize is that we *lose everything* not when we are fed to lions but when we preach another gospel. "For what will it profit a man if he gains the whole world and forfeits his soul?" (Matt 16:26). We should not be surprised when a politician *appeals* to our fears; what should alarm us is when this appeal *succeeds* among those who profess faith in Christ. In every election, what the church has to lose is the integrity of its witness to Christ.

Not to be outdone by the Christian right, the progressive evangelical and "Vote Common Good" founder Doug Pagitt said, "We think there is a real battle going on not only for the soul of the nation but for individuals."[13] That is true, of course, but it has nothing to do with who is in the White House. And anyone who believes this way of thinking, or even preaches it, has forgotten the psalmist's warning, "Put not your trust in princes, in a son of man, in whom there is no salvation" (Ps 146:3). Besides, nations don't have a soul. This trope, heard on both sides, derives from Romanticism, not the Bible, and it inflates a nation's sense of sacredness and divine identity.

Instead of pointing the world to the redeeming God of history, our public pronouncements often give the impression that we are fearful, resentful, and anxious. *They* are pure evil. Even wearing or not wearing a mask in public during a pandemic becomes a political statement. I have heard stories of many believers, even elders, who refused to come to church—not out of fear of the pandemic or personal medical conditions, but in protest against either the church's accommodation or lack of accommodation of guidelines from health officials. Masks have been flags indicating which side you're on. We are really mad at each other, and the angrier we become the higher the ratings and votes soar for those who exploit it. This is not persecution, but folly.

Because they love their neighbors, Christians have been advocates of religious liberty from the beginning not just for themselves but for everyone created in God's image and called to a personal and uncoerced decision concerning Christ. In my calling as a minister of Christ's church, however, I must say that if the U.S. should lose the rights of its great Constitution, there is no need to worry; the church still has the rights of its greater Commission. Christ says, "I will build my church, and the gates of hell shall not prevail against it" (Matt 16:18). Sometimes I have prayed in public worship,

"Thank you, Lord, that we live in a nation that gives us the freedom to preach your gospel." But that's wrong. *Christ* gives us the freedom to preach the gospel, regardless of the consequences. While thanking the Lord for constitutional liberties, I *should* pray with Paul, ". . . that words may be given to me in opening my mouth boldly to proclaim the mystery of the gospel" (Eph 6:19).

Christ has done very well without Caesar's assistance, and even with Caesar's ferocious opposition, in building his church around the world. Every time the Chinese government issues another wave of persecution, the church in China grows. *Foreign Policy*'s Azeem Ibrahim comments, "Statistics are a tricky business in China, but there may be as many as 100 million believers—more than the 90 million members of the Chinese Communist Party. Some, perhaps overly optimistic, estimates see as many as 250 million Christians in China by 2030."[14] This optimistic estimate equals about 75 percent of the U.S. population. Conversely, the church's apostasy has occurred in periods of luxury and a cozy relationship with the empire. The church does not preach the gospel at the pleasure of any administration or decline from preaching it at another administration's displeasure. We preach at Christ's pleasure. And we don't make the policies of this spreading empire of grace, but communicate them from our King, even if we must quietly obey God rather than Caesar.

Caesar has profited by playing to fears of religious persecution. To the extent that evangelicals were willing to be exploited as a political base for short-term privileges, they have lost their cultural moral authority in the long term. But Christ is not ineffective and his gospel is not weak. Jesus came not to Make Israel Great Again, much less to be a mascot for either a Rainbow America or a Christian America. He came to bring forgiveness of sins and everlasting life, to die and rise again so that through faith in him we too can share in his new creation. This is the message that generations of past evangelicals were eager to share with the whole world. The gospel, after all, *is* for the whole world, Jew and Gentile, slave and free, male and female, black, brown, and white, and even Democrat and Republican. In his Great Commission Jesus gave authority to the church to make disciples, not citizens; to proclaim the gospel to all nations, not their own political opinions to their own base; to baptize people in the name of the Father, the Son, and the Holy Spirit, not in the name of America or a political party; and to teach everything that he delivered, not whatever is on their mind.

At his trial, Jesus told Pontius Pilate that he was indeed a king—however, he clarified that he was heir of a greater throne than the Roman prefect could imagine. "My kingdom is not of this world. If my kingdom were of this world, my servants would have been fighting, that I might not be delivered over to the Jews. But my kingdom is not from the world" (John 18:36). The kingdom was *in* the world, sure. Even *for* it. But it was not *from* the world. Pilate does not decide Jesus's fate. It is *his* life: "No one takes it from me, but I lay it down of my own accord. I have authority to lay it down, and I have authority to take it up again" (John 10:18). Jesus predicted the destruction of the Temple in Jerusalem and a long period afterward that would be simultaneously marked by persecution and expansion of his kingdom, his followers armed only with the gospel (Matt 24). Even though these early Christians faced serious persecution, every New Testament command on the subject called them to love and pray for their enemies, even persecutors, with the confidence that Christ is still building his church.

Then why does the appeal to fear work so consistently with many who claim to stand in the line of Jesus's disciples, to whom he said, "Fear not, little flock, for it is your Father's good pleasure to give you the kingdom" (Luke 12:32)? In its present form, the kingdom seems unimpressive. It *is* a "little flock." In many places it suffers under the cross and yet flourishes, while in Europe and the U.S. it is shrinking. Yet there is still a church. Why? Because the kingdom is a gift of the Father's good pleasure. We visit the rubble of the empires of Alexander the Great and the Roman Caesars on vacations. If Christ tarries, America will join the list of kingdoms that were shaken. But there is one kingdom that cannot be shaken, one that we are receiving, not building (Heb 12:28). No other empire has extended so widely throughout the world. In fact, ethnographers followed missionaries to discover new tribes in the modern era. Why? Because every people group in the world must be told the good news.

Stop Craving Cultural Approval

As Christians in the U.S., we are perhaps even more afraid of unpopularity than persecution. Liberal church leaders crave the acceptance of sophisticated elites. For all its talk of "speaking truth to power" and being "prophetic," theological liberalism has long parroted the script of *high culture*: academia, the arts, science, and progressive politics. The only difference between its solemn declarations and secular culture is the lag time. This religious tradition has been almost completely absorbed into the bloodstream of this passing age.

Yet conservative Protestants should not be dancing on any graves; they need to realize that they are digging their own. Evangelical Protestantism has long craved the favor of *pop culture*, especially entertainers, sports celebrities, business, and marketing, along with a generous dose of pop psychology. We have repeatedly heard that evangelicals adored Mr. Trump because he made them feel "proud to be a Christian in America again." So much for, "Let the one who boasts, boast in the Lord" (2 Cor 10:17).

To attract the rich and famous, some megachurch pastors

sport accessories like $5,000 Yeazy sneakers, a $3,000 Gucci jacket, a Louboutin fanny pack worth $1,250, and a Ricci crocodile belt that sells for $2,541. Realizing that any one of these accoutrements cost more than his monthly rent, a parishioner started an Instagram sensation by identifying the wardrobe costs of preachers who think this is what it takes to cozy up to pop royalty.[15] Not surprisingly, these wannabe-celebrity pastors are riddled with scandals, falling like dominos before a watching—and often laughing—world.

On both the left and the right, the culture of many churches in America today is indistinguishable from the world. The only difference is which half of the world. The world seems to sometimes know this better than we do. Why bother with church at all if it seems so much like what they can find in a more authentic form elsewhere?

Rather than being persecuted, we are merely embarrassed and angry that Christian churches and especially the American Protestant establishment do not have the cultural clout that they once held when being a relatively smart WASP (White Anglo-Saxon Protestant) got you into Princeton or when the leadership of government felt obliged to attend the National Prayer Breakfast. The mere waving of Christian symbols by public figures in public places reassures cheering crowds. Whenever Christians want to feel proud and well liked by the world—by power—this always causes a change in the message that, from the kingdom's perspective, is far worse than being persecuted for preaching the gospel.

Chapter 13

LGBTQ+ FEARS

People over Positions

For many today, terms like Feminism, Marxism, Critical Race Theory, and Intersectionality are like flags we're expected either to salute or to burn. I am not an expert on these topics, and I doubt that very many pundits and preachers who invoke these shibboleths, pro or con, are either. These terms are passwords for each club, which is confident that the other club has *nothing* to say worth listening to. Nothing is complicated for either side when religious devotion to ideology replaces reason and common sense.

It is certainly true that Marxism is a worldview. In fact, it is a religion with its own metanarrative, doctrines, rituals, and behaviors. For each Christian teaching there is an antithetical teaching in Marxism. (In fact, interestingly, Marx's learned associate Friedrich Engels made this point, reaching back to the radical Anabaptists as precursors of the communist revolution.) For Marxism, god (i.e., nature) is blind and history is the struggle between oppressor and oppressed. There is no original sin, a fall from a good creation. The world is inherently violent, and it is our job to redeem workers from "original alienation." The communist party is the church and the eschaton is the workers' paradise.

But you have not said everything when you say "Marxist."

Like with abolition and other reform movements, the first wave of feminism was pioneered mostly by evangelicals. The second wave was shaped more by Marxist ideology and the sexual revolution of the seventies, both of which have influenced the LGBTQ+ movement. However, as Carl Trueman demonstrates, the obsession over sexual identity is part of a larger story of expressive individualism in American culture.[1]

It hardly needs noting that the LGBTQ+ agenda has become massively powerful in a relatively short period of time. As a presidential candidate in 2008, Barack Obama said, "I believe that marriage is the union between a man and a woman. Now, for me as a Christian—for me—as a Christian, it is also a sacred union. God's in the mix."[2] By 2012, he had reversed this position. With the Supreme Court decision *Obergefell v. Hodges* on June 26, 2015, same-sex marriage became law nationwide and the White House was draped in rainbow-colored lights. As with other liberation movements, the gay rights agenda was initially propelled by numerous cases of brutality and injustice. However, as a father of four I have seen how the broader agenda has largely spread through social media. An opposite bullying is evident when those who still agree with Obama's 2008 position are reviled as The Most Dangerous People on Earth. I fear the broad attack on the goodness of God's creative design; it ranks near the top of my own failures in trusting the Lord.

Yet we need to distinguish between temptations to which *people* (including Christians) are prone and a *political movement* that celebrates sexual confusion in defiance of "the Law of Nature and Nature's God," to borrow Jefferson's language again. I plead with pastors and elders today to focus on the sheep under their care and not on the Queer movement as such. Just as women have been hurt by our reaction against feminism, sexually confused members of our churches have often become casualties of the culture wars. As Calvin wisely counsels, "A pastor needs two voices, one for gathering the sheep and the other for driving away wolves."[3]

Caring for People by Struggling Together

Many years ago a friend encouraged a young man struggling with same-sex attraction to call me. He was the son of parents who sat on the board of a well-known evangelical family values organization. Discovering the gospel of grace, he came to our organization, the White Horse Inn, as a volunteer and also joined a solid, gospel-preaching church. Eventually returning home, he met cynicism and constant scolding from his parents and the church. His parents, he told me, were embarrassed to have a son who wrestled with this sin. They wanted him to keep it "just between us," but he went to talk to his pastor. One evening, he called to tell me that after he had confessed his continued struggle, his pastor told him that God had "given him up" to his lusts and he had lost his salvation. Despairing, a week later he committed suicide.

Eighty-six percent of LGBTs were raised in a faith community, with more than three-fourths in mostly evangelical "theological conservative religious communities."[4] Given this astonishing statistic, we have to examine our pastoral outlook that in turn shapes the culture of the church and families in it. There are many marvelous examples of grace-oriented repentance to which I could point. Some churches have really read up on the issues and, more importantly, listened to struggling members. But that is not always the case. When someone "comes out" to other members of the church with his or her sexual temptation, too many evangelical pastors and elders react with control instead of care. Their first reaction is, well, *reaction*: To make the church's stand perfectly clear and to keep the "infection" from spreading. This is strange. The frantic believer has no lack of clarity, or even any disagreement, with the church's stand. That is *why* this believer is in a spiritual crisis. But many think that it is their first job as an officer in the culture wars to defend the *position* rather than to care for the *person*. Using the voice for wolves, they instead drive away the sheep.

At this point, though, the daily news-and-culture feeds often take precedence for conservatives, just as liberals do with their digital echo chamber. Where Christ sees a lamb, his ambassador sees a spy for the Others, a political movement poised to destroy the American family right in our midst. It is not surprising that so frequently the victim of this sort of spiritual abuse does in fact become an enemy of the church. Yet the real enemy, Satan, has stolen his way into that church by undermining and overthrowing faith in the gospel.

Members in our own churches and families wrestle with same-sex attraction. Should we just cast them into the flames destined to consume *Them*? No, they are *Christians* who are denying themselves. They are repentant followers of Christ who, like all of us, experience temptation. There are also people whose chromosomes and ovaries are female but have external genitalia that are male. Some people really do experience gender dysphoria and struggle with a transgender identity. Brothers and sisters among us agonize over these issues, usually in isolation.

"Why do people at church think I chose this?", a young woman recently asked me. I don't doubt that peer pressure to design and advertise individual "uniqueness" is part of the broader trend. But this teen did not start feeling this way when she happened upon a transgender website or watched too many hours of CNN and MSNBC. She came from a conservative Christian home, church, and school. "If I could take a pill right now and it would go away, I would," she exclaimed. "I believe the Bible: male and female. But I'm just sure that I am a male. He created everything good, but then there was the fall. I'm broken in body *and* soul." Her church immediately treated it as a discipline issue: She should banish these feelings, as if they were entirely self-chosen and physically unreal.

Yet because we are bodies as well as souls, there is a physical and medical dimension to gender dysphoria. So we have to understand the science as well as the Scriptures if we want to shepherd people and not just issue pronouncements. We need not fear this investigation; understanding yields sympathy for persons, not agreement with conclusions antithetical to biblical truth. The position may not change, but the pastoral care might.

If our first reaction is fear, then we probably either have the wrong theology or our good theology is not fully engaged when it comes to encountering fellow sinners. Jesus's treatment of people in the Gospels is again our standard: "I must come to your house for dinner" (cf. Luke 19:5). In his amazing book *Life Together*, Dietrich Bonhoeffer addresses the danger of imagining (much less, trying to create) a "Community of the Pious" rather than ministering to each other as fellow sinners trusting in Christ and seeking to be his disciples.[5] Let's do this very difficult pilgrimage together!

Such struggles should not surprise us as Christians. Though created "very good," in fact "in the image of God," both "male and female" (Gen 1:26–27), we are fallen in body and soul. Sin is first of all a condition in which we are conceived. Transgression of any kind is unnatural (as created), going against the grain of reality, but sin has corrupted our good nature in every nook and cranny of our existence. Yet actual sins are committed when we indulge sinful temptations rather than accept God's design. This involves daily and deliberate repentance and faith. We all have "besetting sins," but are called to resist rather than embrace them:

> Therefore, since we are surrounded by so great a cloud of witnesses, let us also lay aside every weight, and sin which clings so closely, and let us run with endurance the race that is set before us, looking to Jesus, the founder and perfecter of our faith, who for the joy that was set before him endured the cross, despising the shame, and is seated at the right hand of the throne of God. (Heb 12:1–2)

However, nursed early on by liberal theology, the radical progressive agenda treats these sexual issues not as part of our fallen condition but as part of the biological diversity in an evolutionary development of our species. It is just as natural to be queer, transgender, intersexual, or asexual as it is to be straight and cisgender. Consequently, the confusion, guilt, and shame that people experience cannot be due to anything objective; they are merely subjective feelings provoked by unenlightened oppressors.

From a Christian perspective, however, this counsel is not only contrary to Scripture but is horribly abusive. It demands that a person deliberately deny his or her innate knowledge of reality—even obvious biological facts—in order to become authentic. According to Scripture, everyone knows even apart from Scripture that homosexual acts are unnatural (Rom 1:26–32). When one feels guilt and shame for engaging in these activities, the conscience has not yet been seared. These subjective feelings are still in line with objective reality and with moral sanity, and their *struggle* evidences this.

More importantly, only an objective sin can be objectively forgiven. Essentially, to tell someone that these sins are not really sinful is to withhold the joy of forgiveness from them. When people are denied this relief by abusive counsel, my heart breaks for them just as when they are told that their *brokenness* is not real but something that they have chosen. They instead need to hear that there is an objective problem and an objective solution to their subjective feelings: real sin and real forgiveness from a real God who, in Christ, has absolved all who come to him in repentance and faith. Christ's objective work also provides a basis for a decisive defeat of sin's tyranny; by God's grace we can fight against sin. We have been given the Holy Spirit who works in us to do his pleasure (Phil 2:13). He will never cease in this work, even though we fall and sometimes even quench the Spirit (Phil 1:6). Everyone who trusts in Christ is qualified to hear: "If we are faithless, he remains faithful—for he cannot deny himself" (2 Tim 2:13).

In Romans 1, Christ's apostle treats sexual immorality as a symptom of idolatry. It certainly characterized the Greco-Roman world familiar to him. As he planted churches in major cities and colonies throughout the empire, Paul knew that this would be a flashpoint in a culture whose deep idolatry had come to treat vices as virtues and virtues as vices. So, for example, he tells the Corinthian church,

> Or do you not know that the unrighteous will not inherit the kingdom of God? Do not be deceived: neither the sexually immoral, nor idolaters, nor adulterers, nor men who practice homosexuality, nor thieves, nor the greedy, nor drunkards, nor revilers, nor swindlers will inherit the kingdom of God. (1 Cor 6:9–10)

On the one hand, we should note that Paul does not single out homosexuality as the unpardonable sin. On the other hand, those "who practice homosexuality . . . will not inherit the kingdom of God" any more than those who practice idolatry, adultery, or greed. Believers are tempted and sometimes fall—or even rush—into sin. But it is something else to "practice" that sin like a lawyer practices law or a doctor medicine.

There has been some controversy in evangelical circles over whether we can use the term "gay Christian." This is as much an oxymoron as the other forms of "practicing" sin just mentioned. No one knew better than Paul that believers struggle against these temptations and sometimes give in, but he would never have conceived of a "Christian idolater," an "adulterous Christian," a "greedy Christian" or a "Christian thief." In fact, Paul adds in the next verse, "And such were some of you. But you were washed, you were sanctified, you were justified in the name of the Lord Jesus Christ and by the Spirit of our God" (v. 11).

If you are in Christ, you are a repentant and believing sinner, not a "practicing sinner." You do not say, "I am gay," analogous to "I am a lawyer." That is not what defines you, and it is cruel to tell any believer that it does. What defines us all as believers is that we are "in Christ": washed, justified, sanctified. We are objectively righteous and holy in Christ, while still confessing sins that we commit. We still face temptations, whether gay or straight. We *must* resist them. Yet, as I just mentioned, all of us fall into—and, sadly, even rush into—sins. But this is not our identity. We agree with God's law, that it is good, even when we violate it (Rom 7:16).

Let me conclude this point with a closer look at Paul's crucial teaching in Romans. He exposes Gentile sin. We focus on his mention of idolatry and homosexuality, but he adds that the Gentiles are also "full of envy, murder, strife, deceit, maliciousness. They are gossips, slanderers, haters of God, insolent, haughty, boastful, inventors of evil, disobedient to parents, foolish, faithless, heartless, ruthless" (Rom 1:29–31).

At this point, one might imagine a Jewish reader (or, more likely, hearer) of this epistle cheering him on: "That's those Gentiles, alright. Go get 'em, Paul!" But just when it might seem like a screed of Us versus Them, he turns to Us, his fellow Jews. Sure, the Gentiles are enmeshed in idolatry and immorality. But what about the other things on the list, Paul asks: hatred, anger, arrogance, self-righteousness?

Moreover, Paul observes, there is nothing worse than the hypocrisy of saying "We have the law" while actually practicing the *same sins* as the Others. If Romans 1 is especially relevant to quote to our progressive friends, Romans 2 takes the rest of us to the woodshed: "Therefore you have no excuse, O man, every one of you who judges. For in passing judgment on another you condemn yourself, because you, the judge, practice the very same things" (v. 1). How do those who judge expect to escape God's judgment? In fact, their appeal to the knowledge of God's law—having Judeo-Christian values—is evidence *against* them.

Gentiles sometimes actually do what the law commands because it is written on their conscience, but those who have the written law all too easily break it. Paul says that his brothers according to the flesh, who presume to be the righteous who "rely on the law" (v. 17), fancy themselves "a guide to the blind, a light to those who are in darkness, an instructor of the foolish, a teacher of children, having in the law the embodiment of knowledge and truth" (vv. 19–20).

> You then who teach others, do you not teach yourself? While you preach against stealing, do you steal? You who say that one must not commit adultery, do you commit adultery? You who abhor idols, do you rob temples? You who boast in the law dishonor God by breaking the law. For, as it is written, "The name of God is blasphemed among the Gentiles because of you." (Rom 2:21–24)

Keeping Today's "Us" from Becoming Tomorrow's "Them"

For the first time, membership in a church, synagogue, or mosque has fallen below half of the American population. The Gallup organization mainly attributes this to the rise of the "unaffiliated."[6] Many of these neighbors were reared in our churches, so we need to ponder how and why they not only leave us but resent and often oppose us.

In fact, some of the most ardent opponents of conservative evangelicalism in America were raised in these same churches. Media mogul Ted Turner, who once said that Christianity was "a religion for losers" (a comment he later apologized for) was raised in a fundamentalist home, church, and school.[7] Oprah Winfrey, who was called a "preacher woman" while growing up in a conservative Missionary Baptist church, is perhaps the leading representative of a "spiritual but not religious" perspective. Actress Shirley MacLaine was raised by strict Southern Baptist missionary parents and Hugh Hefner grew up in an equally strict Methodist home. Let me repeat the staggering figure: Eighty-six percent of LGBTs were raised in a faith community, with more than three-fourths in mostly evangelical "theological conservative religious communities."

"Queer Eye" cast member Jonathan Van Ness was not duped by Marxist ideology. He relates that his molestation by an older boy at his church in Quincy, Illinois, set him on a path of sexual and substance addictions.[8] Van Ness quotes Brené Brown: "She says shame is the feeling of, 'If you know all there was to know about me, you wouldn't love me anymore,' which always struck a chord with me."[9] My heart breaks when I read the subtitle of his new autobiography: *A Raw Journey to Self-Love.* After all, beneath the shame is objective guilt that we cannot expiate. What we need is not self-love, but the love of our Creator and Judge who is also our Redeemer, telling us *outside of ourselves* the source of our guilt and the verdict of justification that he renders through faith in his Son. But what love outside of himself did Jonathan Van Ness experience, either in the proclamation of the gospel or through the support of Christians after his sexual assault?

On the list goes. I just assume that people have some firsthand experiences in mind when I hear them rail against "fundamentalism" and "evangelicals." These individuals are just the latest in a long history—going all the way back to the early Enlightenment—of evangelicals (many even studying for the ministry at first) becoming leaders of the opposition to orthodox Christianity.

Of course, not all of these departures can be attributed to churches or families. Many younger people today are influenced more by social media trends and peer pressure than they are by church and home. Some undoubtedly leave us simply because they do not embrace Christian beliefs and ethical convictions (1 John 2:19). It's easy to blame the church for its failures and deflect our own unbelief and unrepentance to its mistakes. For example, I recently heard an interview on NPR in which an actor and the interviewer both recalled being "Psalty the Singing Song Book" as children in church programs. The memory evoked deep anger and resentment toward their respective churches. I don't know their back story, but a lot of similar folks are dropping out of church today, many of them expressing resentment toward the same things. There are two evidence-based reasons why church dropout is a huge problem today: a growing ignorance of Christian truth and a subculture that is failing to adequately foster intergenerational discipleship.

First, many evangelicals today have a superficial understanding of even basic Christian doctrines and therefore have lost the key rationale for discipleship in the church and in their callings in the world. A Pew study found that atheists and agnostics were better informed about religions (followed closely by Jews and Mormons) than Christians were, including Christianity itself.[10] Ligonier's 2020 "State of Theology" study showed the astonishing level of ignorance, confusion, and even outright rejection of central beliefs among professing evangelical Christians.[11] Unsurprisingly, a majority of U.S. respondents agreed with the statement, "Religious belief is a matter of personal opinion; it is not about objective truth."[12] However, over half of evangelical respondents also said, "God accepts the worship of all religions."[13] If the faith is reduced to whatever I feel, experience, or want to believe, then of course its truth claims won't be taken seriously. For example, there is no need to understand what the Bible teaches about the Trinity if my view of God is just something that bubbles up from within me. If I don't see any practical usefulness for the historic Christian view of Christ—one person in two natures—then I will stick with resources that cater to how I already feel and think. Limiting our diet to junk food, we do not grow into healthy and mature adult believers. If one's religious background is "moralistic, therapeutic deism," it's not such a large step to a vague, New Agey spirituality that affirms his or her lifestyle regardless of whether its beliefs can be defended. It's "true for me."

"Evangelical," from the Greek word for "gospel" (*euangelion*), was what the leaders of the Protestant Reformation wanted to be called. Reformers had already come and gone crying out against the moral and spiritual state of the church, but Luther directly struck at the church's heart because its doctrine, particularly the gospel, was at stake. If "faith comes by hearing . . . the word of Christ" (Rom 10:17) and that word of Christ or gospel is garbled by other words, then the church becomes just another branch of this dying age rather than the branches of the Living Vine. In short, when Christ's doing, dying, and rising are front and center, there is a church, an embassy of Christ's kingdom in the world. When we preach ourselves—moralism, self-help therapy, politics, or whatever—there might be a religious or spiritual organization, but not the church of Christ.

The two most important emphases of the Reformation were justification (being declared righteous before God) in Christ alone through faith alone and Scripture alone as the arbiter of Christian doctrine and practice. However, the meaning of "evangelical" changed over time, especially in America. After his time in the U.S. in 1930, Dietrich Bonhoeffer described evangelicalism as "Protestantism without the Reformation." On the 500th anniversary of the Reformation in 2017, a majority of U.S. Protestants (52%) sided with the Roman Catholic view that both good deeds and faith in Christ are required for justification before God. Only 23% even knew that Protestants traditionally teach that salvation comes through faith alone and 45% erroneously thought that both Protestants and Catholics teach that doctrine. They are also split over *sola scriptura*: the Reformation's insistence that while tradition is important, Scripture is the sole arbiter of faith and practice. A slight majority of Protestants (52%) deny this. Finally, only 44% of U.S. evangelicals affirm both justification through faith alone and *sola scriptura* as the norm for faith and practice.[14] Studies show that the *practicing* theology of most Americans, across all denominations, is "moralistic, therapeutic deism."[15]

Christians are swimming against a powerful tide of opposition today, catechized daily by Facebook, Twitter feeds, and cable news gurus. For centuries, children were taught Scripture at home with the aid of a catechism (a question and answer format). I remember growing up with Bible memorization that included "sword drills." But a lot of these traditional habits are now falling to the wayside. We cannot take for granted that even those who have grown up in the church know what they believe or are aware of the basic plot line and central message of Scripture.

Even more unlikely is that these Christians know *why* they believe. The teenage years are made for questioning; this period of time is the prelude to young people owning the faith for themselves. This is not the time to use mere memorization to try to help your teenagers make up for their lack of familiarity with the

Bible and Christian doctrine. It is the perfect time to listen to their doubts and struggles, instead of reacting in shock or merely exhorting them to read the Bible and pray more. Even more than dating tips and hipster programs, this is when teenagers need arguments and evidences for their faith—before they go to college and encounter opposing beliefs.

Second, while many who abandon evangelical churches do not know enough even to apostatize properly, what they did know was a particular culture. It is this culture, more than anything else, that they are rebelling against. In many cases theology is secondary. They may agree with the creed, but the culture is suffocating. Of course, they're not just rebelling *against* the Christian subculture. They're also being shaped by a relativistic, consumeristic individualism which pervades modern societies.[16] However, let me note two issues in our churches that younger people are rebelling against: politics and hypocrisy.

Politics: In line with Gallup and Pew, the authors of *The Secular Surge* note that thirty years ago the percentage of Americans identifying as having no religious affiliation was 1 in 20. Now it is 1 in 4 and growing—and politics plays a large role in this. The authors said in an interview, "... if you're not sympathetic to the Republican Party, you don't want anything to do with religion." But younger generations are just as wary of religious leaders who dabble in progressive politics.[17] They don't need to hear more political pronouncements from pastors, but a richer, fuller, and more biblically grounded faith that can inform their pilgrimage in this world.

Hypocrisy: Some younger people have left the church because they rejected God's law and gospel. But others have left because they have been scolded for sins they struggle with while reading the sordid headlines about Christian leaders who preached one thing and practiced another. A fair number have seen their own pastor fall into sin and his protectors cover up the evidence. Young people with a tender conscience and greater sympathy for victims of abuse, oppression, and violence see hypocrisy where many of us older generations see fidelity. They see how we exclude, dishonor, and even shame women in our circles. They witness a kind of masculinity that is sometimes more cultural than biblical. They have seen evangelical leaders preach moralism while winking at (male) adulterers and abusers. And even if some young people do not personally wrestle with same-sex attraction or gender dysphoria, they know people who do. And they are offended by the way we talk about Them.

The Way Forward

As a minister today, my greatest fear is not of Them but of Us. I am afraid that tomorrow's most vocal acolytes of Them may well be people who once belonged to Us—that instead of communities of faith, our churches were incubators of resentment where young people only experienced a superficially Christian subculture. I pray that our churches are the place where you can count on the gospel being proclaimed every Sunday, forming embassies of grace and creating a fellowship of forgiven and repentant sinners that welcome Them as Us. This is not a subculture that swings from shunning to sentimental "affirmation," but a gospel-driven communion of real repentance and real forgiveness.

But there is good news—literally, the gospel of Christ. Jesus did not die for us when we got our act together, but while we were his enemies (Rom 5:10). In fact, long before we chose him, he chose us (John 15:16)—before the world was even created (Eph 1:4). And by "us" I mean sinners who have been forgiven, washed, and renewed and yet still battle besetting sins, including the fear of Them. This new Us—the body of Christ from every nation, culture, ethnicity, and political and socioeconomic location—exists only because we have Christ alone as our head.

There is more to recovering our sanity than knowing doctrine. The church is not just a school; it's a family. It is in the actual life of the local church where doctrine meets life, where the gospel proclaimed and administered in baptism and the Supper forms intergenerational fellowship. Many evangelicals have gone from the nursery to children's church to youth group to college ministry without ever really having been nurtured in the life of the congregation. Their main relationships were with peers rather than with mature believers. Many, especially among younger generations, are now being catechized every day with their smartphones, while the church has let them down both in teaching *and* in incorporation into real person-to-person, embodied social life together.

Since younger people increasingly know fewer older folks, their peers play a greater role in their formation. So their view of adults tends to be defined more by social stereotypes than by actual relationships. If younger people felt more connected to the church in the first place, both in conviction and in fellowship, it would be harder for them to drift away or "leave loud" when scandals hit. And older generations might become more understanding of contemporary challenges instead of grumbling to each other about the daily news and "young people today."

Imagine what this new Us could mean in American society right now. There can be local churches that proclaim this good news and live in light of it, convinced that it is God's kindness that leads all of us to repentance (Rom 2:4). A recent study is surprisingly encouraging: While only 9 percent of the general population is open to returning to the faith they've abandoned, "76% of LGBT people are open to returning to their religious community and its practices." And only 8% of these said that this would require a change in theology or convictions about sexual ethics, while the remaining 92% simply wanted to be loved and given real time instead of being shunned or ignored. In other words, "*92 percent* would be open to return *even without that faith community changing their theology*."[18] Was this not how Jesus led disciples who routinely failed to understand his mission and even denied him? He did not condemn Peter, but restored him. We all come to the Lord's table in repentance and faith, but never with perfect trust and obedience. And those who cannot come to the Lord's table yet in repentance and faith should be nevertheless welcomed into the gathering of the Lord's people and into their homes for hospitality—with the hope that they too will be granted repentance.[19] Love comes first. "We love because he first loved us" (1 John 4:19). Looking up beyond the crowd into a tree, Jesus tells the fearful but hopeful observer, "Zacchaeus, hurry and come down, for I must stay at your house today" (Luke 19:5).

Instead of demonizing Them, what if we saw Them as Us, beggar to beggar, and together raised our eyes to the Lord who is our help (Psalm 121)? Then perhaps instead of continuing to populate the growing opposition to Us, we could be havens of repentance and faith. Evangelicals often pray for revival. We do need one, but it may not be the sort of revival that many today have in mind. *Christians* need to come back to God and his Word even on Sunday, that brief sabbath from the clamor and clashing swords of the week. *That* would be a revival. Then we would have something to say from another King and his kingdom that could bring repentance and faith to a fearful and angry world.

Chapter 14

RACIAL FEARS

Redefining "Us"

As John Perkins argues so well in *One Blood*, Christians don't actually believe that there can be *racial* division because God "made from one man every nation of mankind to live on all the face of the earth" (Acts 17:26).[1] There is one race with many ethnicities (*ethnê*: peoples or nations). It is this basic truth that grounds the gospel. God the Son assumed *human* nature to be the Savior of the world. And he is building his new humanity around himself instead of Adam through the preaching of the gospel, making disciples from "all nations" (*panta ta ethnê*, Matt 28:19). Our problem is that we keep trying to build societies and sometimes even churches around ourselves and "our people" (*ethnos*). But the biblical drama redefines what "our people" means: the one human race with its redemption and reconstitution found in Christ.

We worship a sovereign God who can do anything. However, barring a sweeping spiritual revolution, it seems unlikely that a society that worships autonomy (self-rule) and expressive individualism is going to suddenly give all that up for the reign of Christ. Jesus says that when he returns he will "give justice to his elect . . .

speedily. Nevertheless, when the Son of Man comes, will he find faith on earth?" (Luke 18:7–8). We feel the weight of this question especially right now, don't we? Yet we are promised that Christ is building his church. We were once not his people, but "were by nature children of wrath, like the rest of mankind"(Eph 2:3). We were Them, God's enemies. So we want those who do not yet know the Lord to join Us on this pilgrimage of repentance and faith to the Holy City.

But how can "We" begin to better reflect here and now the design of the Savior who purchased a people from every tribe and tongue (Rev 5:9)? Jesus said, "By this all people will know that you are my disciples, if you have love for one another" (John 13:35). What a testimony it would be to the world if Christ's love for us could bind us together across ethnic, cultural, and political boundaries!

Ironically, as our neighborhoods become more diverse, our relationships become thinner while our sociopolitical identity with Us becomes thicker. Our own private world is narrowing even as the public world expands, significantly defined by politics. Where would conservative evangelicals get to know liberal Jewish people or even evangelical Korean, Chinese, Indian, and Ethiopian believers? Where do African American and Latino Christians mix and mingle with white believers, and vice versa? The answer should be the church. Merely pointing this out cannot change things, though. It is God's kindness that leads us all to repentance (Rom 2:4). And repentance never ends until we are glorified.

In his remarkable book, *Right Color, Wrong Culture*, Bryan Loritts points out that "black" is not just a color but a culture. Playing himself in the sitcom *The Fresh Prince of Bel-Air*, Will Smith moves from West Philadelphia to his aunt and uncle's posh family. He could not be more different from his pompous cousin, Carlton. This is a good example, Loritts observes, of the clash of cultures that goes far beyond skin color.[2] No churches I am familiar with would ever intentionally exclude nonwhite visitors or members; on the contrary, they would extend a warm welcome. In fact, many white-majority churches want greater ethnic diversity. However, one often feels like the mom who brings the kids to her fastidious mother-in-law's house. Grandma is delighted to see the grandkids, as long as they realize that it is *her* house. Don't break the teacups and make sure that nothing is out of place. Like the Fresh Prince's new home in Bel-Air, the culture of Grandma's house during the stay is what it is and will not change. It's not surprising that the kids sigh when we inform them that we'll be visiting again.

Throughout the latter half of this book, I have been trying to apply biblical categories to our various fears. In recent chapters we've been looking at our fear of Each Other. This chapter focuses on fears of losing a dominant, familiar, and privileged culture. There is not only white violence, of course. Sadly, interracial hostilities spread into all ethnic communities, especially where "outsiders" trespass. This is more often a subtle and even unrecognized but powerful fear of full *social* equality that many of us bring with us when we go to church. If you have some doubts about this description of fear, I understand. But I will demonstrate that it exists and offer partial but crucial solutions based on God's Word.

Much of my engagement here focuses on black-white unity, but I also have broader relationships in Christ's body in mind. When I was growing up, in popular culture Native Americans were the Indians who threatened decent folk expanding west. We were the cowboys defending the homestead and advancing the settlements. It never occurred to me that what we called "discovery" and "settlement" included violent theft of land and ethnic cleansing of people who had lived there for centuries. Based on the idea of an imaginary covenant with God, who gave us all the land "from sea to shining sea," the doctrine of Manifest Destiny justified such atrocities. Happily, though, my grandparents—born in the 1880s—had sharp memories and they lived with us, indulging my constant request for stories. Born in "Indian Territory" (before Oklahoma statehood), my grandmother saved several Native American children from the U.S. Cavalry by hiding them in flour barrels. She also recalled her uncle being saved from the white Kansas "Jayhawkers" by a Comanche warrior. One of my aunts also worked as a missionary on a Navajo reservation. None of them cared much for the Cavalry.

Throughout the history of the U.S., Asians were generally viewed with suspicion and frequently endured violent attacks. In 1871, a mob of five hundred men in Los Angeles massacred nineteen Chinese men in "Negro Alley." Fifteen of these victims, most of whom had been shot to death earlier, were also hanged. All convictions were later overturned. Shortly after Pearl Harbor, President Franklin D. Roosevelt ordered people of Japanese descent to be sent to concentration camps set up across California. Most were U.S. citizens, while the rest had been denied citizenship by law because they were born in Japan. Hollywood also represented Asians as secretive, running backroom businesses of ill repute. Even today, in the wake of COVID-19, which has been routinely and intentionally dubbed the "China Virus," Asian Americans have endured physical violence—in some cases, even death. A nonpartisan research center reported that even though hate crimes in general dropped 7% from 2019 to 2020, hate crimes targeting Asian Americans in sixteen major U.S. cities rose by 150% during that same period.[3] On March 18, 2021, eight Asian women were murdered in Atlanta. Ten days later, in Manhattan, an elderly woman was brutally assaulted, punched, and kicked with racial epithets while onlookers did nothing. She was on her way to church.

Latinos have also been targets of racial violence and stereotype-based disadvantages, especially when Central and South American immigrants (including refugees of political violence) were labeled as rapists and thugs by a U.S. president. Not even a U.S. judge was immune from this president's racial innuendos.[4]

My focus here is not general society, however, but the impact of these social rituals on Christian discipleship. What does it mean when a young man yelling "Go back to China!" to an Asian American woman at the supermarket parking lot (she was Korean) is in church on Sunday singing, "In Christ Alone"? Or when a group of Christians at an informal get-together engage in racial slurs and stereotypes that would perhaps be seen as inappropriate in the church narthex? If Jesus moved next door, would we welcome him or bristle at his Jewish eccentricities? We may try to keep the social and spiritual hemispheres of our brain distinct from each other, but the former inevitably creates neurological pathways into our patterns of behavior and the culture of our churches. How do we get the traffic moving in the other direction?

I do not see myself as a self-loathing victim of white guilt. I am grateful for my ethnic heritage. Like yours, my ancestry includes the good, the bad, and the ugly. We are all sinners. And we are also artists and doctors, janitors and lawyers, and poets and politicians as God's image-bearers and by his common grace. Sometimes we are the oppressor, and sometimes we are the oppressed. In America, however, my ancestors and I have not experienced the short end of the stick. Even as a kid in a lower middle-class family, I enjoyed privileges that some of my neighbors lacked.

When we focus only on slavery and Jim Crow, it is easy to dismiss the complicated web of injustice and exclusion in our own day. "Well, *I* don't have any slaves and I've never lynched anyone or burned a cross on a neighbor's lawn." That is what Others have done. Yet whites such as myself have grown up in neighborhoods defined by redlining (real estate rules that kept minorities in separate communities), police violence, and mass incarceration of black men as well as the often condescending policies of white liberals who create public housing ghettos.

Sin isn't just actions but is also a condition in which I am born and act out in ways that reflect sinful patterns of my particular tribe. I can say with Isaiah, "I am a man of unclean lips, and I dwell in the midst of a people of unclean lips; for my eyes have seen the King, the LORD of hosts!" (Isa 6:5). From a God-centered rather than self-centered perspective, I am a part of the problem—even in ways I'm not aware of, however indirectly. And, as a believer, I realize that while *civil* justice remains a priority, judgment begins in the house of God, the only real commonwealth in the proper sense of the term. Isaiah, after all, was referring to the people of God with the designation "people of unclean lips." Like you, I have some thoughts as a citizen about policy matters concerning racial justice and the different histories—real and imagined—that generate different stances.[5] However, my focus here is on what Scripture clearly and authoritatively calls us to in Christ's body.

It's Pretty Black-and-White: Why Is Sunday Still the Most Segregated Day of the Week?

When the media talks about "evangelicals," it typically has in mind white Christians who identify, however vaguely, with certain religious beliefs but is for the most part a subset of the Republican Party. This is not quite fair. Most evangelicals can be found in the Global South (especially Africa and Central and South America) and in Asia (especially China and South Korea). In the U.S., survey after survey shows that Black, Latino, and Asian Protestants align with evangelical rather than liberal doctrines and share evangelical convictions about personal morality. So it is pretty obvious that the label "evangelical" has acquired a more cultural and ethnic resonance than a theological one. And then BLM and MAGA folks funnel personal antagonism into the Manichean divide between Us and Them.

What really divides African American and white evangelicals today? Many of the latter assume that black people do not want to live in their neighborhoods or go to their churches and schools. They also might view African Americans as theological and political liberals, since they always vote Democratic. But the reality is surprising. Let's look at the facts.

First, nearly 80% of African Americans self-identify as Christian (as do 77% of Latinos and 70% of whites). Eighty-three percent say they believe in God with absolute certainty, compared with 61% of white Americans.[6] More than half of African Americans attend church at least once a week, pray daily, and believe in God "with absolute certainty," according to Pew. Even those who identify as *unaffiliated* are as likely to believe in God and to pray daily as *affiliated* mainline Protestants and Catholics.[7] So the divide cannot be religious. In an exit poll for an election in Alabama, 76% of blacks self-identified as born-again or evangelical, compared with 72% of whites.[8]

Theological conservatives by and large supported racial segregation and theological liberals typically promoted racial justice. The young Martin Luther King Jr. was an evangelical by conviction, but was not accepted at white evangelical seminaries. So he attended Crozer Seminary. After an initial attraction to the Social Gospel, he sought to return to his roots.[9] We can wish that he had been welcomed at a more theologically orthodox seminary. We may wish that more white evangelicals had joined his nonviolent protests even in the face of retaliatory attacks. However, this did not happen. On the contrary, most of those who perpetrated violence against black brothers and sisters were singing hymns on Sunday. African American preachers who shared evangelical convictions found allies in their cause of justice among theological liberals. What is surprising, therefore, is not the presence of theological modernism in some black churches, but the remarkable fidelity of most African Americans to the Christian faith in spite of their difficult history among fellow believers.

Second, African Americans by and large also share evangelical convictions about family values. Political researcher Allison Calhoun-Brown observes, "Despite the fact that African Americans hold evangelical beliefs, belong to evangelical denominations, and show high levels of religiosity, Black Evangelicals do not mobilize with the Christian Right." She adds that "the major reason for this is not primarily a lack of conservative positions on family values issues," but "major differences" in "symbolic political attitudes."[10]

According to Pew, 42% of the members of historically black Protestant denominations believe that abortion should be illegal in most if not all cases. That is a lower percentage than evangelicals (63%), but higher than mainline (mostly white) Protestants (35%).[11] Across all religious groups in America, as in society generally, acceptance of homosexual behavior has grown significantly, especially since 2007. In that year, 90% of evangelicals said that their faith "strongly discourages" or "forbids" homosexuality, but in 2020 that number had fallen to 65%. However, nearly half of those who belong to historically black denominations still share the traditional Christian view, in comparison with only 35% of mainline Protestants.[12]

Perhaps most surprisingly of all, as I noted in Chapter 11, African Americans are even more likely than any other ethnic group to embrace the narrative of America as a Christian nation. Even though white Christian nationalism uses this narrative to oppose black empowerment, African Americans draw strength from it for the goal of greater inclusion in the American dream.[13]

Not surprisingly, black Protestants are more moderate

Democrats, while white evangelicals are uber-Republicans.[14] White conservative Protestants (i.e., evangelicals) are, as David French explains, "very, very Republican." It is not merely about abortion and issues of sexuality and gender. Rather, the majority are uber-Republican down the line.[15] White evangelicals were more likely than any other demographic group (70%) to say that recent police shootings of black men "are isolated events rather than part of a pattern."[16] Negative attitudes toward interracial marriage have plummeted since 1967, when it was made legal in the U.S. However, Pew Research found that white evangelicals (19%) are still the most likely of any group to say that interracial marriage is "bad for society," more than twice the number of the general population (7%), while 13% were "very comfortable" with marriage outside the faith.[17]

We now see polarization even on points that were once broadly shared by most Americans. But once more these differences turn mostly on fear of the ethnic Other. Christian charity used to undergird the ideal of welcoming strangers as they passed the Statue of Liberty announcing with her silent lips,

> Give me your tired, your poor,
> Your huddled masses yearning to breathe free,
> The wretched refuse of your teeming shore.
> Send these, the homeless, tempest-tost to me,
> I lift my lamp beside the golden door![18]

In 2020 most Americans still said that America has an obligation to welcome political and religious refugees. However, when asked whether a policy against admitting refugees would be a good idea, "white evangelical Protestants stand out as the only religious group among whom a majority favor this policy (40% oppose; 58% favor)."[19] Statistically, white evangelical support for the Republican Party turns on immigration more than abortion.[20]

Divisions cannot therefore be attributed to anything specifically Christian. On the contrary, *in the name of Christianity*, an essentially ethnic and sociopolitical movement has drawn its battle lines against many, including black and brown fellow Christians who hold the same evangelical beliefs. While in this sense *narrowing* the definition of a true Christian, this movement also *broadens* the tent to include non-Christians who share its political values.

Culture, not religion or even politics per se, is the driver. For example, desegregation played a major part in the founding of private Christian schools, especially in the South. A lot has changed, to be sure, but the church's legacy of racism continues to have enormous influences in the wider culture. Imagine being a nonwhite simply wanting to hear God's Word, receive the Supper, pray, and become part of a local family of gospel-driven believers, but nearly 20% of the congregation does not approve of your interracial marriage. And then also consider the myriad assumptions in the background, sometimes in the foreground, that make you feel like "this is someone else's house." The same is true in reverse. If cultural prejudices are the obstacle to Christian unity, then they have to be arrested, interrogated, and taken captive to the obedience of Christ (2 Cor 10:5).

There has been a lot of reporting on "white evangelicals" that is inaccurate and unfair. Nevertheless, it seems true for both sides that cultural hegemony is more definitive than Christian doctrine and practices. As noted earlier, a growing number of professing Christians in the United States seem to be ignorant of basic doctrines or hold religious beliefs that are antithetical to the faith. Yet there is overwhelming unity on cultural attitudes and public policies. This suggests that our churches—white, black, Latino,

Asian, etc.—are more like cultural enclaves than gospel-creating embassies of grace.

"How could a Christian be a Democrat?", many evangelicals ask. But it is just as reasonable to ask why so many evangelicals are committed wholesale to a Republican agenda while so many black and brown brothers and sisters are more selective in their support of Democratic policies. In short, the deep divisions among believers are not over doctrine and practice, or even over abortion and family values, but are ethnic, cultural, and sociopolitical.

Recovering Biblical Coordinates

In order to repent, we need to return to biblical coordinates. When we speak of "We" as believers, whom do we have in mind? Even when we talk about not wanting to offend "outsiders," who are the "outsiders"—and "insiders"? Is the church's ministry touching our hearts on these vital issues so that our daily lives are shaped by the vision of Christ's kingdom in the New Testament?

The church as an institution created by the triune God through his Word returns to the inerrant Scriptures not only to determine its own affairs but to discover the ultimately authoritative coordinates for how we should think about all matters that Scripture addresses. To that extent, Scripture must determine our faith and practice not only when we are gathered together as God's people but also when we are in our home, our work, the marketplace, the neighborhood, and the voting booth. There are at least four biblical coordinates worth considering.

First, God's Word tells us that all people are created in God's image and likeness. Our God himself is three persons—Father, Son, and Holy Spirit. "So God created man in his own image, in the image of God he created him; *male and female* he created them"

(Gen 1:27, emphasis mine). Diversity is God's idea; it is not part of the fall but originates in creation itself. This image-bearing identity is common to all humans, no matter where they live or what culture they inhabit. "And he made from one man every nation of mankind to live on all the face of the earth, having determined allotted periods and the boundaries of their dwelling place" (Acts 17:26).

Second, "all have sinned and fall short of the glory of God" (Rom 3:23). Sin consists not only as actions of one person toward another, but first of all as a condition (original sin) in which all people share equally even from birth (Ps 51:5; Rom 5:12–21; Eph 2:1–5). We are all sinners and sinned-against, perpetrators and victims in a tangled web of selfishness. This is an essential point in contemporary debates because on both sides there is a tendency toward Pelagianism—the ancient heresy that rejects the seriousness of sin as a universal condition.

Sin is, first of all, an inherited and universal condition and then, secondarily, acts that we commit. To restrict sin to individual behaviors violates the biblical doctrine of original sin. We all fail to love God and our neighbor not only individually but collectively. Because we are all sinners, even the best of our economic, social, and political systems are corrupted by sin and perpetuate systematic injustices. Power itself does not corrupt. Rather, corruption clings to all of our hearts. Inherently selfish, we seek others who are like us to reinforce our power and prejudices against others.

Such group "narcissism" is not distinctive of one ethnic group or nationality, but is especially rampant without adequate legal and political restraints on power and with the weakening of religious, civic, and other local institutions. Because sin is a universal condition, humans tend to justify and to even work collectively to form societies that reflect and reinforce narcissistic ambitions. We see an example of this in the Tower of Babel (Gen 11).

Once majorities have institutionalized collective narcissism, future generations are conditioned to perpetuate them as a normal rather than malignant state of affairs. Consequently, a fully biblical view of original sin does not allow us to reduce the sin of racism to particular acts of some individuals.

At the same time, it is also unscriptural to identify sin only with structures and systems, deflecting personal responsibility for our actions. Unjust laws and systems do not make us unjust and just laws do not make us good (Matt 12:33; 15:11). Unjust systems may encourage us to sin or give others leeway to sin against us in specific ways. However, the tendency among many today to treat sin as merely structural or systemic contributes to the deflection of personal responsibility for behavior contrary to God's revealed will.

Both extremes—reducing sin to merely the acts of some individuals or to a system—allow us to deflect sin to others. In the former case, I can say, "I am not racist; I don't hold slaves or use demeaning slurs." In the latter, I can say, "I am a victim of those sinners who built this system and keep it going." Instead, a biblical piety calls us to recognize that we are all sinners from conception although we have sinned collectively and individually in importantly different ways. When we measure ourselves not by our own ethnic group or nationality but by who we are before God, respect for our common humanity—created good yet fallen—replaces self-justification as a starting point for conversation.

Third, although God works through different covenants, the moral character of God does not change. On the political left and right, there is a history of appealing (selectively) to the Law and the Prophets as if their conditional promises and threats pertained to any modern nation.

Israel was the only nation that had a covenant with God. "But like Adam they transgressed the covenant . . ." (Hos 6:7). There is no offer in Scripture to any nation today to enter into a covenant with God.

The idea of America being God's special people in covenant with him, a "holy nation," is a heresy. It violates the doctrine of "one holy, catholic, and apostolic church." Peter declares, "But you are a chosen race, a royal priesthood, a holy nation, a people for his own possession, that you may proclaim the excellencies of him who called you out of darkness into his marvelous light" (1 Pet 2:9). These were the designations given to Israel under the old covenant (Exod 19:6), but now they apply to the worldwide body of Christ.

As I mentioned earlier, this unbiblical ideology of an American covenant provided spiritual justification for many of the evil deeds our nation committed. Yet, ironically, a similar notion has often echoed in the civil rights movement, as if America had a special relationship with God and could become more fully the "shining city on a hill"—the phrase John Winthrop had used in founding the Massachusetts Bay Colony. However, this quotation from Matthew 5:14 only applies to Christ's flock gathered from the world, not to geopolitical entities. The national covenant God made with Israel has become obsolete (Heb 8:13) and cannot be applied to civil religion, lest it plague churches across the political spectrum. In contrast, the new covenant is far greater in its promises, blessings, and mediator.

Nevertheless, God's heart has not changed from the Old Testament to the New. God created all things for his glory—"The Lord is good to all, and his mercy is over all that he has made" (Ps 145:9). Psalm 82 expresses God's lordship over Israel, judging her judges who have failed to execute their vocation. Notice that it ends on an eschatological note, anticipating the day when such righteous judgment will be brought to the whole earth:

God has taken his place in the divine council;
    in the midst of the gods he holds judgment:
"How long will you judge unjustly
    and show partiality to the wicked? *Selah*
Give justice to the weak and the fatherless;
    maintain the right of the afflicted and the
        destitute.
Rescue the weak and the needy;
    deliver them from the hand of the wicked."

They have neither knowledge nor understanding,
    they walk about in darkness;
    all the foundations of the earth are shaken.

I said, "You are gods,
    sons of the Most High, all of you;
nevertheless, like men you shall die,
    and fall like any prince."

Arise, O God, judge the earth;
    for you shall inherit all the nations!

Jesus took this Psalm on his lips when he proclaimed himself as the Good Shepherd-King who is judging the false shepherds of Israel in John 10. And in the book of Revelation, this judgment of all the nations—the world system represented by "Babylon the great"—is anticipated (Rev 18). In fact, mention is made of the merchants whose cargos included "slaves, that is, human souls" (v. 13). "The merchants of these wares, who gained wealth from her, will stand far off, in fear of her torment, weeping and mourning aloud" (v. 15).

From Genesis to Revelation, God's righteousness, holiness, and justice are unchangeable:

- "Blessed are those who have regard for the weak" (Ps 41:1 NIV).
- God "will deliver the needy who cry out, the afflicted who have no one to help. He will take pity on the weak and the needy and save the needy from death. He will rescue them from oppression and violence, for precious is their blood in his sight" (Ps 72:12 NIV).
- "Defend the weak and the fatherless; uphold the cause of the poor and the oppressed. Rescue the weak and the needy" (Ps 82:3–4 NIV).

To imagine that we can repeat the theocracy or bring in the consummated reign of Christ through social justice is the height of arrogance. The civil laws of Israel are as obsolete now as the ceremonial ones. However, God's unchanging moral will is still revealed in the Ten Commandments, and this will is to be proclaimed to all people, including rulers and authorities, as God's standard.

To single out just one indictment through the prophets based on God's moral law, the book of Isaiah begins,

> When you come to appear before me,
>   who has required of you
>   this trampling of my courts?
> Bring no more vain offerings;
>   incense is an abomination to me.
> New moon and Sabbath and the calling of
>   convocations—
>   I cannot endure iniquity and solemn assembly.
> Your new moons and your appointed feasts

my soul hates;
they have become a burden to me;
I am weary of bearing them.
When you spread out your hands,
I will hide my eyes from you;
even though you make many prayers,
I will not listen;
your hands are full of blood.
Wash yourselves; make yourselves clean;
remove the evil of your deeds from before
my eyes;
cease to do evil,
learn to do good;
seek justice,
correct oppression;
bring justice to the fatherless,
plead the widow's cause. (Isa 1:12–17)

Words like "oppression" and "injustice" were not invented by "woke" Social Justice Warriors, but by God. These words assume that sin is not just interpersonal but also systemic: social, judicial, economic, educational, etc. God lashes out at "you cows of Bashan" who "oppress the poor and crush the needy and say to your husbands, 'Bring us some drinks!'" (Amos 4:1 NIV). "'I will tear down the winter house along with the summer house; the houses adorned with ivory will be destroyed and the mansions will be demolished,' declares the LORD" (Amos 3:15 NIV).

All of these messages from God through the prophets are to his holy nation that has become profane. However, in the New Testament Jesus announces a new regime in which there is no distinction between holy and common nations:

> *You have heard that it was said,* 'You shall love your neighbor and hate your enemy.' But I say to you, Love your enemies and pray for those who persecute you, so that you may be sons of your Father who is in heaven. For he *makes his sun rise on the evil and on the good,* and *sends rain on the just and on the unjust.* (Matt 5:43–45, emphasis mine)

For now, the unjust seem to be roaming freely. But judgment day is coming. This is still the day of salvation, of the unjust being justified and of the dead being raised to newness of life.

It is precisely because the Bible is so clear in both its commands and its promises that slaves found it empowering and enslavers often, for that reason, considered it dangerous. Imagine a jihadist wanting to excise from the Qur'an any sections that might encourage slaves to rebel against their masters. There are no examples, because Islam has never had trouble justifying slavery, at least in the Qur'an or in Muhammad's example. However, in 1807 a curious work was published, *Select Parts of the Holy Bible for the Use of the Negro Slaves in the British West-India Islands.*[21]

We recall Thomas Jefferson's slimmed-down version of the New Testament, deleting all references to miracles and the divinity of Christ. The people who put together this edited version may well have held a high view of the supernatural, but their self-interest trumped the Word of God. The Bible evidently had dangerous ideas that had to be omitted for the perpetuation of an institution that, paradoxically, many professed Christians regarded as biblically justified. Excised from this *Slave Bible,* for example, is the exodus narrative (emancipation from Egypt) and Galatians 3:28, which is a beautiful fulfillment of that type.

There were some who thought that Paul's refusal to empower slaves to rebel (especially in Philemon) reduced his authority. Yet, as Frederick Douglass pointed out, Roman slavery was quite different and, in any case, Roman Christians would never have participated in a system based on kidnapping and torture. He instructed,

> What do you do when you are told by the slaveholders of America that the Bible sanctions slavery? Do you go and throw your Bible into the fire? Do you sing out, 'No union with the Bible!' Do you declare that a thing is bad because it has been misused, abused, and made bad use of? Do you throw it away on that account? No! You press it to your bosom all the more closely; you read it all the more diligently; and prove from its pages that it is on the side of liberty—and not on the side of slavery.[22]

A veteran of the Revolutionary War and the nation's first black ordained minister, the Congregationalist Lemuel Haynes (1753–1833) appealed to the "inalienable right to freedom" enshrined in the Declaration of Independence. Though this charter was written by a slaveholder, Haynes was convinced that it provided principles against which current practice could be weighed. On this basis, Haynes issued his own declaration of independence: slavery is unjust. If it is wrong to belong to an empire that taxes without representation, then it is surely wrong to exclude from the "inalienable rights" of humanity those who have been kidnapped from another country.

For Christians, Haynes explained that the Apostle to the Gentiles spoke of all walls of race being broken down in Christ. Even if the curse on Ham had anything do with black people (which it did not), there is no ethnic curse in the new covenant.[23] Defenders of slavery had twisted Scripture, edited it, or simply kept it from fellow believers. And yet black leaders and pastors knew that the Bible itself was the solution rather than the problem. Nevertheless, this legacy of corrupting the biblical message by cultural ideologies remains with us.

My hope is that we—both blacks and whites—can shift entirely from the "Christian America" story to the "in Christ" story that believers share together. Let me give you an example from someone who understood the distinction between the City of God and the City of Man and was therefore able to appeal not to the myth of a Christian nation but to God's reign in justice (in the earthly city) and in grace (in the heavenly one).

Jourdon Anderson and Seeking Justice

Just after the end of the Civil War, African American Jourdon Anderson received a desperate letter at his home in Dayton, Ohio. It was from his former master Colonel P. H. Anderson, in Big Spring, Tennessee, pleading with Jourdan to help him save his failing business. Jourdon's reply, dated August 7, 1865 and later printed in the *New-York Daily Tribune*, is noteworthy. "I have often felt uneasy about you," he divulges. Yet the letter breathes a refined spirit of kindness. Reminding Colonel Anderson that he had "shot at me twice before I left you," he adds, "I did not want to hear of your being hurt, and am glad you are still living." He asks his former master to greet his family on his behalf. "Give my love to them all, and tell them I hope we will meet in the better world, if not in this." Jourdon even catches the colonel up on his life since leaving Big Spring. His kids "go to school and are learning well," especially his son Grundy. "The teacher says Grundy has a head for a preacher. They go to Sunday-School, and Mandy and me attend church regularly."

But now to the colonel's plaintive request: "Now, if you will write and say what wages you will give me, I will be better able to decide whether it would be to my advantage to move back again." Clearly, Jourdon has a sense of himself that is quite apart from that of a former slave, reasoning with his former master on new terms—man to man—only a year after his release by Union troops. The colonel promises him his freedom, but Jourdon replies that "there is nothing to be gained on that score, as I got my free-papers in 1864 from the Provost-Marshal-General of the Department of Nashville." Jourdon and Mandy have added up the unpaid wages. At twenty-five dollars a month over thirty-two years for him and two dollars a week for Mandy for twenty years, plus interest (and even deducting certain clothing and medical expenses), he arrives at "$11,680." If the colonel agrees to this, says Jourdon, "it will make us . . . rely on your justice and friendship in the future." In other words, this is not going to be even close to the relationship that they had before. If Jourdon and Mandy return to Colonel Anderson, it will be as business partners. "If you fail to pay us for faithful labors in the past we can have little faith in your promises in the future."

Jourdon grounds his claim not only in temporal justice but in God's judgment:

> We trust the good Maker has opened your eyes to the wrongs which you and your fathers have done to me and my fathers, in making us toil for you for generations without recompense . . . any more than for the horses and cows. Surely there will be a day of reckoning for those who defraud the laborer of his hire.

Jourdon also asks if his younger daughters, "now grown up, and both good looking girls," will be safe from the sexual abuse that two of his older daughters experienced at the hands of "their young masters." Finally, he inquires if Colonel Anderson knows of any freedmen's schools in the area, since "The great desire of my life now is to give my children an education, and have them form virtuous habits." Jourdon even adds a P.S. to the letter: "Say howdy to George Carter, and thank him for taking the pistol from you when you were shooting at me."[24]

Besides its beautiful testimony to Jourdon's character, the letter offers a window into a very different era when, even in the immediate aftermath of slavery, it was possible to imagine a new, just, and humane relationship between perpetrators and victims of violent injustice. Colonel Anderson may have been, like many other masters, a professing Christian who nevertheless twisted the Scriptures to justify his own prejudices and interests. Yet Jourdon definitely reads his life through a God-centered lens. Only God can release the colonel of his guilt, but Jourdon can release him from his crimes against him. Christians must forgive, but this does not obligate them to restore an abusive relationship. The colonel may be forgiven by God, yet he must not only promise to do better in the future, but he must also make amends for his offenses—not to God, but to Jourdon and Mandy. The colonel must simply reimburse them for their labor. Jourdon does not see himself as a former slave, the colonel's inferior, but as a defrauded business partner.

At the end of the day, Jourdon will go on with his life. In fact, he never did return to Big Spring. He did not need his former master's approval, repentance, or even justice in order to authenticate himself as a free man. Placing ultimate justice in God's hands, Jourdon was able to surrender any vendetta he might lawfully have harbored, Yet he would not help the colonel unless justice was served. I am not reducing justice to interpersonal relationships. Societal wrongs must be socially made right. But political, legal, and judicial change is downstream from the cultural attitudes that make bad laws and policies seem plausible in the first place. Protests are both a sign of a healthy democracy and a powerful force in advancing justice. But the clarity, charity, and resolve of Jourdon Anderson toward his former master is where the deepest change begins.

The Civil War ended the institution of slavery, but what did emancipation really mean? Reconstruction was mostly about politically reaccommodating the South, not about the plight of ex-slaves who now had to fend for themselves, often in conditions indistinguishable from slavery. One sad example follows: As the Civil War was drawing to a close, General William T. Sherman and U.S. Secretary of State Edwin M. Stanton met with twenty black pastors and local lay leaders in Savannah, Georgia. They asked the delegation what would help restore dignity and empowerment to the ex-slaves. "Forty acres and a mule" was their reply. As a result, Sherman issued Special Field Orders, No. 15 (January 16, 1865), with President Lincoln's approval. It would have allotted 400,000 acres of former slave-owners' land to emancipated families, but Lincoln's successor Andrew Johnson revoked it upon taking office after Lincoln's assassination.[25]

Fourth, biblical eschatology promises neither a gradual perfection of humanity (nor perfect union in America) nor the "late, great planet earth," but the renewal of the whole creation that groans with us for this liberation (Rom 8:18–30). When Jesus returns, all will be made right. That doesn't keep us from being active citizens, trying to make things more just for our fellow citizens and neighbors. But it does mean that whatever good we have in this age is fleeting, temporary, and cannot even be compared with Christ's consummation of his kingdom. Christians testify to this kingdom, the only empire that "cannot be shaken," which we are "receiving," not building (Heb 12:28). Therefore, we must resist all attempts to assimilate this kingdom to any nation, party, ethnic group, or policy agenda.

When "We" Come to Church

"This is the way 'we' do it." "This is how 'we' see things." "Do you want to join 'our' church? You're more than welcome." So, who is "we"? We often just don't know how racial hegemony in the church is itself part of the long history of overt, structural, legalized, moralized—and, sadly, theologized—sin. Remember, sin is not just what we have *done* but what we have *not* done. Sloth—simply ignoring people different from us—is a major part of our failure. Are we deliberately *undoing* ingrained patterns of exclusion? We also have a hard time figuring out how this hegemony influences the background prejudices which we are often not even aware of except perhaps in hindsight. Racism is both explicit and implicit as well as structural and interpersonal, and, as Martin Luther King Jr. emphasized, it hurts the perpetrator and privileged as well as the victim.

The effect of social media and twenty-four-hour cable news is pervasive. Neighborhoods are now more divided than ever by race and especially by economic status and political affinities. As the opportunities shrink for everyday community across this divide, we hunker down in our demographic bunkers with Facebook "friends," our favorite social media pundits, and either FOX or CNN. The greatest tragedy, however, is the impact of this balkanization on our churches. Even talk of repentance and reconciliation *in the church* between offended parties strikes some Christians as a slippery slope of mission creep, although myriad political issues are still fair game.

There is a strange tradition in American Protestantism of politicians being given the pulpit. This de-sacralizes—literally, desecrates—the place from which God is supposed to address *his* people. When this occurs, a church becomes no longer the site where the King of kings gathers and addresses his people from every tribe but is instead just another agent of further division. If it was true before, it is even more evident now that many churches have become little more than the Republican or Democratic Party at prayer. When the fear of God and the Father's mercy toward us in Christ are recovered as the focus of everything, cultural and political differences will properly become secondary. Then church will indeed be a holy assembly, claimed, created, and multiplied by the word of the Lord.

Our cultural prejudices, which are not all wrong, are difficult for us to recognize. When I studied in England, friends thought I had a strange accent. I had never imagined such a thing; Californians don't have a distinctive accent. But apparently we do to other cultures that even speak the same language. It is easy for me to discern the cultural "distinctiveness" in nonwhite churches while imagining that cultural distinctives (especially Northern European) are absent in white-majority churches. Even when we don't intend to display them, those tacit assumptions—cultural, political, socioeconomic—can make a brother or sister feel like "this is not my home" even if they share the same faith and practice.

So, how far would we be willing to go—black and white, Latino and Asian, First Nations, Pacific Islander and Indian, African and European—to make our "Us" more reflective of the catholic (that is, universal) Us that Christ is building? Are we willing to submit to mutual correction as well as encouragement? Without imitating the fear-driven purity codes of "cancel culture," all of us might hear ourselves in a new light. Our prayers would be more reflective of the multiethnic and global church, "a shining city upon a hill," than the petitions of a subculture. Even styles of worship that have nothing to do with essential biblical elements of worship but are only circumstances that depend on wisdom can become an obstacle of which we aren't even aware. "It's just how *we* do it." That is true for all of our churches, regardless of ethnicity. How far are we willing to go for love?

Cultural backgrounds are not just unavoidable. They are intrinsic to the difference that God's providence has generated. Many-in-One, One-in-Many: An analogy of the Trinity, the distinctness of persons is not absorbed into the unity of Christ's body. Nobody should be expected to leave their embodied, cultural, and ethnic particularity at the door. The challenge is to incorporate brothers and sisters of *different* cultural backgrounds into *one body*. Doing this is not optional, and it takes work. Everyone has to surrender tribe pride to gospel unity.

There is no more important question if we want to talk about Revelation 5:9 and the possibility of us imagining now what that heavenly worship will be like.

> And they sang a new song, saying,
>
> "Worthy are you to take the scroll
> and to open its seals,
> for you were slain, and by your blood you ransomed
> people for God
> from every tribe and language and people and
> nation,
> and you have made them a kingdom and priests to
> our God,
> and they shall reign on the earth." (Rev 5:9–10)

That is a great hymn. This is the "Us" that *should* be in our minds and hearts.

I need to briefly mention two things from this marvelous passage. First, the saints haven't made themselves a kingdom but have been *made* a kingdom of priests *by* the Lamb, and it is not a sociopolitical empire but a gospel Word-and-Sacrament kingdom. It's not a rerun of the old covenant theocracy, so conservatives can stop using Israel as a template for a Christian America and progressives can stop using it as a template for achieving social justice in a secular nation. Both sides must resist the temptation to use eschatological language ("God's nation" or "the Beloved Community") for any temporal society. Rather, Christ's kingdom is a global empire that incorporates all who are baptized into it and receive its royal Lamb by faith. It's not the place where we "get out the vote," but where we come away from CNN or FOX for a holiday, a sabbath rest from Babylonian captivity, praying for the earthly city but not finding our ultimate good in it. Marching to Zion does not consist in accumulating more judges or defunding the police but in being made part of the new creation as the rays of the *age to come* break in on this present and fading age.

Second, this passage tells us that Christ has ransomed with his blood "people from every tribe and language and people and nation." On the one hand, this underscores that beyond a generic "humanity" the people for whom Christ died are from Kenya and Korea, France and Fiji. They are Scandinavian and Sioux, Dalits and Dutch. They don't stop being who they are in the cultural and ethnic identities that God's good providence has given them. They come into Christ's kingdom *with* all of this, the good and bad of it. That's the real world, the new creation, the kingdom of priests. It's the real *e pluribus unum*: "out of many, one."

Where Does This Unity Start?

As the apostle Paul teaches us in Ephesians, the unity of the body of Christ is objective, grounded in God's gracious election and redemption in Christ. The thickest barrier, dividing Jews and Gentiles, has been broken down because "one new person"—Christ as head with his body—has appeared on the stage of history. We are now called to work at visibly maintaining the unity that we already have in Christ, "with all humility and gentleness, with patience, bearing with one another in love, eager to maintain the unity of the Spirit in the bond of peace. There is one body and one Spirit—just as you were called to the one hope that belongs to your call—one Lord, one faith, one baptism, one God and Father of all, who is over all and through all and in all" (Eph 4:2–6). Though simultaneously justified and sinful, like each of us, the church cannot resignedly throw up its hands in the face of the racial division that threatens its call to visible unity in faith and love. We have to press on, growing in sanctification together, "eager to maintain the unity of the Spirit in the bond of peace."

The strategy of the 1980's and 1990's was "homogeneous church growth." People like to worship with people who are like them, the theory goes, and if only we kept churches segregated then those churches would grow more quickly. But this assumes that I choose myself and then I choose whom I call brother and sister. The problem with this theory is that God chose me in Christ *and* chose for me my ultimate family: this church that Christ purchased with his blood from every race and ethnicity to be united in him—and in him alone. We do remain temporary citizens of Babylon. We pray for that city, as the exiles were told to do (Jer 29:6–8). But we have been *given* an inheritance, *made* a kingdom of priests, and *given* a kingdom. This frees us up to take our temporary citizenship seriously, but not *too* seriously. "Therefore let us be grateful for receiving a kingdom that cannot be shaken, and thus let us offer to God acceptable worship, with reverence and awe, for our God is a consuming fire" (Heb 12:28–29).

Racism, therefore, opposes the gospel. It narrows the saving work of Christ to the realm of the individual, instead of recognizing that the gospel is a sweeping act of God that not only rearranges our relationship to him but also to one another. Because we are reconciled to God by grace alone through faith alone in Christ alone, any other identification marker is at least implicitly another gospel; something other than Christ is the tie that binds. This was the controversy over the inclusion of Gentiles that threatened to divide the nascent church in Acts. Must they be circumcised and keep kosher? Is ethnic identity the tie that binds, or is it Christ alone? Thankfully, by God's grace the church of the apostles heeded the "new thing" that Christ was creating right in the middle of this present evil age.

Ecclesiology, the doctrine of the church, is therefore closely related to soteriology, the doctrine of salvation. "Catholic" means universal—the elect from every nation and people. We cannot consistently say that we cling to Christ alone for our personal salvation while we deny the catholicity of the church in him.

It is certainly true that the church as a divine institution has no authority or competence to solve the myriad and complicated political and cultural issues of our day. However, the church is also scattered to be salt and light in a variety of vocations in the world. The church cannot bind consciences beyond Scripture: It cannot tell an engineer how to build an office complex or the voter which candidate he or she must choose. But it is hopefully shaping the broader and deeper horizon for all of life.

We can be encouraged when conservative denominations issue public apologies for racism and other sins. However, the most important confession and absolution happens in church. In a powerful essay, Carl Trueman reminds us that we crave absolution from the world more than from God.[26] But the world cannot absolve us of our sins. Only God can, and in doing so he reconciles us with brothers and sisters we have offended. In the string of public confessions or pronouncements from denominations or prominent preachers, when was the last time one began with, "Against you, you only, have I sinned . . ." (Ps 51:4)? We desperately want the world to love us, whether the cultural right or the cultural left, whether high or pop culture. But where is that in the Bible? Didn't Jesus say, "Hey, they hated you, so where did you get the idea that they would love you any more? Is a servant greater than his master" (cf. John 15:20)?

It is *in the church* where we need to recover the fear of God. That is where judgment begins. Imagine what things might be like in the United States today if the churches had immediately opposed slavery in New England and other colonies? What if they had exercised the keys of Christ's kingdom? What if slaveholders had been disciplined in the usual way? After serious attempts to exhort, teach, and correct, unrepentant slaveholders would be excommunicated. As everyone knows, American slaves were kidnapped in Africa and brought in chains on disease-ridden ships. God warned Israel, "Whoever steals a man and sells him, and anyone found in possession of him, shall be put to death" (Exod 21:16). If America were in covenant with God and one were to consistently apply the old covenant laws to the U.S., both slave traders and slave owners would have been executed by the state. So why weren't they at least disciplined in the church? And why are there still some conservative Christians today who cast nostalgic glances at Southern antebellum society? By the way, I am convinced that anyone who is directly involved in the murder of the unborn and the sale of their body parts is in the same position today. Or in the sex slave trade today that has exploded into a global industry.

Once we regain the fear of God—indeed, of Christ as well (he's not just the friend of sinners but the judge of all)—and face up to who we are before him, coming with empty hands to receive his Son, we'll begin to lose this fear of the world. We will not be embarrassed when the unkempt widow sings off-key with the gusto of heartfelt conviction or when the building is drab or if we have never had a brush with greatness and our pastor has never been photographed with anybody in the news. The faithful preaching of the Word, baptism, and the Lord's Supper; the gracious care, encouragement, and warnings of elders and the wider body; the extension of Christ's love for temporal needs through the deacons; common prayers, singing, confession of our faith and of our sins, Christ's declaration of forgiveness, and even God's greeting at the beginning and his benediction at the end—all these will seem so marvelously familiar and new to us at the same time. And then we will begin to not need the world's affection any longer.

CONCLUSION

Walking Each Other to the City of God

With cable news screens filled twenty-four hours a day, seven days a week, now joined by the perpetual noise of social media, no society in history has been as exposed as ours to natural disasters, health crises, corruption, divisions, war, and violence. An earthquake somewhere, a tsunami or flood somewhere else, melting glaciers, an explosion detonated in a mall far away, and shots of children starving somewhere all converge together to barrage our senses. Our sympathy is strained by our sheer exposure to events attended by vivid footage. Everything becomes vague since we do not have any feel for the context or factors we need in order to treat it as more than a meme. We become numb to it all. That's the downside of exploiting our fears. After all, how outraged or terrified can a person be in one day?

Can we turn it all off on Sunday? Just turn it off completely? Can we come away to the Lord's family and feast together on his Word and revel in that miracle that God is performing on earth called the church? Then Monday might look a little different.

Can we imagine the possibility of Christians—of various ethnicities, political parties, cultural backgrounds, and socioeconomic locations—joining arm in arm on the way to the City of God? I am prone to wander off the path, often in ways that I'm not aware of. I need brothers and sisters with different backgrounds and experiences to guide me: younger and older, wealthier and poorer, and with distinctive cultural heritages that help me to see my blind spots. And, of course, they need me too for the same reason.

Can there be a sense, as Augustine perceived, that the best commonwealth in this age is but a parody of that final refuge of God's pilgrims? As we fix our eyes on Christ, we discover that even this world looks different. Precisely in fearing God we can embrace our life, callings, citizenship, families, and neighbors as important but not ultimate, and as means of loving God rather than as idols that fail us. As we raise our eyes *together* to heaven, our sanity can be restored.

> For your name's sake, O Lord,
> pardon my guilt, for it is great.
> Who is the man who fears the Lord?
> Him will he instruct in the way that he should choose.
> His soul shall abide in well-being,
> and his offspring shall inherit the land.
> The friendship of the Lord is for those who fear him,
> and he makes known to them his covenant.
> My eyes are ever toward the Lord,
> for he will pluck my feet out of the net.
> Turn to me and be gracious to me,
> for I am lonely and afflicted.
> The troubles of my heart are enlarged;
> bring me out of my distresses.
> Consider my affliction and my trouble,
> and forgive all my sins. (Ps 25:11–18)

ACKNOWLEDGMENTS

We raise our eyes to heaven together with others, and I am grateful for my wife Lisa and my young adult children as well as to friends who have helped me along this path. Among close friends who have done this over the years, I am especially grateful to Dan Bryant, Derek Lewis, Mark Green, Eric Landry, Julius Kim, Jeff and Carla Meberg, Ryan Glomsrud, and Ben Sasse. Ben, in particular, has written insightfully on various themes in this book, especially in *Them.* Unless I am able to directly trace defects to my friends, I of course bear responsibility for any remaining weaknesses.

I am also grateful to the remarkable team at Zondervan, especially to Ryan Pazdur, whose expert editorial skills significantly improved this book, and to Jesse Hillman's knack at relating content to design. Daniel Saxton, a former student and now an assistant editor at Zondervan, saved me considerable embarrassment by his sharp eye, encyclopedic knowledge, and instinct for clarity.

NOTES

Foreword

1. T. S. Eliot, "East Coker," in *T. S. Eliot: The Complete Poems and Plays, 1909–1950* (Orlando, FL: Harcourt Brace & Company, 1980), 125–26.

Chapter I: A Pandemic of Fear

1. Jean M. Twenge, *iGen: Why Today's Super-Connected Kids Are Growing Up Less Rebellious, More Tolerant, Less Happy—and Completely Unprepared for Adulthood—and What That Means for the Rest of Us* (New York: Atria, 2017).
2. "America's Top Fears 2018," Chapman University, October 16, 2018, https://blogs.chapman.edu/wilkinson/2018/10/16/americas-top-fears-2018/.
3. "Suicide in Children and Teens," American Academy of Child and Adolescent Psychology, No. 10 (June 2018), https://aacap.org/AACAP/Families_and_Youth/Facts_for_Families/FFF-Guide/Teen-Suicide-010.aspx.
4. F. B. Ahmad, L. M. Rossen, and P. Sutton, "Provisional Drug Overdose Death Counts," National Center for Health Statistics, 2021, https://www.cdc.gov/nchs/nvss/vsrr/drug-overdose-data.htm.
5. "Results from the 2017 National Survey on Drug Use and Health: Detailed Tables," Substance Abuse and Mental Health Services Administration, September 7, 2018, https://samhsa.gov/data/sites/default/files/cbhsq-reports/NSDUHDetailedTabs2017/NSDUHDetailedTabs2017.pdf.
6. Edmund S. Higgins, "Is Mental Health Declining in the U.S.?", *Scientific American* (January 1, 2017), https://scientificamerican.com/article/is-mental-health-declining-in-the-u-s/.

7. Madison Czopek, "No, the CDC Hasn't Stopped Calling COVID-19 a Pandemic," Politifact, September 10, 2020, https://politifact.com/factchecks/2020/sep/10/facebook-posts/no-cdc-hasnt-stopped-calling-covid-19-pandemic/.
8. Robinson Meyer, "The Unprecedented Surge in Fear about Climate Change," The Atlantic, January 23, 2019, https://theatlantic.com/science/archive/2019/01/do-most-americans-believe-climate-change-polls-say-yes/580957/.
9. IPCC, 2013, "Summary for Policymakers," in T. F. Stocker et al., eds., *Climate Change 2013: The Physical Science Basis. Contribution of Working Group I to the Fifth Assessment Report of the Intergovernmental Panel on Climate Change* (Cambridge, UK and New York, NY: Cambridge University Press), https://www.ipcc.ch/report/ar5/wg1/.
10. NASA, October 14, 2021, https://climate.nasa.gov/evidence. The specific numbers are daily updated on the home page of the website.
11. R. J. H. Dunn et al., eds., "Global Climate" in "State of the Climate in 2019," *Bulletin of American Meteorology* 101,no. 8: S86–S98.
12. Statistics can be found at the CAL FIRE website, https://fire.ca.gov/stats-events/.
13. Francis Schaeffer, *Pollution and the Death of Man* (Wheaton, IL: Crossway, 2011).
14. Heather Long and Andrew Van Dam, "America Is in a Depression. The Challenge Now Is to Make It Short-Lived," *Washington Post*, April 9, 2020, https://washingtonpost.com/business/2020/04/09/66-million-americans-filed-unemployed-last-week-bringing-pandemic-total-over-17-million/.
15. Emily Pandise, "One Year into Pandemic, Main Street Bankruptcies Continue," NBC News, May 15, 2020, https://nbcnews.com/business/consumer/which-major-retail-companies-have-filed-bankruptcy-coronavirus-pandemic-hit-n1207866.
16. "The 2019 Long-Term Budget Outlook," Congressional Budget Office, June 25, 2019, https://cbo.gov/publication/55331.
17. Ben Sasse covers this ground with statistical evidence and shrewd

interpretive insight in *The Vanishing American Adult: Our Coming-of-Age Crisis—and How to Rebuild a Culture of Self-Reliance* (New York: St. Martin's Press, 2017). He also treats this issue in *Them: Why We Hate Each Other—and How We Can Heal* (New York: St. Martin's Press, 2018), 46–74, 219–38.

18. See Frank Furedi, *Politics of Fear: Beyond Left and Right* (New York: Continuum, 2005) and Corey Robin, *Fear: The History of a Political Idea* (Oxford, UK: Oxford University Press, 2006).
19. Bobby Azarian, "Fear and Anxiety Drive Conservatives' Political Attitudes," *Psychology Today*, December 31, 2016, https://psychologytoday.com/us/blog/mind-in-the-machine/201612/fear-and-anxiety-drive-conservatives-political-attitudes.
20. See Sasse, *Them*, 75–105.
21. David French, "Do Pro-Lifers Who Reject Trump Have 'Blood on Their Hands'?", *The French Press* (blog), *The Dispatch*, August 23, 2020, https://frenchpress.thedispatch.com/p/do-pro-lifers-who-reject-trump-have.
22. Jeremy Stahl, "How Many House Republicans Believe the Jews Attacked California with a Space Laser?", *Slate*, January 29, 2021, https://slate.com/news-and-politics/2021/01/marjorie-taylor-greene-kevin-mcarthy-jewish-space-lasers.html.
23. John Newton, "Glorious Things of Thee Are Spoken," *Trinity Psalter Hymnal* (OPC/URCNA, 2017), #403.

Chapter 2: What Does It Mean to Fear God?

1. Sherry Turkle, *Alone Together; Why We Expect More from Technology and Less from Each Other* (New York: Basic Books, 2012); Robert D. Putnam, *Bowling Alone: The Collapse and Revival of American Community* (New York: Simon and Schuster, 2020).
2. The example is taken from Steve Bruce, *Secularization: In Defence of an Unfashionable Theory* (Oxford, UK: Oxford University Press, 2011), 44.
3. John Calvin, *Institutes of the Christian Religion*, ed. John T. McNeill,

trans. Ford Lewis Battles (Philadelphia: Westminster Press, 1960), 1.4.2.

4. See G. C. Heider, "Moloch" in Karel van der Toorn, Bob Becking, and Pieter W. van der Horst, eds., *Dictionary of Deities and Demons in the Bible*, 2nd ed. (Leiden: Brill, 1999), 581–85.

Chapter 3: Eyes toward Heaven

1. Walt Whitman, "Song of Myself," in *Walt Whitman: Complete Poetry and Collected Prose*, ed. Justin Kaplan (New York: Library of America, 1982), 188, 211–12, 236, 246.

Chapter 4: The Wisdom in Fear

1. C. S. Lewis, *The Silver Chair* (New York: HarperCollins, 2002), 20–21.
2. Friedrich Nietzsche, *Thus Spake Zarathustra*, trans. Thomas Common (Ware, UK: Wordsworth, 1997), IV.67 (p. 257).
3. Robert J. Lifton, "The Protean Self" in *The Truth about the Truth*, ed. Walter T. Anderson (New York: Putnam, 1995), 130–35.

Chapter 5: Fears Relieved

1. David Zahl, *Seculosity: How Career, Parenting, Technology, Food, Politics, and Romance Became Our New Religion and What to Do about It* (Minneapolis: Fortress, 2019).
2. John Calvin, *Commentaries on the Epistle of Paul the Apostle to the Hebrews*, trans. John Owen (Grand Rapids: Baker, 1996), 110.

Chapter 6: The "Sting" of Death Removed

1. An insightful Stanford Medical School study shows that our cells not only die from the usual apoptosis but from necrosis, pyroptosis ferroptosis, and NETtosis. Hanae Armitage, "How Your Cells Can Die: The Good, the Bad, and the Leaky," *Scope* (blog), Stanford Medicine, August 22, 2018, https://scopeblog.stanford.edu/2018/08/22/how-your-cells-can-die-the-good-the-bad-and-the-leaky/.

2. Lisa Miller, "The Christian Mystery of Physical Resurrection," *Newsweek*, March 24, 2010, https://www.newsweek.com/christian-mystery-physical-resurrection-69435.
3. Lisa Miller, "U.S. Views on God and Life Are Turning Hindu," *Newsweek*, August 14, 2009, https://www.newsweek.com/us-views-god-and-life-are-turning-hindu-79073.
4. It is worth watching Johnny Cash's rendition: Johnny Cash, "AIN'T NO GRAVE (Can Hold My Body Down), YouTube video posted February 5, 2010, https://youtube.com/watch?v=66QcIlblI1U.
5. *Origen: On First Principles*, trans. G. W. Butterworth (Gloucester, MA: Peter Smith, 1973), 2.11.7; cf. 2.3, 2.10, 3.6, 4.4.
6. Peggy Lee, "Is That All There Is?", 1969, YouTube video, https://www.youtube.com/watch?v=LCRZZC-DH7M.

Chapter 7: Suffering Isn't Bad Karma

1. "What Lessons Do Americans See for Humanity in the Pandemic?", Pew Research Center, October 8, 2020, https://pewforum.org/essay/what-lessons-do-americans-see-for-humanity-in-the-pandemic/.
2. C. S. Lewis, *The Problem of Pain* (New York: HarperCollins, 1996), 91.
3. Bob Smietana, "Mental Illness Remains Taboo Topic for Many Pastors," Lifeway Research, September 22, 2014, https://lifewayresearch.com/2014/09/22/mental-illness-remains-taboo-topic-for-many-pastors/.
4. Ben Sasse, *Them: Why We Hate Each Other—and How We Can Heal* (New York: St. Martin's Press, 2018), 19–45.
5. Sasse, *Them*, 22–23, 25.
6. Sasse, *Them*, 167–200.
7. John Newton, "The Lord's Day," *Hymns and Spiritual Songs for the Use of Christians* (Philadelphia: John W. Scott, 1803), 64.

Chapter 8: A Secure Future

1. See for example Sir Keith Thomas, *Man and the Natural World: Changing Attitudes in England, 1500–1800* (Oxford, UK: Oxford University Press, 1996).

2. On this point see especially David VanDrunen, *Politics after Christendom* (Grand Rapids: Zondervan Academic, 2020), 56–180.

Chapter 9: Stewards, Not Saviors

1. Quoted in Jürgen Moltmann and Douglas Meeks, *The Open Church: Invitation to a Messianic Life-Style* (London: SCM, 1978), 42.
2. Christine Gutleben, "The Development of Evangelical Perspectives on Animals," The Humane Society, https://humanesociety.org/sites/default/files/docs/development-of-evangelical-perspectives-animals.pdf.
3. Matthew Scully, *Dominion: The Power of Man, the Suffering of Animals, and the Call to Mercy* (New York: St. Martin's Press, 2003).
4. Gutleben, "Development of Evangelical Perspectives on Animals."
5. Isaac Watts, "Joy to the World," in *Joy to the World: or, Sacred Songs for Gospel Meetings*, ed. T. C. O'Kane, C. C. M'Cabe, and Jno. R. Sweney (New York: Phillips & Hunt, 1879), 1.
6. Klaus Schwarzwäller, "The Bondage of the Free Human," in Joseph A. Burgess and Marc Kolden, eds., *By Faith Alone: Essays on Justification in Honor of Gerhard O. Forde* (Grand Rapids: Eerdmans, 2004), 50–51 (emphasis mine).

Chapter 10: Why We Fear Each Other

1. "New Initiative Explores Deep, Persistent Divides Between Biden and Trump Voters," UVA Center for Politics, September 30, 2021, https://centerforpolitics.org/crystalball/articles/new-initiative-explores-deep-persistent-divides-between-biden-and-trump-voters/ (emphasis mine). I found this reference in this illuminating reflection by David French, "A Whiff of Civil War in the Air," *The French Press* (blog), *The Dispatch*, October 3, 2021, https://frenchpress.thedispatch.com/p/a-whiff-of-civil-war-in-the-air.
2. Bob Woodward, *Fear: Trump in the White House* (New York: Simon and Schuster, 2018).
3. Doug Pagitt, *Outdoing Jesus: Seven Ways to Live Out the Promise of "Greater Than"* (Grand Rapids: Eerdmans, 2019).

4. Lachlan Markay (@lachlan), "Inbox from the NRCC," Twitter, March 29, 2021, 11:47 a.m., https://mobile.twitter.com/lachlan/status/1376561685398482948. See also Aidan McLaughlin, "Top GOP Campaign Committee Now Begging Supporters to Sign Up for Trump's Future Social Media Website," Mediaite, March 29, 2021, https://mediaite.com/trump/top-gop-campaign-committee-now-begging-supporters-to-sign-up-for-trumps-future-social-media-website/.
5. Jonathan Haidt, *The Righteous Mind: Why Good People are Divided by Politics and Religion* (New York: Vintage, 2012).
6. For example, there are three angels, appearing as men, who appear to Abraham to announce the judgment of Sodom. Yet one of them is identified as Yahweh himself (Gen 18:1, 22, 33), and the other two rescue Lot and his family while the Angel of the Lord returns to heaven to execute the judgment in chapter 19. Similarly, in Zechariah 3 Yahweh judges and the Angel of Yahweh mediates but is also identified as Yahweh.

Chapter II: "Christian America" versus the Body of Christ

1. Andrew L. Whitehead and Samuel L. Perry, *Taking America Back for God: Christian Nationalism in the United States* (New York: Oxford University Press, 2020), 41.
2. Whitehead and Perry, *Taking America Back for God*, 41–42.
3. The January 2021 storming of the U.S. Capitol provides an excellent illustration of how America has been viewed as a special nation. As shown in Luke Mogelson's remarkable video posted on YouTube by *The New Yorker* on January 17, 2021 (https://www.youtube.com/watch?v=270F8s5TEKY), both the rioters and the police referred to the Capitol as sacred. When Jacob Chansley, the so-called "QAnon Shaman," entered the Senate, a policeman asked him to leave because "this is like the sacredest place." "I know," Chansley responded (at minutes 6:45–6:50).

   At around 8 minutes into the video, the rioters invoke the name of Jesus Christ and say a prayer over a minute long "in this sacred space," describing the nation as being "reborn." It's apparent that the rioters feel they are not "desecrating" the Capitol but rather purifying it and hallowing it much like what Old Testament kings such as Hezekiah and Josiah did for the Jerusalem temple after it had been desecrated by their evil predecessors.

4. Thomas Jefferson, "Reply to the Danbury Baptist Association," in *The Papers of Thomas Jefferson, Volume 36: 1 December 1801 to 3 March 1802*, ed. Barbara B. Oberg (Princeton: Princeton University Press, 2009), 258, https://jeffersonpapers.princeton.edu/selected-documents/danbury-baptist-association-0.
5. Thomas Jefferson in a letter to William Short in 1819, in *Thomas Jefferson: Writings*, ed. Merrill Peterson (New York: Library of America, 2011), 1430. According to Epicureanism, advocated by Lucretius, the world consists of nothing but randomly swerving atoms. The gods are not involved in this world at all. There is no divine creation in the past or divine judgment in the future, so we can relax and just enjoy this life. Lucretius also emphasizes that religion is the invention of priests to control society with the fear of death.
6. "Treaty of Peace and Friendship, Signed at Tripoli November 4, 1796," in *Treaties and Other International Acts of the United States of America, Vol. 2, Documents 1–40: 1776–1818*, ed. Hunter Miller (Washington, DC: Government Printing Office, 1931), https://avalon.law.yale.edu/18th_century/bar1796t.asp. An excellent book analyzing this treaty and other aspects of how the Founding Fathers regarded religion is Frank Lambert, *The Founding Fathers and the Place of Religion in America* (Princeton: Princeton University Press, 2003).
7. Montesquieu, *The Spirit of the Laws*, Book 11, Chapter 6, "On the constitution of England," trans. and ed. Anne M. Cohler, Basia Carolyn Miller, and Harold Samuel Stone (Cambridge, UK: Cambridge University Press, 1989), 157.

8. John Calvin, *Institutes of the Christian Religion*, ed. John T. McNeill, trans. Ford Lewis Battles (Philadelphia: Westminster Press, 1960), 4.20.8.
9. Lee Ward, *Modern Democracy and the Theological-Political Problem in Spinoza, Rousseau, and Jefferson* (New York: Macmillan, 2014), 25–26.
10. John Witherspoon, "Man in His Natural State," in *The Works of the Rev. John Witherspoon*, vol. 2 (Philadelphia: William W. Woodward, 1800), 302. A helpful article putting Witherspoon's thinking in context is Ian Speir, "The Calvinist Roots of American Social Order: Calvin, Witherspoon, and Madison," *Public Discourse*, April 13, 2017, http://thepublicdiscourse.com/2017/04/19116/.
11. James Madison, "The Federalist No. 51," in *James Madison: Writings*, ed. Jack N. Rakove (New York: Library of America, 1999), 295 (emphasis mine).
12. Madison, "The Federalist No. 10," in *James Madison: Writings*, ed. Jack N. Rakove (New York: Library of America, 1999), 163 (emphasis original).
13. Madison, "The Federalist No. 51," 295.
14. "The State of Theology, Statement 11," Ligonier Ministries, 2020, https://thestateoftheology.com/data-explorer/2020/11.
15. John Calvin, "The Many Functions of God's Law," in *Sermons on Galatians*, trans. Kathy Childress (Edinburgh: Banner of Truth, 1997), 3:19–20.
16. See David VanDrunen, *Natural Law and the Two Kingdoms: A Study in the Development of Reformed Social Thought*. Emory University Studies in Law and Religion (Grand Rapids: Eerdmans, 2009).
17. Luther's views on the "two kingdoms" are well known, but Calvin urges the same distinction in the *Institutes* (see especially 2.15.3; 4.5.17; 4.20.1, 8).
18. Martin Luther, "On Temporal Authority," *Luther's Works*, American Edition, vol. 45, ed. Walther Brandt, (Philadelphia: Fortress Press, 1968), 88–95.
19. Calvin, *Institutes*, 4.20.23.

20. Carlos Eire, *War Against the Idols: The Reformation of Worship from Erasmus to Calvin* (Cambridge: Cambridge University Press, 1986), 288.
21. James Madison, "Memorial and Remonstrance Against Religious Assessments," in *James Madison: Writings*, ed. Jack N. Rakove (New York: Library of America, 1999), 29–36.
22. Records of the Proceedings of Hanover Presbytery from the Year 1755 to the Year 1786 [typed copy by George S. Wallace, 1930], 326–27. Cited by the editors at the National Archives, Founders Online at https://founders.archives.gov/documents/Madison/01-08-02-0163.
23. Scott Horton, "Calvin and Madison on Men, Angels and Government," Harper's Magazine, November 14, 2009, https://harpers.org/blog/2009/11/calvin-and-madison-on-men-angels-and-government/.
24. Patrick Henry, "'And I Don't Care What It Is': The Tradition-History of a Civil Religion Proof-Text," *Journal of the American Academy of Religion* 49, no. 1 (March 1981): 41.

Chapter 12: Religious Liberty: Cancel Culture and Persecution

1. "40% of Millennials OK with Limiting Speech Offensive to Minorities," Pew Research Center, November 20, 2015, https://pewresearch.org/fact-tank/2015/11/20/40-of-millennials-ok-with-limiting-speech-offensive-to-minorities/.
2. Tyler Kingkade, "Americans Are Split Along Party Lines Over Whether Schools Should Punish Racist Speech," *Huffington Post*, January 4, 2016, https://huffpost.com/entry/poll-campus-racism_n_568342b9e4b0b958f65ac433.
3. Evette Alexander, "First Amendment Vitals: Taking Gen Z's Pulse on Free Expression and Inclusion," Knight Foundation, May 13, 2019, https://knightfoundation.org/articles/first-amendment-vitals-gen-z-free-expression-inclusion/.
4. John Villasenor, senior fellow at the Brookings Institution, provides an insightful evaluation of the data and trends: John Villasenor,

"Views among College Students Regarding the First Amendment: Results from a New Survey," *FixGov* (blog), Brookings Institution, September 18, 2017, https://brookings.edu/blog/fixgov/2017/09/18/views-among-college-students-regarding-the-first-amendment-results-from-a-new-survey/.

5. U.S. National Archives and Records Administration, "Declaration of Independence: A Transcription," America's Founding Documents, https://archives.gov/founding-docs/declaration-transcript.
6. An example is Bret Weinstein, a professor of evolutionary biology. A staunch liberal, his advocacy for inclusion and diversity was turned against him by a mob of students when he disagreed with the decision to have a "day away" when white people could not be on campus. The story is recorded here: "Campus Argument Goes Viral as Evergreen State Is Caught in Racial Turmoil (HBO)," VICE News, YouTube video, June 16, 2017, https://youtube.com/watch?v=2cMYfxOFBBM. Weinstein's wife, a professor at the same college, was also dismissed for alleged racism.
7. Tom Gjelten, "A 'Scary' Survey Finding: 4 in 10 Republicans Say Political Violence May Be Necessary," NPR, February 11, 2021, https://npr.org/2021/02/11/966498544/a-scary-survey-finding-4-in-10-republicans-say-political-violence-may-be-necessary.
8. Sarah Pulliam Bailey, Susan Svrlurga, and Michelle Boorstein, "Jerry Falwell Jr. Resigns as Head of Liberty University, Will Get $10.5 Million in Compensation," *Washington Post*, August 25, 2020, https://washingtonpost.com/education/2020/08/25/fallwell-resigns-confirmed/.
9. J. Gresham Machen, *Christianity and Liberalism* (1923; Grand Rapids: Eerdmans, 2009).
10. H. Richard Niebuhr, *The Kingdom of God in America* (1937; Middletown, CT: Wesleyan University Press, 1988), 193.
11. Martin Luther, *Commentary on the Sermon on the Mount*, trans. Charles A. Hay (Philadelphia: Lutheran Pub. Society, 1892), 190–91.
12. Aliza Nadi and Ken Dilanian, "In Closed-Door Meeting, Trump Told Christian Leaders He Got Rid of a Law. He Didn't," NBC

News, August 28, 2018, https://nbcnews.com/politics/elections /trump-told-christian-leaders-he-got-rid-law-he-didn-n904471.

13. Rebecca R. Bibbs, "Vote Common Good Hopes to Prevent Reelection of Donald Trump," *The Herald Bulletin*, March 10, 2020, https://heraldbulletin.com/news/vote-common-good -hopes-to-prevent-reelection-of-donald-trump/article_514c1f5c -626b-11ea-90e7-b7a652d6c49d.html.
14. Azeem Ibrahim, "The CCP Is Scared of Christianity," *Foreign Policy*, July 1, 2021, https://foreignpolicy.com/2021/07/01 /chinese-communist-party-scared-of-christianity-religion/.
15. Sarah Pulliam Bailey, "Preachers and Their $5,000 Sneakers: Why One Man Started an Instagram Account Showing Churches' Wealth," Washington Post, March 22, 2021, https://www .washingtonpost.com/religion/2021/03/22/preachers -sneakers-instagram-wealth/.

Chapter 13: LGBTQ+ Fears: People over Positions

1. The acronym LGBTQIA stands for Lesbian, Gay, Bisexual, Transgender, Queer, Intersexual, Asexual. Carl Trueman provides a cultural history of the sexual revolution in *The Rise and Triumph of the Modern Self* (Crossway, 2020).
2. "Full Transcript: Saddleback Presidential Forum, Sen. Barack Obama, John McCain; Moderated by Rick Warren," Vote Smart, August 17, 2008, https://justfacts.votesmart.org/public -statement/658545/full-transcript-saddleback-presidential-forum -sen-barack-obama-john-mccain-moderated-by-rick-warren /#.VSbObJTF938.
3. John Calvin, *1 and 2 Timothy and Titus*, Crossway Classic Commentaries, ed. Alister McGrath and J. I. Packer (Wheaton, IL: Crossway, 1998), 184.
4. Andrew Marin, *Us Versus Us: The Untold Story of Religion and the LGBT Community* (Colorado Springs: NavPress, 2016), 1, 6–7.
5. Dietrich Bonhoeffer, *Life Together: The Classic Exploration of Christian Community* (San Francisco: HarperOne, 2009).

6. The latest Gallup survey, tracking an eight-decade trend, shows that membership in houses of worship has fallen from 70% in 1999 to 47% in 2020. Jeffrey M. Jones, "U.S. Church Membership Falls Below Majority for First Time," Gallup, March 29, 2021, https://news.gallup.com/poll/341963/church-membership-falls-below-majority-first-time.aspx.
7. Ann O'Neill, "The Reinvention of Ted Turner," CNN, November 17, 2013, https://www.cnn.com/2013/11/17/us/ted-turner-profile/index.html.
8. "Van Ness' Battle with Abuse and Addiction," *The Week*, October 11, 2019, https://pressreader.com/usa/the-week-us/20191011/281814285603770.
9. Jonathan Van Ness, *Over the Top: A Raw Journey to Self-Love* (New York: HarperOne, 2019), 6.
10. J. J. Sutherland, "Survey: Atheists, Agnostics Know More about Religion Than Religious," NPR, September 28, 2010, https://npr.org/sections/thetwo-way/2010/09/28/130191248/atheists-and-agnostics-know-more-about-bible-than-religious.
11. "The State of Theology," Ligonier Ministries, 2020, https://thestateoftheology.com.
12. "The State of Theology, Statement 31," Ligonier Ministries, 2020, https://thestateoftheology.com/data-explorer/2020/31.
13. "The State of Theology, Statement 3," Ligonier Ministries, 2020, https://thestateoftheology.com/data-explorer/2020/3.
14. "After 500 Years, Reformation-Era Divisions Have Lost Much of Their Potency," Pew Research Center, August 31, 2017, https://pewforum.org/2017/08/31/after-500-years-reformation-era-divisions-have-lost-much-of-their-potency/.
15. Christian Smith and Melinda Lundquist Denton, *Soul-Searching: The Religious and Spiritual Lives of American Teenagers* (New York: Oxford University Press, 2009); Christian Smith and Patricia Snell, *Souls in Transition: The Religious and Spiritual Life of Emerging Adults* (New York: Oxford University Press, 2009).
16. See Christian Smith and Keri Christoffersen, *Lost in Transition:*

The Dark Side of Emerging Adulthood (New York: Oxford University Press, 2011).

17. David E. Campbell, Geoffrey C. Layman and John C. Green, *The Secular Surge: A New Fault Line in American Politics* (Cambridge: Cambridge University Press, 2020). The quotation is from an RNS interview: Jana Riess, "'Allergic to Religion': Conservative Politics Can Push People Out of the Pews, New Study Shows," RNS, March 12, 2021, https://religionnews.com/2021/03/12/allergic-to-religion-conservative-politics-can-push-people-out-of-the-pews-new-study-shows/.
18. Marin, *Us Versus Us*, 65–74 (emphasis mine).
19. Rosaria Butterfield vividly describes what this looks like in *The Gospel Comes with a House Key* (Wheaton, IL: Crossway, 2018).

Chapter 14: Racial Fears: Redefining "Us"

1. John M. Perkins, *One Blood: Parting Words to the Church and Race and Love* (Chicago: Moody, 2018).
2. Bryan Loritts, *Right Color, Wrong Culture: The Type of Leader Your Organization Needs to Become Multiethnic* (Chicago: Moody Press, 2014).
3. Rich McKay and Gabrielle Borter, "For Asian-Americans, Atlanta Shooting Sows Fresh Fear After a Year of Mounting Discrimination," Reuters, March 17, 2021, https://reuters.com/article/us-crime-georgia-spas-fear/for-asian-americans-atlanta-shooting-sows-fresh-fear-after-a-year-of-mounting-discrimination-idUSKBN2B934A.
4. Federal judge Gonzalo Curiel, born in Indiana, was referred to as a "Mexican" by Mr. Trump in a case against Trump University. David A. Graham, "Gaffe Track: Trump's Attack on a 'Mexican' Judge," *The Atlantic*, May 31, 2016, https://theatlantic.com/notes/2016/05/gaffe-track-trumps-attack-on-a-mexican-judge/484877/.
5. See, for example, Jemar Tisby, *The Color of Compromise: The Truth about the American Church's Complicity in Racism* (Grand Rapids: Zondervan, 2019); Michael Emerson and Christian Smith,

Evangelical Religion and the Problem of Racism in America (New York: Oxford University Press, 2000).

6. David Masci, "5 Facts about the Religious Lives of African Americans," Pew Research Center, February 7, 2018, https://pewresearch.org/fact-tank/2018/02/07/5-facts-about-the-religious-lives-of-african-americans/.
7. "A Religious Portrait of African Americans," Pew Research Center, January 30, 2009, https://pewforum.org/2009/01/30/a-religious-portrait-of-african-americans/.
8. Michelle Boorstein, "The Stunning Difference between White and Black Evangelical Voters in Alabama," *Washington Post*, December 13, 2017, https://washingtonpost.com/news/acts-of-faith/wp/2017/12/13/there-was-an-enormous-gap-between-black-evangelical-voters-and-white-evangelical-voters-in-alabama/.
9. Marshal Frady, *Martin Luther King Jr.: A Life* (New York: Penguin, 2002), 20–22.
10. Allison Calhoun-Brown, "The Politics of Black Evangelicals: What Hinders Diversity in the Christian Right?", *American Politics Quarterly* 26, no. 1 (1998): 81–109 (here at p. 81).
11. "Views about Abortion," Pew Research Center, https://pewforum.org/religious-landscape-study/views-about-abortion/.
12. "Views about Same-Sex Marriage among Members of the Historically Black Protestant Tradition Who Believe in Hell by Religious Denomination," Pew Research Center, 2014, https://pewforum.org/religious-landscape-study/compare/views-about-same-sex-marriage/by/religious-denomination/among/belief-in-hell/believe/religious-tradition/historically-black-protestant/. See also Paul A Djupe, "American Religion Is Becoming More Gay-Accepting," *Religion in Public* (blog), June 23, 2020, https://religioninpublic.blog/2020/06/23/american-religion-is-becoming-more-gay-accepting/.
13. Andrew L. Whitehead and Samuel L. Perry, *Taking America Back for God: Christian Nationalism in the United States* (New York: Oxford University Press, 2020), 41.

14. Amina Dunn, "5 Facts about Black Democrats," Pew Research Center, February 27, 2020, https://pewresearch.org/fact-tank/2020/02/27/5-facts-about-black-democrats/.
15. David French, "The Cultural Consequences of Very, Very Republican Christianity," *The French Press* (blog), *The Dispatch*, Nov. 15, 2020, https://frenchpress.thedispatch.com/p/the-cultural-consequences-of-very.
16. "Summer Unrest over Racial Injustice Moves the Country, But Not Republicans or White Evangelicals," PRRI, August 21, 2020, https://prri.org/research/racial-justice-2020-george-floyd/.
17. On the first statistic, see also Tobin Grant, "Opposition to Interracial Marriage Lingering among Evangelicals," *Christianity Today*, June 24, 2011, https://www.christianitytoday.com/news/2011/june/opposition-to-interracial-marriage-lingers-among.html. On the second, see "Religious Switching and Intermarriage," in *Asian Americans: A Mosaic of Faiths*, Pew Research Center, July 19, 2012, https://pewforum.org/2012/07/19/asian-americans-a-mosaic-of-faiths-religious-switching-and-intermarriage/.
18. Emma Lazarus, "The New Colossus," November 2, 1883, https://www.nps.gov/stli/learn/historyculture/colossus.htm.
19. "Immigration after Trump: What Would Immigration Policy That Followed American Public Opinion Look Like?," PRRI, January 20, 2021, https://prri.org/research/immigration-after-trump-what-would-immigration-policy-that-followed-american-public-opinion-look-like/.
20. Ryan P. Burge, "For White Evangelical Republicans, Approval of Trump Is about Immigration More Than Abortion," *Religion in Public* (blog), August 27, 2020, https://religioninpublic.blog/2020/08/27/for-white-evangelical-republicans-approval-of-trump-is-about-immigration-more-than-abortion/.
21. I am grateful to my student, C. J. Francis, for making me aware of this slave bible (as well as the Frederick Douglass and Lemuel Haynes quotes) in his "Modernity and Apologetics" paper (Westminster Seminary California, Spring 2021).

22. John R. McKivigan, Julie Husband, and Heather L. Kaufman, eds., *The Speeches of Frederick Douglass: A Critical Edition* (New Haven: Yale University Press, 2018), 180.
23. Ruth Bogin, "'Liberty Further Extended': A 1776 Antislavery Manuscript by Lemuel Haynes," *The William and Mary Quarterly* 40, no. 1 (1983): 94–95.
24. Jourdon Anderson, "Letter from a Freedman to His Old Master," *New-York Daily Tribune*, August 22, 1865, https://chroniclingamerica.loc.gov/lccn/sn83030213/1865-08-22/ed-1/seq-7/.
25. See Eric Foner, *Reconstruction: America's Unfinished Revolution, 1863–1877* (New York: Harper Perennial Modern Classics, 2014), 70.
26. Carl R. Trueman, "Woke Repentance," *First Things*, August 25, 2020, https://firstthings.com/web-exclusives/2020/08/woke-repentance?fbclid=IwAR1miZxhJ-dd7jPev0ve5Q-uE7NpUzYfsESBCXSbtboahRJdQ5_2MRw8hSE.